Fort Worth

OUTPOST ON THE TRINITY

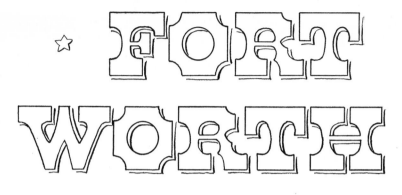

☆ FORT WORTH

OUTPOST ON THE TRINITY

BY OLIVER KNIGHT

Norman :   UNIVERSITY OF OKLAHOMA PRESS

Library of Congress Catalog Card Number: 53–8817

Copyright 1953 by the University of Oklahoma Press
        Publishing Division of the University
        Composed and printed at Norman, Oklahoma, U.S.A.
        by the University of Oklahoma Press
        First edition

To my Grandmother

who knew Texas when it was a frontier

Preface

FORT WORTH is like a young hellion who has matured into an unwonted respectability. Behind it is a tradition of adventurers and highbinders of every stripe who made things happen in pursuing fortune as the town progressed through a series of dramatic episodes, several of a boom nature. Since other western towns went through similar periods and then receded under competition from newer towns farther west, the reasons for Fort Worth's survival and growth lie quite as much in the personalities of its people as in its economic circumstances.

Within three generations it has advanced from a remote army post to a major city where the first nonstop flight around the world began and ended. During the intervening years it passed through several colorful periods that coincided with the principal phases in the development of the Southwest. It gained a toe hold because it was a good day's journey closer to the cattlemen and the buffalo hunters than were other towns, and thus it became a supply base for the southwestern frontier. Too, the word *fort* had a psychological value in making it the point of departure for westbound immigrants heading into the Comanche country and for trail drivers going north. Besides that, Fort Worth was a good place for hell-raising, particularly during the feverish boom years that succeeded the Civil War, and West Texans still look upon it as the place to go for a ripsnorting good time. During the wild seventies and later, it acquired economic and geographical significance because of its railroads. Fundamentally it is a town of cattle and oil, where industry has only recently been recognized as of great importance, and it has remained peculiarly close to the soil.

But the economic circumstances do not tell the whole story. The full picture comes into focus only with the personalities of the men who came empty-handed into a new country where they were determined to make their fortunes. The merchants, investors, and workingmen were just as adventurous in their own right as the cowboys, buffalo hunters, gunmen, gamblers, and opportunists who created the excitement upon which more stable men built. Their daring, initiative, independence, chicanery, and devotion gave Fort Worth a peculiar vitality, a characteristic which it retains today.

However, Fort Worth does not have the supercharged atmosphere of a city that is conscious of itself. Nor is it particularly conscious of culture. Rather, the people go ahead with their own culture, letting their lives revolve quietly around their homes, their churches, and their schools. It is a town of easygoing informality, with only a faint trace of old-family traditions. But in their businesses and shops the people of Fort Worth have kept alive the legacy of the ebullient West. They call their town the place "Where the West Begins," "Cowtown," and "Panther City." With its own distinctive flavor and personality, Fort Worth is paradoxically a metropolitan country town.

It is also a town with a vivid past, where the present is considered of much greater importance. This book is an attempt to tell the story of Fort Worth in human terms, with emphasis upon economic and political development. The book had its origin as a reportorial assignment on the *Fort Worth Star-Telegram* when the author was assigned to work on a special historical edition in 1949 under the direction of Cullum Greene, now Sunday editor. In the course of that assignment, the author came to feel that there was a definite need for a single-volume history of Fort Worth; thus the book grew from a city-room assignment.

As the work progressed, the author found himself indebted for wise guidance, counsel, and information to James R. Record, managing editor of the *Star-Telegram;* Phil North, executive assistant managing editor; Mack Williams, now managing editor of the *Denton Record-Chronicle;* Dr. Rex Z. Howard; J. S. Ibbotson and his fine staff at the Fort Worth Public Library; the Lewis Historical Publishing Company for permission to quote from Captain Paddock's histories; and especially to Cullum Greene.

Nor could the book have been written without the understanding and historical insight of my wife whose generous assistance made all phases of the work easier, in editing, in proofreading, and particularly in indexing.

All but two of the photographs were made available through the courtesy of the *Fort Worth Star-Telegram.* The two exceptions are the photographs of General Harney, which came from the National Archives, and of the city from the air, which came from the Fort Worth Chamber of Commerce. My thanks go to all three for their courtesy.

OLIVER KNIGHT

Norman, Oklahoma
September 10, 1953

Contents

Preface : vii

I   Saber and Musket : 3
II   The Stolen Courthouse : 26
III War and Evil Days : 46
IV   Thundering Hooves : 59
V   Boom Town : 66
VI   Blood, Lust, and Gold : 87
VII Vice and Reform : 112
VIII "Queen City of the Prairie" : 123
IX   Transition : 150
X   A Bold New Century : 167
XI   The Golden Goddess and a Lucky Lady : 195

APPENDICES

A   Military Orders and Correspondence
     Relating to the Establishment
     and Occupation of Fort Worth : 231
B   County Officers Since 1849 : 247
C   Congressmen Since 1849 : 258
D   State Legislators Since 1853 : 261
E   City Officials Since 1873 : 268

Bibliography : 279

Index : 283

List of Illustrations

Map of Twiggs' and Worth's lines, *facing page* : 11
General W. J. Worth : 18
General W. S. Harney : 19
Map of Fort Worth in 1853 : 25
Middleton Tate Johnson : 34
Press Farmer : 35
Captain E. M. Daggett : 50
A. B. Norton : 51
Major K. M. Van Zandt : 82
Captain M. B. Loyd : 83
Fort Worth in 1880 : 98
Fort Worth in 1949 : 98
Mule car in 1881 : 99
Captain B. B. Paddock : 130
Long Hair Jim Courtright : 131
Tarrant County Courthouse
    destroyed by fire in 1876 : 162
Tarrant County Courthouse razed in 1894 : 162
Tarrant County Courthouse since 1894 : 163
Aerial View of Fort Worth in 1953 : 178
Amon G. Carter : 179

Fort Worth

OUTPOST ON THE TRINITY

CHAPTER I

Saber and Musket

TTACK was imminent. Excitedly the bugler lipped his instrument and sent the call to arms ringing across the Fort Worth parade ground. With sabers clanking against their high boots, dragoons rushed from stable, orderly room, and hospital. With muskets ready, infantrymen tumbled from barracks and cook shack in response to the brisk, imperative bugle call. Ordered into line by Major Ripley Arnold, the soldiers took their places in formal battle array and waited.

Less than a mile to the northwest the enemy was in full view. Angry Comanche and Caddo braves were demonstrating in savagery and fury. Yelling taunts at the soldiers, they raced back and forth on their half-wild war ponies, defiantly shaking musket and bow in the direction of the army post that sat high on a bluff overlooking the Trinity River.

The threatened attack had developed first as an intertribal conflict; now, all of a sudden the isolated army outpost faced a screaming war party. Early on that day in 1850, a band of the cannibalistic Tonkawas had been surprised by Chief Towash and his band of Comanches and Caddos. The Tonks fled to the fort where Arnold gave them sanctuary in the commissary which stood about where Weatherford and Houston streets now intersect. His orders specifically directed him to maintain peace among the tribes.

However, Towash and his braves considered that giving the Tonks asylum was an undeserved interference. Furious at losing captives, the Comanches and Caddos assembled and began making warlike gestures toward the fort.

Arnold quickly mustered his feeble forces—Company F, Second Dragoons, and Company F, Eighth Infantry. The Companies F were so understrength that the two formed a contingent of not more than one hundred men. Minute by minute the tension grew. Watching and waiting, the soldiers saw a brave ride forward from the Indian force, waving something above his head. They made it out to be a rag that was serving as a flag of truce.

The brave rode up the slight rise to the fort, where he talked with Arnold, demanding release of the Tonks. The Major refused. The Indian wheeled his pony and galloped back to his forces. The crucial moment would come when he reported Arnold's answer to Towash. Abe Harris, who was sergeant major of the infantry company, said this is what happened:

"They were yellin' out there at the head of Robinson's branch like red devils. The major he ordered us into line and said if fight was what they wanted, fight it was, and Sergeant McCauly who had charge of the big gun [the post's lone howitzer] brought it out and unlimbered it at the northwest corner of the square at the head of Houston Street. The major he told the rag messenger that he was not in the habit of serving up his guests for breakfast, at least to strangers, and that they might be prepared for a fight.

"The Injuns were about three hundred strong, and let me tell you we fellers in blue were but a squad in comparison to them, but we had the gun, and were sure they had never heard her bellow, so while the Injuns were scattered around over the bottom there over the bluff looking northwest, the major said to McCauly, 'Sergeant, touch her off and graze the heads of the big bucks over there in the valley if you can without hitting them, but if you should hit one, mind you, there will be no love lost, even if you take his head smooth smack off!'

4

"So the sergeant he pulled the lanyard, and boom! room! doom! rang the shrapnel over the heads of the bucks, and scatter, clatter, scatter, clatter went the Injuns hither and thither, scared out of their wits."[1]

The boom of the strange gun and the angry swish of hot metal above their heads took the fight out of Towash's militant braves, but to save face they demanded food from Arnold. He gave them three beeves.

With a single cannon shot the soldiers of Fort Worth had carried out the mission for which they were assigned to the wild frontier of Northwest Texas—to break up Indian raids. At no other time since the fort was established on June 6, 1849, had the Indians threatened. In this the garrison was fortunate because the fort was usually understrength. The nearest reinforcements were fifty miles away. Circumstances that caused the army to place a fort in such a remote region dated back to 1848.

In 1848 Mexico had just been defeated in a war that was ignited by the annexation of Texas, and with the cessation of hostilities, Americans were ranging westward across the continent in search of adventure and fortune. Hundreds of them, restless and ambitious, were rolling through the woodlands and over the prairies into the virgin vastness of Texas. Their path menaced by lawless white men and Indians painted for war, the immigrants looked to the government for security.

In turn, the government, freed from an exacting involvement in Mexico that had drained home defenses, posted toughened troopers of the regular army on the infant state's uneasy frontier. To command the troops on Texas station, the War Department assigned Major General William Jenkins Worth, a hot-tempered soldier risen from the ranks, whose talent as a tactician qualified him especially for such a potential trouble zone as the Southwest. Like his troops fresh from Mexico, General Worth as a division commander had smelled gunpowder and seen the saber red. He arrived at army head-

[1] Quoted in *Fort Worth Register,* June 1, 1902.

5

quarters in sun-baked San Antonio in January, 1849, to take charge of the Eighth and Ninth Military Departments—Texas and New Mexico.

On the crude map of his sprawling command western Texas was shown to be the country of the Lipans and the Comanches. The Lipans were of the Apache family, although not as warlike as their New Mexico cousins. The Comanches were fierce and indomitable, like the Seminoles in Florida that Worth, then a colonel, had subdued in 1842. Then his mission had been to prosecute an outright war against Indians. Now his mission was to protect northern Mexico against hostile Indians from West Texas, to escort wagon trains, and to mark new trails across the wild lands. But primarily he was to safeguard the western line of settlement in Texas, to protect both Indian and settlers from each other.

In accepting this mission, Worth faced a disheartening tactical situation. Upon assuming command, he reasonably could have expected to find troops stationed at key points along the five hundred miles of frontier between the Red River and the Río Grande, plus several hundred more along the border that he was also to defend. On the contrary, however, he found only meager forces bunched on a short, thin, poorly marked line in the center of the state. Even after reinforcement he had a mere one thousand troops in Texas, a limited force that was nonetheless approximately 10 per cent of the United States Army—an army in 1849 of 10,320 officers and men. His troops were distributed among the twenty-eight companies of the Eighth Infantry, First Infantry, Fourth Artillery, and Second Dragoons.[2] Because foot soldiers were useless against the fleet, mounted Plains Indians, Worth placed his greatest reliance in his one mobile regiment, the Second Dragoons.

The dragoons had been formed less than twenty years

[2] Lena Clara Koch, "Federal Indian Policy in Texas 1845–1860," *Southwestern Historical Quarterly*, Vol. XXIX, No. 1 (July, 1925), 19–35; Charles C. Little and James Brown, *American Almanac for 1850*, 116.

before as a special Indian-fighting force, usually in the field as cavalry, but also trained to fight as infantry. The Second Regiment of Dragoons, organized by Congress on May 23, 1836, to bolster the army in fighting the Seminoles, had brought glory to their banners in Florida and still more in Mexico. When the Mexican War ended, the regiment had remained on duty below the border for several months while awaiting a new detail. On September 24, 1848, General Zachary Taylor—commanding the army's western division from Baton Rouge—ordered part of the regiment to take position on the Texas Frontier.[3]

Entering the new state, the regiment had become part of the Eighth Military Department, commanded by Major General David Twiggs, Worth's predecessor. Twiggs had been a division commander at Monterrey, but he had missed the first day of battle because he had taken a strong dose of medicine the night before.[4] From his headquarters at Galveston, Twiggs issued Order No. 2 on November 7, 1848, which sent four companies of dragoons to Ranger stations where they relieved the volunteers who had held the line during the war.

The first dragoon company went to Conner's Station on Richland Creek between the present towns of Hillsboro and Corsicana; the second, to Ross's Station on the Bosque River west of the Brazos and only a few miles from the first company; the third, to McCulloch's Station fifty miles above Austin on the Colorado River; and the fourth, to a station on the Medina ten or fifteen miles above Castroville.

Along with instructions that commanders cultivate friendly relations with the Indians, Twiggs specified that the natives be contained north and west of a line connecting the Ranger stations. For effectuation of his policy, Twiggs's tactical position, employing even fewer men than Worth subsequently

[3] Theo F. Rodenbough, *From Everglades to Canyon with the Second Dragoons*, 18; Robert E. Riegel, *Young America*, 59 and 69.
[4] Robert Selph Henry, *The Story of the Mexican War*, 150-52, 358-61, 382-83.

used, was inadequate. It was based in its entirety upon a line of weak and isolated posts extending from Conner's Station, a few miles north of Waco, to the Medina River, a short distance above San Antonio. The Ranger stations were backed up by clusters of infantry at Fredericksburg, Austin, and San Antonio.

Twiggs had left two huge stretches of Texas without military protection. One was the wedge-shaped domain bounded by San Antonio, Corpus Christi, and Laredo. Indian, Mexican bandit, and renegade white all preyed upon defenseless settlers in this great sweep of territory. The other was in the north of Texas. From Conner's Station to the Red River was a wide-open frontier about 150 miles long, with nothing to discourage the swift attack of Comanches and Kiowas upon the fast appearing homes, farms, and towns in the North Texas wilderness. The Comanches and Kiowas lived in Indian Territory, periodically sweeping south to make war upon their traditional enemies, the Texans. The exposed wing of civilization included the blossoming village of Dallas and the giant Peters Colony where settlement had begun in 1843 under a contract with the Republic of Texas.[5]

In general, that was the unhappy situation Worth faced when he took command at San Antonio in 1849. Within a month after his arrival, he redeployed his thin forces, strengthening his line. For the border he created the Río Grande District to cover the area between Laredo and Fort Polk on the Gulf. For the western line he created the Frontier District, which extended from northern Texas to the Río Grande at a point opposite Presidio, Mexico, midway between Laredo and Eagle Pass. Responsibility for the Frontier District was placed in the able hands of Brevet Brigadier General William S. Harney, commander of the Second Dragoons, who maintained headquarters in Austin at the Harney Place, a half-mile north of the State House.[6]

[5] *Corpus Christi Star,* Dec. 16, 1848, p. 1.
[6] Orders No. 13, Headquarters, 8th and 9th Military Depts., Feb. 14,

At the same time, Worth dotted the western fringe of settlement with a north-south line of fortifications manned by soldiers withdrawn from the Ranger stations. Placing one strong force in the extreme north, he ordered, on February 8, 1849, that Dragoon Companies F and I evacuate their respective positions at Ross's and Conner's stations and consolidate at a permanent post at Towash Village on the Brazos River, near the present town of Hillsboro.[7]

Command of both companies fell to Brevet Major Arnold, captain commanding Company F, a professional soldier with several citations for valor, who brought the two companies together and established a post which he called Camp Thornton. The official title, however, was seldom used; the post constantly was referred to as Towash Village, a name taken from a near-by Indian chief and his encampment.

Establishment of the post at Towash Village did little to change the general situation in North Texas. About all Arnold's command could do was to watch Towash and block any Indian expeditions down the Brazos valley toward the more populous sections of Texas. Peters Colony and Dallas still were without a buffer against the Comanches. Yet Worth was not unmindful of their plight.

Determined to give the northern settlers protection, Worth, on February 14, 1849, ordered Harney to make a personal survey of North Texas for a new fort site somewhere between Towash Village and Fort Washita—a long-established post a few miles north of the Red River, above the present town of Denison, Texas.[8]

Beginning his inspection tour in early March, Harney first

1849, National Archives, War Department Records, Office of the Adjutant General, Orders 8th and 9th Military Departments. (Designation for War Department records in the National Archives hereafter will be abbreviated to NA, WDR, OAG.)

[7] Orders No. 9, Feb. 8, 1849, NA, WDR, OAG, Orders 8th and 9th Mil. Depts.; Report of Brig. Gen. Harney, May 1, 1849, NA, WDR, U. S. Army Commands, Department of the West, Letters Received.

[8] Orders No. 13, Feb. 14, 1849, loc. cit.

9

reached Arnold's post at Towash Village, which he considered unfit for a dragoon post. It was on a sandy ridge surrounded by a swamp and lacked adequate grazing land. Harney directed Arnold to move Companies F and I six miles north to José María Village, an encampment of Anadarko Indians, where a new post was built a few miles west of the present town of Hillsboro. Harney named the new post Fort Graham.[9]

NEW MEXICO

OKLAHOMA

Fort Washita

Fort Worth   o DALLAS

Fort Graham

Fort Gates   o WACO

Trinity River

Fort Crogaan

Fort Martin Scott   o AUSTIN

MEXICO

o SAN ANTONIO   GALVESTON

Fort Lincoln

Fort Inge

Presidio

Fort Duncan

LAREDO   CORPUS CHRISTI

---- *Twiggs' Line*
—— *Worth's Line*

FORT POLK

He then carried out the remainder of his assignment, which took him on a long horseback ride through the western Cross Timbers and over the great prairie of North Texas. At the end of his trip, he recommended that a post be established on the West Fork of the Trinity River.[10] Evidently without waiting for Worth's concurrence, Harney told Arnold to pro-

[9] Report of Brig. Gen. Harney, *loc. cit.*
[10] *Ibid.*

ceed immediately with selection of the exact site for the new fort that would be the northern anchor of the army's first chain of forts across Texas.

Riding at the head of his blue-uniformed dragoons, Arnold marched from Fort Graham early in May, 1849, moving forward to meet Middleton Tate Johnson, Worth's comrade-in-arms from Mexico, who as a colonel commanded a small Ranger detachment in North Central Texas. His home was Johnson Station, a few miles southeast of present-day Fort Worth, where he had built a two-story log home, a blacksmith shop, sorghum mill, gristmill, and a store. Johnson Station was the military, social, business, and political headquarters for North Central Texas. After Arnold discussed his mission, the lettered and gracious Johnson suggested that the post be placed a few miles to the northwest where two arms of the Trinity joined to form the main stream.

Early on the morning of May 8, 1849, Arnold and his dragoons left Johnson Station to explore the Trinity for a suitable site, accompanied by Johnson and Texas Rangers Simon B. Farrar, Charles Turner, Joe Parker, and W. B. Echols. Their route took them through a wild and beautiful country blanketed by brilliant flowers and bountiful with mustang, deer, turkey, bear, wolves, and small game. After a few hours' ride they forded the sparkling, clear Trinity. In the lowlands on the south side of the stream, near the juncture of the two forks, Arnold found the place where he thought the fort should be built. He and his detachment then returned to Fort Graham.[11]

While Arnold was locating the site for the new fort, Worth died from Asiatic cholera in San Antonio, and Harney succeeded to temporary command of the department. As department commander Harney issued the order that resulted in establishing the new post—Orders No. 16, Headquarters,

[11] Alphonso Freeman, one of Major Arnold's dragoons, quoted in *Fort Worth Register*, Jan. 19, 1902; letter of Simon B. Farrar, *Fort Worth Star-Telegram*, Oct. 30, 1949, Homes Section, p. 2.

Frontier District, Austin.[12] The directive was forwarded to Arnold, who spent the rest of May getting equipment and supplies in order for the move northward. By June he was ready to leave.

Through the misty half-light of dawn on June 4, 1849, the marching command rang down the line of Company F, and Arnold reined his white horse to the north, his company falling in behind him. Two days later the company reached the site selected a month earlier, establishing an outpost which Arnold named Camp Worth in honor of the late general. Although the War Department delayed formal designation as a fort until November 14, the post from the start was referred to as Fort Worth. In filling out his post return—an army report form—for the month of June, 1849, Arnold wrote:

> Fort Worth established on the south side of the West Fork of the Trinity River in the Republic (or county) of Navarro. Thirty five miles west of "Dallas" (a Postoffice). Co. F, 2nd Drags. arrived at Fort Worth 6 June 1849.[13]

Arnold's West Fork is known as the main stream today.

Both Worth, whose name was perpetuated in the Trinity outpost, and his admirer Arnold were professional soldiers who achieved distinction in the same campaigns, Florida and Mexico.

Worth was born in Hudson, New York, on March 1, 1794, the son of a middle-class family, in whose midst he grew up to become a store clerk. Escaping from the humdrum of commercial routine when the War of 1812 flared, he marched away as a private. Although without benefit of formal academic training or proper instruction in military matters he

---

[12] Philip C. Brooks, chief archivist (1950) of the War Records Branch of the National Archives, is authority for the designation of the order directing the establishment of Fort Worth, a copy of which he says has never been found.

[13] Post Return for Fort Worth for the month of June, 1849, by Bvt. Maj. R. A. Arnold, NA, WDR, OAG, Post Returns.

was a major by brevet and an intimate of the arrogant, egocentric General Winfield Scott by the time England capitulated.

Worth remained in the army to pursue a promising military career. In March, 1820, he went to West Point as commandant of cadets, where he inaugurated the high standards of bearing and drill precision that mark the Academy. When the Cherokees were removed from Georgia in 1838, he was Scott's chief of staff. In the same year he was placed in command of the newly formed Eighth Infantry. As a staff officer and then as a regimental commander, he sat on the side lines and watched while the army sent general after general into Florida to subdue the Seminoles who defied the United States' determined plan of moving all Indians westward. After ten generals had been humbled by the Seminoles, the army gave Worth direction of the campaign.

Taking command of the forces in Florida in 1840, he hammered the Seminoles with a series of blows, defeating them within two years. When the war with Mexico erupted, he joined Taylor's force assembling in Texas and marched to Monterrey, where as a brevet brigadier general he commanded a division attacking the city. With an encircling movement against the western fortifications, he split the city's defenses, enabling Taylor to pierce Monterrey with the main effort of the attack.

When Scott took personal command for a sea-borne invasion and a march upon Mexico City, Worth joined his column. Again as a division commander, he was the first man ashore at Vera Cruz in the first joint army-navy amphibious attack in American history. After the coastal areas were cleared, it was time to advance upon Mexico City. Then it was that Worth's friendship for Scott turned to pique because the latter allowed Twiggs's division to lead the column.

Nearing Mexico City, the army ran into Santa Anna's grouping of southern defenses. First the invaders encountered Lake Chalco, and thought for a while they would be forced to cross the lake in boats because of unfavorable terrain along the shore. But Worth found a southern route for a quick, surprise march that upset the whole set of Mexican defenses. Scott claimed credit for the maneuver and so enraged Worth that their already soured friendship turned to enmity. Worth remained in Mexico City until June 12, 1848; his was the last division to leave.[14]

Arnold, who was born January 17, 1817, near Pearlington, Mississippi, was admitted at the age of seventeen to West Point, where he was graduated in 1838 as a classmate of Pierre Beauregard, who was to become the brilliant artillerist of the Civil War. Upon graduation Arnold began his military career with combat in Florida. After a few months he was sent home on recruiting duty, where he courted and eloped with blue-eyed Catherine Bryant, the sixteen-year-old daughter of a United States marshal in Bay St. Louis, Mississippi. He then returned to Florida.

Through gallantry he earned a promotion to first lieutenant on February 1, 1841. On April 19, 1842, he was engaged in the rout of Tustenuggee's band in the Big Hammock of Pilaklikaha. During the pursuit, he and eight men were separated from the company and found themselves facing a superior and well-posted enemy force. He fought his way out with such skill that Worth recommended him for brevet of captain.[15]

After the Florida war he was in garrison at Baton Rouge and Fort Jesup, Louisiana, until 1845, when he moved into Texas with the Army of Occupation. The next year he participated in the first two battles of the Mexican War—Palo Alto and Resaca de la Palma, on May 8 and 9, 1846. For "gallant and meritorious" conduct while serving on the regimental staff during those two battles, Arnold was breveted major. Because of another tour of recruiting duty in the States, he

[14] Edward S. Wallace, "General William Jenkins Worth, the American Murat" (Ph.D. dissertation, Boston University, 1948), 1 ff.
[15] Rodenbough, *From Everglades to Canyon,* 453.

missed the final months of conflict. But by the time the war was over he had rejoined his regiment, moving with it into Texas in November, 1848.[16] He took his company first to Ross's Station on the Bosque, then to Fort Worth on the banks of the Trinity.

After a short occupancy of the river-bottom encampment, Arnold became dissatisfied with the site because the river overflowed the camp. As an alternative he moved the command in August to a bluff, from which the weather-stained Criminal Court building rises today.

The dragoons erected log and mud buildings in a rectangle, without a stockade. They chopped trees in the lowlands, dragging them to the camp site. A crude sawmill converted a few logs into green lumber that furnished siding for the post hospital and roofing for a few buildings. Two slender cottonwoods were joined by an iron band to form a flagpole that stood as a sentinel over the broad valley of the Trinity, lined with cottonwood, elm, oak, and hackberry, and over the rolling prairie that to the southward lay muffled in a sea of waving grass high enough to reach a rider's stirrups.

Strategically, Arnold hardly could have selected a better location for an outpost, for the position was a central point from which he could strike to protect sparsely settled territory to the east, north, and south against Indian forays. To the east, Dallas, less than fifty miles distant, with a population of nearly three hundred, needed protection. Nine miles east of the fort was Birdville, inhabited by perhaps fifty persons and surrounded by scattered farms. To the north, Denton County had a developing pattern of settlement. To the south, settlements were thicker and thicker—a rich target that might tempt raiding parties unless the saber and musket of the United States Army barred the path.

Fifty-six miles south was Fort Graham. Beyond Fort Graham in the line of western defense were Fort Gates, near the present Gatesville; Fort Croghan, near Burnet; Fort Martin

16 *Ibid.;* Kate Arnold Parker quoted in *Fort Worth Register,* June 1, 1902.

Scott, two miles from Fredericksburg; Fort Lincoln, fifty miles west of San Antonio on the Río Seco; Fort Inge on the Leona, three miles south of Uvalde; Fort McIntosh, near Laredo; and Fort Duncan, near Eagle Pass.[17]

While Arnold's strategic position was excellent, his practical military position was hardly tenable. His company strength was credited at one officer and forty-two men, whereas the authorized strength was three and eighty-six. But his actual strength was far below either. In June, 1849, he had only twenty-five privates for duty and not another officer in his command, a force so small he was unable to maintain scouting parties. He asked for replacements from the cavalry depot at Carlisle Barracks, Pennsylvania, sarcastically remarking that he would like soldiers, not more recruits like those sent out the previous November with neither carbine nor saber training.[18] During the summer his position worsened. On September 1, with nineteen privates for building, scouting, and escorting at "this extreme frontier post," he wrote: "In case of difficulty with the Indians on this frontier I should be in rather a feeble condition."[19]

Truly, Arnold and his men were on the western rim, in an area seen by few white men before them. The first settlement had been Bird's Fort (later known as Birdville), established in 1840 by Colonel Jonathan Bird and about twenty Rangers as a northern defense for more southerly settlements. Near Bird's Fort delegates of Sam Houston signed a treaty with tribal chiefs setting a line of demarcation between the lands of white men and red. And in 1847 Johnson Station was placed on the map. Earlier even than Johnson, two trappers— Terrell and Lusk—reached into the Fort Worth area, the first white men to penetrate that particular section. At a spring that now is a lagoon in Botanic Garden they were captured by Indians and held prisoner for over a year.

[17] J. C. McConnell, *West Texas Frontier*, 67–72.
[18] Letter from Arnold to Maj. Gen. Roger Jones, Adj. Gen., June 15, 1849, NA, WDR, OAG, LR.
[19] Arnold to Jones, Sept. 1, 1849, NA, WDR, OAG, LR.

When the dragoons moved to the bluff to build their fort, they found a newcomer—Press Farmer, from Roan County, Tennessee—living in a tent on the present site of the Tarrant County courthouse with his wife, Jane, and their baby daughter, Susan Ann. Arnold and Farmer made a mutually advantageous arrangement whereby the Tennessean was named sutler, performing some of the duties that today are divided between post exchange and quartermaster. In the sutler's store he sold biscuits, button polish, perhaps a twist of Climax chewing tobacco, and other soldier necessities. Too, he contracted with settlers to furnish food for the men and forage for the animals. Being sutler made him the first merchant.

Because his command lacked a surgeon, Arnold contracted with Dr. J. M. Standifer, who had served troops north of Waco Village, as surgeon for Fort Worth, making him the first physician. The doctor brought his wife and three daughters to Johnson Station and built a home there, where four servants cared for the women during the week while he worked at the fort; he spent his week ends at Johnson Station.[20]

Being on the frontier as a soldier and bearing the colors of a nation progressing toward greatness were adventures. Living was made zestful by the danger attendant upon weekly patrols to the Red River and by other expeditions from the fort. Guard duty, the honeywagon detail, shining leather, polishing buttons, cleaning arms, jumping the ditch and bar, dismounted exercises, drills with musket and saber—all formed a routine that kept the men busy from dawn till dark. Yet garrison life was dull.

For an infraction of rigid army regulations, punishment was harsh, and Arnold was a commander adept at devising punishment to fit the crime. One time he sentenced a soldier, guilty of stealing a pig, to remain the entire day on the hot parade ground with the dead pig suspended from his neck.[21]

[20] Reminiscence of the former Julia Standifer in *Research Data, Fort Worth and Tarrant County* (Texas Writers Project), I, 116–17 (hereafter referred to as *Research Data*).

[21] Dr. Carroll M. Peak in *Research Data*, I, 198.

Adventure was compensation for the privation, hardship, and danger, since soldier pay was meager. The pay ranged from eight dollars a month for a private to sixty a month for a major, who also received four dollars for rations and two for servants. Arnold once wrote the War Department urging that he be given more than four dollars a month for rations because as post commander he was forced to entertain the many "Citizen Gentlemen" who were passing through the country.[22]

Some of the "Citizen Gentlemen" picked home sites and settled near the fort, while others were in the steady stream of transients who encouraged the establishment of civilian business enterprise. Henry Daggett, fresh from the Shelby County commotion—known as the War of the Regulators and Moderators—came with Archibald F. Leonard to open the first civilian store. Their store, placed in a live-oak grove northeast of the fort because army regulations forbade a civilian business within one mile of a military post, offered a temporary diversion for the soldiers. But the novelty of having a store wore off, and the only thing to look forward to was the weekly dragoon express bringing letters, newspapers, and parcels from the post office at Dallas. Later the mail came from Waco, which was the post office for both Forts Worth and Graham.

For the first few months Company F of the Second Dragoons, with Arnold as the only officer, constituted the garrison, until Washington responded to his appeals for reinforcements. On October 6, 1849, Company F of the Eighth Infantry, commanded by Captain Robert P. Maclay of Pennsylvania, who was to serve the Confederacy as a brigadier general, augmented the garrison. The infantry company's first lieutenant was James Longstreet, also destined for glory under the Stars and Bars, who happened to be on detached service in the north and did not rejoin his company while it was at Fort Worth. Maclay brought in thirty-nine foot soldiers

[22] Arnold to Maj. George Deas, Asst. Adj. Gen., 8th Mil. Dept., July 30, 1849, NA, WDR, OAG, LR.

General W. J. Worth

General W. S. Harney

and another officer, Second Lieutenant John Bold, a young South Carolinian. More new faces arrived on Christmas Day when Second Lieutenant Samuel H. Starr of the Second Dragoons rode in with eighteen recruits from Carlisle Barracks.[23] With the additional forces Arnold maintained patrols and escorts and completed the fort. Upon completion, the fort contained three sets of officers' quarters, two of clapboards and one of logs, each containing two rooms with a passage between; barracks, constructed of logs and puncheons with dirt floors and mud chimneys, for 120 men; a hospital and the adjutant's office, each of frame construction with a shingled roof and stone chimney; and a stable of split logs, roofed with clapboards.

Supplies were drawn from New Orleans through Houston, and hauled to Fort Worth at three dollars a hundred pounds. Two other roads, one to Austin and one to Shreveport, also led from the fort. There was little that the surrounding country could supply to the satisfaction of the troops except fresh beef, which was plentiful. Local flour was an inferior grade. "Cow pease" were substituted for beans. Hard soap was unobtainable, but in their big black wash kettles farmers made soft soap which they sold to the army at a price the quartermaster considered prohibitive.[24]

Nevertheless, the fact that some commodities could be had locally, less than a year after establishment of the fort, was evidence of the stability troops had lent the section and the settlement their presence encouraged. Even a lawyer, Charles Harper from New Hampshire, arrived to establish a practice.

Then the Texas Legislature decided to make a county of the land surrounding the fort, the dominant spirit in the formation of the new county being General Edward H. Tar-

[23] "Fort Worth, Texas," NA, WDR, OAG, Reservation File; Arnold to Jones, Oct. 6 and Dec. 27, 1849, NA, WDR, OAG, LR.

[24] *House Executive Document No. 2*, 32 Cong., 1 sess., 27–271; Starr to Maj. Gen. George Gibson, commissary general of subsistence, April 22, 1851, NA, WDR, Office of Quartermaster General.

rant, who represented Navarro and Limestone counties in the Third Legislature, meeting in 1849. An old Indian fighter and onetime member of the Texas Congress, Tarrant had a special fondness for the northern part of Navarro County, where he had eliminated a major Indian threat with a surprise attack upon an encampment on Village Creek near Fort Worth in 1841.

As the Third Legislature convened, he pointed to the growing population around Birdville, the establishment of Fort Worth, and the mushrooming of farms west of the fort as reason enough to add a new county to Texas' existing seventy-nine counties. Agreeing with Tarrant, Representative William M. Cochran of Dallas and Denton counties, a member of the committee on county boundaries, introduced on November 9, 1849, a bill creating an unnamed county from the northern portion of Navarro.

The next day the bill was amended to name the new county for Tarrant. On December 17, it was passed by the House and forwarded to the Senate, where passage was voted two days later. Next it went for signature to Governor George T. Wood, who was working feverishly in the frame capitol to clear his desk before the end of his term. The Governor signed the bill into law on December 20, 1849, and Tarrant County came into being. As an interim governing body, Vincent J. Hatton, W. R. Rogers, Johnson, Sanders Elliott, and a man named Little were appointed commissioners.[25]

Tarrant County was one of twenty-six carved from the original Peters Colony that was set aside for development when the Republic of Texas contracted in 1843 with Peters and Company to bring in at least 250 families a year, in return for every alternate section of land. With promotional zeal, Peters and Company advertised glittering promises of free land, riches, and contentment. To entice settlers, the company promised to build a cabin for each family. Most of the settlers thus attracted were farmers from Missouri, Illinois,

25 B. B. Paddock (ed.), *Northern and Western Texas*, I, 205.

Indiana, Kentucky, and Tennessee. In close little knots, settlements suggested points of origin—each named for the home country, such as Indiana Colony, Missouri Colony, and so forth.

Discontent rumbled through the colony within a few years when settlers learned that the Republic was granting 640 acres to family heads and 320 to single men, while Peters gave but half that. Discontent gave way to fury with another disclosure. The local manager for Peters, Henry O. Hedgecoke, was charged with trying to steal even the half-grants by entering slanderous remarks on titles which could be forfeited through moral turpitude. Angry settlers formed an "army" of about one hundred men, with John J. Good of Dallas at their head, and advanced on Hedgecoke's office at Stewardsville in Denton County. From him they wrested papers pertaining to the land and forced him and his daughter into flight. Not until 1853 was the title muddle cleared up by the legislature.[26]

Gradually the wilderness gave ground in the Fort Worth vicinity. Only a few months after the first dragoons arrived, a horseman rode over the county in 1850, taking the census and writing the names of the county's 664 inhabitants in a fine, formalized hand. Fort Worth's population was not listed separately. In April, 1850, the first sermon was preached at the fort, at Arnold's invitation, by Rev. John Allen Freeman, who four years earlier had helped establish the Lonesome Dove Baptist Church as the first church in the area.

Mrs. Arnold and the children arrived in the summer of 1850 from Washington, where they had wintered. Mrs. Arnold's piano and the Major's children playing on the parade ground were symbolic of the change taking place. Adolphus Gounant, a French refugee whose home was near the fort, taught music to the children in the commander's quarters. Kate, one of the Arnold children, had a pet antelope that was the delight of the youngsters. Sometimes her father mounted his white horse and galloped after the animal in

26 *Research Data*, I, 1371–81.

playful chase. Yet what happiness the Arnolds could wring from the cold and barren army life was spoiled when two of the younger children, Sophie and Willis, died at the fort.[27]

More and more as time went on, civilization warmed itself beside the fort. On August 5, 1850, the first county election was held to select officers, who would succeed the temporary officials appointed the preceding December, and to choose a county seat. Birdville, as the largest settlement in the county, was chosen. A ramshackle wooden building was the first courthouse. The first court held in Fort Worth was convened in November by Judge O. M. Roberts, of Tyler, later governor of Texas. Roberts, judge of the Fifth Judicial District, had exchanged districts for a time with Judge Bennett H. Martin, whose Ninth Judicial District embraced Tarrant County.[28]

Although civilians and civil government were becoming more important with each passing week, Fort Worth still was first and foremost an army post. Arnold's Company F and Maclay's Company F constituted the entire garrison until April 6, 1851, when the infantry was shifted to Fort Gates, leaving Arnold's company alone at the fort. An inspecting officer found it to be an inefficient company, composed of Germans who were "indifferent" riders and in need of instruction.[29]

On June 17, 1851, Arnold and his company rode away from Fort Worth, marching to Fort Graham. They were relieved by Companies F and H of the Eighth Infantry, under Captain J. V. Bomford, who was to become a brigadier general in the Federal Army during the Civil War. The infantrymen did not like what they found at the fort. A reporting officer called the officers' quarters miserable, the barracks scarcely habitable, the hospital "a mere shell." On January 8, 1852, Company F of the Second Dragoons returned to Fort

---

[27] Kate Arnold Parker, *loc. cit.; Research Data,* I, 100.

[28] *Fort Worth Star-Telegram,* Oct. 30, 1949, Merchandising Section, p. 16.

[29] Inspection Report of Col. Samuel Cooper, 1851, NA, WDR, OAG, LR.

Worth, freeing the infantry for duty elsewhere, and garrisoned the post until August 13, when Arnold again was relieved, this time by Brevet Major Hamilton W. Merrill and sixty-four troopers from Company B, Second Dragoons.[30]

With his company, Arnold moved to Fort Graham and violence. The post surgeon at Fort Graham was Dr. Josephus M. Steiner, with whom Arnold soon clashed. The two had no respect for each other and did not speak even at social gatherings.

Bad blood lay behind the enmity of Arnold and Steiner. Steiner detested the way Arnold handled his children. Once when a young lieutenant came to the fort to investigate the alleged sale of government horses for which proceeds had not been turned in by Arnold, Steiner helped him prepare the report. The investigation occurred while Arnold was in the field. Upon his return, the Major asked a noncommissioned officer about the doctor's action during the investigation, and then said: "Damn him, he is the man that made the report and is trying to disgrace me and my family. I will put him out of the way. He shall not live to give evidence against me."

On the evening of September 5, 1853, Steiner, while calling upon a sick officer, became engaged in a loud argument with drunken Lieutenant Bingham, whom he found there. Other officers rushed to the cabin, trying without success to quiet the two before Arnold should hear them. But Arnold, always the stern disciplinarian, heard the commotion. Barging into the cabin, he silenced the quarrel and ordered the participants to quarters. Before leaving, Steiner yelled furiously that he would kill Arnold if the Major tried to arrest him.

The next morning Arnold sent Lieutenant Richard Anderson to arrest both Steiner and Bingham. Angrily Steiner threw the arrest order on the floor and rushed out toward the commanding officer's quarters. Arnold was waiting in the passageway of his home. Steiner demanded to know why he had

[30] Bold's report of public buildings at Fort Worth, Oct. 5, 1851, NA, WDR, QMG; Fort Worth, Texas, *loc. cit.*

been placed under arrest. "Drunkenness and falsifying," answered Arnold. Steiner hotly replied that the Major was wrong and had insulted him. Gunfire followed. Eyewitnesses disagreed over who drew first. But it was agreed that Arnold fired first, missed Steiner with two bullets, and "burst a cap" on the third. Steiner put four bullets into Arnold, who fell in the passageway, dying within the quarter-hour.

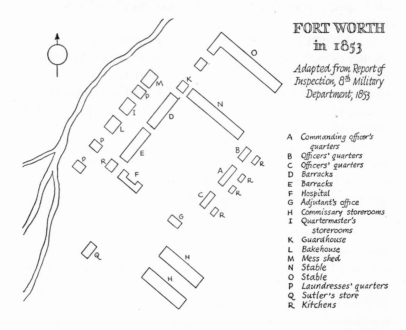

FORT WORTH
in 1853

Adapted from Report of Inspection, 8ᵗʰ Military Department, 1853

A   Commanding officer's
    quarters
B   Officers' quarters
C   Officers' quarters
D   Barracks
E   Barracks
F   Hospital
G   Adjutant's office
H   Commissary storerooms
I   Quartermaster's
    storerooms
K   Guardhouse
L   Bakehouse
M   Mess shed
N   Stable
O   Stable
P   Laundresses' quarters
Q   Sutler's store
R   Kitchens

The army wanted to try Steiner, insisting that it was a case for court-martial. Civilians, however, forcibly took Steiner from military custody, and kept him away from uniformed search parties. When the trial opened, the Hillsboro courthouse was surrounded by armed civilians, ready to fight the soldiers if necessary to protect Steiner. He was acquitted.[31]

In 1854, through the efforts of his old friend Gounant,

[31] A. Y. Kirkpatrick, *The Early Settlers Life in Texas and the Organization of Hill County,* 45–48; *Texas State Gazette,* Nov. 15, 1853; Rodenbough, *From Everglades to Canyon,* 453; Report of Lt. Richard Anderson in *Fort Worth Star-Telegram,* Oct. 30, 1949, Historical Section, p. 4.

Arnold's remains were removed to Fort Worth. Upon the night of arrival the casket rested in the smithy of Richard King. The next day he was reinterred in Fort Worth with Masonic rites, the first such funeral in the town's history.[32] Mrs. Arnold, who lived until 1894, was buried at Marlin.

After Arnold and his troopers had marched away from Fort Worth in 1852, Merrill and Company B garrisoned the post. On September 7, 1853, the fort was inspected by Lieutenant Colonel W. G. Freeman, who reported the command was well trained, mounted on sixty horses that were the finest in any Texas garrison, was armed with muskets, sabers, and Colt revolvers, and cultivated an eight-acre garden. For five cents a pound the post quartermaster bought local beef, which was issued as rations about once a week. Flour and meal were bought from near-by mills.[33]

During the years since Arnold and his jaunty dragoons first rode on to the bluff overhanging the Trinity, waves of settlers had shoved the frontier forever westward. As the line of settlement jabbed farther into the copper range side of West Texas, a new line of forts was built farther west. As Fort Worth had held the north of the first line, Fort Belknap, near the present town of Newcastle, held the north of the new line. Because of new conditions, orders went forward to Merrill to move his command to Fort Belknap, one hundred miles away, on September 17, 1853. Fort Worth was abandoned.

For four years it had served as a buffer between Indian and white man, playing a role of immeasurable importance in permitting the pioneer development of North Texas. But abandonment did not mean that the fort would fall into decay and ruin. For when the troops left, "Citizen Gentlemen" began converting the fort into a town.

[32] *Fort Worth Telegram*, March 15, 1903, p. 11.
[33] Report of Inspection of 8th Mil. Dept. 1853, NA, WDR, OAG, Miscellaneous File 282.

CHAPTER II

The Stolen Courthouse

FTER THE soldiers left, Fort Worth survived only because of the great migratory movement westward. Soon the crumbling army buildings received settlers from the old states who made them into homes and business establishments. The village that grew up around the old parade ground lay athwart the natural route to western Texas. Some of the newcomers were from Missouri and the old Northwest Territory, but most were from the Southern and border states. Most of them were of Colonial American descent, although a few were European immigrants.

They were of all types. Cultured, sophisticated men came to replace fortunes lost during evil times in the East. Untutored, brawny men came because they were dissatisfied with labor conditions in the East. Farmers came in quest of fertile fields. Some men came simply because they wanted the freedom of open sky and unfenced woodland, but all were attracted by the free land that Texas gave homesteaders.

The newcomers halted in Fort Worth for various reasons. Some had gone as near Indian country as they cared to, others found ready-made habitations in the old fort, and many visualized what would come eventually from a town at the crossroads of western trade.

Some of the soldiers remained in Fort Worth when their enlistments were up. Francis Knaar stayed on as a blacksmith, Louis Wetmore cut the first street through waist-high grass with a dragstone made of limestone, and Abe Harris lived out his life in the new community. The former soldiers joined forces with the civilians who had followed the lure of a bright, new country—men like Johnson, Farmer, and Henry Daggett. Following Henry Daggett came his brothers from East Texas, C. B. and Eph. The latter, known as Captain Daggett from his Mexican War days when he had captured Santa Anna's silver washbasin, realized that the town needed a hotel. As it happened, the biggest and best building was the old army stable. He took it over, converted it into a hotel, and later sold it to Lawrence Steele. For a dinner bell, Steele imported a large bell made in England in 1782, which now is in the Masonic Temple.

Julian Feild arrived from Harrison County and, with W. J. Masten, a Methodist preacher from Dallas, opened a general store in an abandoned army cabin. Coffee and sugar from Shreveport and salt from Grand Saline were hauled to their store in lumbering ox-wagons.

Soon after his arrival in 1854, Feild became ill. Because the community had no doctor, a young Dallas physician was called to treat him—Dr. Carroll M. Peak, recently arrived from Kentucky. When the townsmen persuaded Dr. Peak to establish his practice in Fort Worth, he moved into a former barracks with his bride. He became one of the forceful figures in the city's early history, and in 1858 he was joined by the town's second physician, Dr. W. P. Burts.

A young man just out of college, John Peter Smith, arrived from Kentucky as the first schoolteacher. Eventually he became wealthy, one of the first men to make his fortune in the new country. Among the homespun pioneers there appeared a polished and sophisticated planter, Colonel Nathaniel Terry, a former lieutenant governor of Alabama who moved west after he was defeated for governor. He built a plantation-style home in the Cold Spring vicinity north of the fort. He traveled in a rig, and his dress commonly included a beaver hat.

A young lawyer, J. C. Terrell, stopped in Fort Worth en

route to the California gold fields, and chanced upon an old schoolmate from Boonville, Missouri, Dabney C. Dade, also a lawyer. Terrell decided to remain. The two established one of the earliest law partnerships.

Immigrant wagons rolling west prompted a rivalry between Fort Worth and Dallas that would endure for a century. When the wagons bypassed Dallas, rumbling on toward Fort Worth, Dallas men began intercepting the settlers with tales of danger ahead. Fort Worth retaliated by having horsemen meet the wagon trains east of Dallas to lead them to Fort Worth along a road that skirted the rival town.

One of the families met by Dallas alarmists was that of Stephen Terry, who came in 1854 from Kentucky. The family stopped for the night in Dallas, where they received callers. "Indians will scalp you if you go to Fort Worth," the Terrys were told. These attempts to belittle the town angered Mrs. Terry. "I'd just as soon be scalped by Indians as stay here and be eaten up by mosquitoes," she retorted. "Besides, if wild Indians were thirty miles away, you wouldn't be here."[1] The Terrys left Dallas the next morning, settling a few days later in Fort Worth.

The favored transportation was a wagon pulled by oxen, in one or more spans. The animals were directed by a bullwhacker, who strode beside the team with a four-foot length of hickory in his hand to whack the oxen's rumps now and then to goad them forward. He might be wearing a canvas overcoat painted on the outside to break the chill winds, a broad-brimmed black hat, and high boots. The woman in the wagon might be dressed in a plain gingham dress buttoned down the front for easier access to her breast at the baby's mealtime.

Commercial passenger transportation was soon available. In response to demands from men wanting transportation to the gold fields, the Southern Pacific mail route opened a stage

[1] Mrs. Elizabeth Terry Chapman, *Fort Worth Star-Telegram*, Oct. 30, 1949, Automobile Section, p. 2.

line from St. Louis to San Francisco on a route that passed near Fort Worth.[2]

The first homes were chinked, single-room log cabins with two doors and one or two small windows. Some roofs were thatched, others sodded, and others covered by split logs. The pioneer housewife cooked in the one fireplace that also provided the only heat against bone-chilling northers whistling across the prairies. She poked a round iron hook above the flame tips to lift thick lids from metal pots steaming with food.

The one room was the center of life. There the family slept, worked, cooked, ate, and played. Meals were taken from a roughhewn table. Beds were lowered from the ceiling or the wall. A spinning wheel and sometimes a piano stood on the earthen floor. In bad weather the pioneer man joined his family before the fire to patch harness or helped his wife with the candlemaking. Sometimes the itinerant shoemaker sat beside the hearth, making footwear for the family from home-tanned leather and shoestrings from rawhide. Other clothing was rough and homemade, too. Women carded wool, spun linsey, wove their own fabrics, and colored them with dyes made from herbs, roots, and the bark of the bois d'arc tree. A woman could consider herself dressed up if she wore a cameo pin on a dotted swiss or black alpaca dress.[3]

Corn and wheat were ground into meal and flour in a hollowed log by means of a pestle suspended from a pliant sapling.[4] More frequently the grain was taken to a custom mill for grinding. The settlers often got fifty bushels of wheat to the acre on five or six acres, cut the grain with a cradle, and tramped and fanned it out. Then once or twice a year they made a week's trip to Dallas to have it ground, coming home with enough flour to last for many weeks. Game and half-wild hogs supplied meat. When a beef was killed, a rare event, a

2 B. B. Paddock (ed.), *Fort Worth and the Texas Northwest*, II, 834.
3 *Research Data*, I, 203–205.
4 *Ibid.*, I, 128–30.

quarter would be swung up to the limb of a tree so that it would be beyond the reach of wild animals and would remain sweet for weeks. Sugar was almost unknown; sorghum molasses was the usual sweetener.[5]

Life was full of chores, burdens, and dangers. West of Fort Worth lived a man named Malloy and his two motherless children, aged five and seven. Suddenly he became seriously ill, and, realizing that he would probably die during the night, he called the two children to his bedside. He told them what might happen, and cautioned them to remain in the house until sunup because of the wolves that were abroad at night. The next morning, he said, they were to get Uncle Johnny Kinder, who lived near by. Malloy did die, and the children followed his instructions. Kinder justified his faith in him and saw to it that he received decent burial and that his children were provided for.

A favorite among the settlers, Kinder was renowned for his marksmanship with a rifle. Once when he was standing on the Fort Worth parade ground, talking with the soldiers, an officer began to tease him about his shooting and suggested that he shoot a wing feather from a buzzard circling overhead. Uncle Johnny raised his rifle, aimed, and fired. A feather drifted earthward. Saying he did not want to leave the buzzard overbalanced, he fired again. A feather from the other wing floated into the air.[6]

After a time there were enough people in the vicinity to warrant the opening of the trade-ways to East Texas, where lumber was obtained for the houses that were beginning to replace the log cabins. Typical of frontier construction, the combination home and law office built by Terrell and Dade was a single-story building of two rooms, with a fireplace in each. One room was for cooking and sleeping, the other for a law office. An open passageway, sometimes called a dog-trot, between the rooms was characteristic of early construc-

[5] Paddock (ed.), *Northern and Western Texas,* I, 205.
[6] *Research Data,* I, 125 and 310.

tion. In it were stored saddles, fishing tackle, and other gear.[7] Housebuilding was occasion for a house-raising, where neighbors pooled their efforts to erect a house in a day. At house-raisings whisky was always in demand, but the favorite refreshment consisted of cider and gingerbread, when cider was available.

Otherwise the settlers had little time for entertainment. But when an opportunity arose, they made the most of it. Music, furnished by piano, fiddle, guitar, and banjo, was the principal diversion. Dancing was infrequent, but families and sometimes their neighbors would gather in the evening quiet to hear a piano or tap their toes in time with a fiddler swaying to the nostalgic tunes sawed from a coveted instrument.

The favorite fiddler was Uncle Jack Durrett, a courtly old fellow who came west after inheriting and spending two fortunes. Uncle Jack loved talking, fishing, and playing old mountain airs like "Dilcy Hawkins." In the evening the men often congregated on the square to listen to his tunes.

The first piano was brought to Fort Worth by Mrs. Arnold when she joined the Major in 1850. Another came a few years later with the family of Dr. M. L. Woods when they built a home in White Settlement, near Fort Worth. At first the Indians were afraid of the piano, certain that the keys were the teeth of a wild animal that made strange noises. Gradually, however, they came to like the sounds, and each trip to town found them bolder. Finally, they would enter the house, motion toward the piano, and say, "Peck, gals, peck." Another early piano was brought by Mr. and Mrs. John A. Mitchell from Tennessee in 1856.[8]

To meet the demand for liquid refreshment, Noel Burton in the early fifties opened the first saloon, a package store where he prohibited drinking on the premises and limited sales to one pint to a customer.

[7] J. C. Terrell, *Reminiscences of the Early Days of Fort Worth*, quoted in *Research Data*, I, 273–75.

[8] *Research Data*, I, 124, 304–305.

By the sixties he had been supplanted by Ed Terrell, who was operating the First and Last Chance Saloon, a crackerbox building one block west of today's courthouse on Weatherford Street, then the east-west-road. The First and Last Chance consisted of a small, dingy room with a few shelves on the west wall for whisky, peach brandy, gin, and bitters. On the plain, varnished bar stood a wooden pail filled with water for those who liked a chaser. Along the west wall was a bench where customers lounged and, in the wintertime, absorbed some of the warmth from a box stove in the center while listening to Uncle Jack or Jess Ferguson fiddle. The First and Last Chance after a time had competition in Tom Prindle's Saloon and the taproom of Steele's Tavern. "Hospitality was only thirty cents a gallon, with a corn stopper."[9]

Politics also afforded a welcome chance for the outlanders to come together and share in the excitement of a good stump debate. Fort Worth first experienced an important political rally on July 4, 1857, when Sam Houston, then serving as United States senator, and Hardin Runnels arrived in the course of their respective campaigns for governor.

Houston was the house guest of Colonel Terry, who would in a few years, ironically enough, be a member of the state convention which would depose Houston as governor and declare Texas free of the federal compact. Runnels was the guest of Johnson at Johnson Station. On the night before the barbecue for the two candidates, a wagonload of watermelons was placed in the chill waters of Cold Spring. Next morning servants barbecued beef, pork, and chickens, and piled food on improvised tables.

At the speaking, Terry introduced Houston and Johnson presented Runnels. Runnels was running as a Democrat, and at that time was leading the forces which called for a showdown with the North even if it meant secession. Houston, who once had bolted to the Know-Nothings and then bolted again, was in the field as an independent, insisting upon Union

[9] *Ibid.*, I, 56, 124, 276, 307.

solidarity. Each candidate was cheered lustily by his follow-
ers. Later a grand tournament was held for men and women
riders, who speared hoops suspended from a wire.[10]

The need for companionship and formal association
brought ten Masons together on a warm April evening in
1854 to organize the first Blue Lodge. John M. Crockett came
from Dallas to preside at the first meeting, held in Feild's
small store. Feild, whose name is perpetuated in another
lodge, was installed as worshipful master. Later, on April 21,
the first stated meeting of this initial group, Lodge No. 148,
was held. In 1857 the first Masonic hall was built—a boxlike
structure at East Belknap and Grove. The Masons met upstairs, making the lower floor available for school and church.

Organized religion was slow in taking root. Ordinarily,
when a settler moved in, he had no close neighbors and was
too far away from a church to attend services. Consequently
the family received religious instruction beside the hearth.
As more settlers arrived, they built their homes as close as
possible to the first families. Out of these loosely knit com-
munities came men and women of like faith who grasped
at the opportunity of meeting for worship.

In first one home and then another they met, an elder
layman directing the services. As the country grew, the circuit
rider found the community and placed it on his regular round,
going from home to home to conduct services. After the home
as a place of worship came the brush arbor. As the number
of persons in a community increased, small churches were
built in the country. At these country churches a full guard
of men took post outside to protect the worshippers against
the threat of lurking Indians. Generally, organized religion
fared better in the rural areas than in Fort Worth.

Because of its sparse population, by the mid-sixties Fort
Worth had only small congregations of Disciples of Christ,
Methodists, Episcopalians, and Baptists. Only two places
were available for services—the Masonic Hall and a small con-

[10] *Ibid.*, I, 207.

crete building at Belknap and Lamar streets, the latter a crude structure with a rough pulpit and hard cottonwood slabs for pews. The two buildings were used by all denominations fortunate enough to find a preacher.[11]

The first denominational church was organized in the summer of 1855 by the Reverend A. M. Dean, a Disciples of Christ minister who had a farm some distance away. He was shocking grain in Colonel Terry's fields near Fort Worth when several of the Disciples invited him to preach in the village. Shortly afterwards he founded the First Christian Church,[12] services being held in the home of Dr. Peak until a concrete building was constructed at Belknap and Lamar streets, about 1857. The congregation soon outgrew the new building, however, and began meeting in the Masonic Hall. After Dean left, the pulpit was filled by a succession of early-day preachers. One was B. F. Hall, a Collin County dentist who preached when not pulling teeth. Another was Dr. Mansell Mathews, a nomadic preacher who with his family of forty and their flocks and herds, annually trekked north and south following the grass.

In the mid-fifties a Methodist society functioned, served by Rev. Lewis J. Wright and Rev. William Bates, circuit riders from Denton County. Rev. Walter South knew the Fort Worth group as part of the Grapevine Mission prior to 1855, the year that Rev. John W. Chalk preached the first sermon in the Methodist church. Within a year the church was considered strong enough for formal recognition. At the Texas Conference at Gonzales in 1856, the Fort Worth District was created, with Rev. James G. Johnson as presiding elder and Rev. Fountain P. Ray in charge of the Fort Worth Mission. For several years services were held in the Masonic Hall.

Episcopal services began in 1850, when the Rt. Rev. Alexander Gregg, Bishop of Texas, rode in from South Texas, dismounted, and held a service. For the next twelve years

[11] *Ibid.*, I., 216.
[12] *Ibid.*, I, 199.

Middleton Tate Johnson,
who helped select the site of Fort Worth

Press Farmer, the army sutler

itinerant priests visited the distant village, and then Rev. Thompson L. Smith commenced regular services.

Just as the Methodist church first sprang from a rural church, so did the Baptist. Indeed, the first Baptist church came from the first Christian outpost ever planted in the county. In 1844 all the members of a small Baptist church in southern Missouri decided to migrate to Texas. Packing their wagons with their belongings and the records of their church, they headed southwest toward the brave new Republic. Some were turned back by the hazards of travel, but others stuck to their purpose, arriving late in the year in southern Denton County, near the present Tarrant County line.

After a few months James Gibson and James Halford visited their old home in Missouri with tales of Texas that captured the imagination of a young divine, John A. Freeman, who forthwith started for Texas. He arrived in the Denton County community about the same time as Rev. Joshua Hodges, an experienced preacher whose gospel fires were as bright as young Freeman's.

A Sabbath service was arranged in Gibson's home. First Hodges and then Freeman preached. So impressed was the audience that Freeman alternated with Hodges as preacher when regular services began. The fireside services led in time to a meeting in Charles Throop's log cabin on the north side of Denton Creek, where twelve Baptists presented letters and formed the Lonesome Dove Church. Some accounts claim that the name chosen was the same as that of the church left behind in Missouri, others that it was chosen because this was thought to be the first Protestant church established west of Waco, without another between it and the Pacific. On Sunday, July 19, 1846, Freeman was ordained in the home of James Halford. The congregation decided to build a church, choosing a site several miles to the south, near Grapevine, in Tarrant County. There the church was built the next year with Freeman and David Myers as copastors.

As the countryside became more thickly populated, members in areas comparatively remote from the church petitioned for separation. The elders granted these requests, and additional churches came into being with some regularity. On the third Sunday in June, 1850, the Lonesome Dove Church dismissed several members, granting them the privilege of establishing a new church at the head of Bear Creek. Freeman, Myers and J. Fyke then formed the Mount Gilead Baptist Church in northeastern Tarrant County. Mount Gilead was the first church actually organized in the county— although Lonesome Dove had been the first in the county, it had been organized in Denton County. Both churches were still active in 1953. One of the early missionaries was Noah T. Byars, in whose blacksmith shop at Washington-on-the-Brazos the Texas Declaration of Independence had been signed in 1836. He made his home near Birdville as a Baptist missionary.

Despite fruitful labors in the rural areas, the peripatetic Baptists did not establish a church in Fort Worth until the sixties. The first is believed to have been started in 1867 by Rev. W. W. Mitchell and A. Fitzgerald. At any rate, the church was active a year later, for in 1868 the Fort Worth group petitioned for membership in the West Fork Baptist Association.[13] Other Protestants, Roman Catholics, and Jews were to make their appearance later.

Commerce began to sputter like a wood fire coming to life. Evacuation of the fort in 1853 had allowed Daggett, then in complete control of the store he had started with Leonard, to move his establishment to the edge of the parade ground that had become the public square. Then came Feild and Masten with their store. There was not a great deal of business for these early stores. The settlers grew almost all of the food they ate and supplied most of their own clothing. But they did depend upon the stores for staple groceries and for

[13] D. D. Tidwell, "A History of the West Fork Association" (Th. D. dissertation, Southwestern Baptist Theological Seminary, 1940), 5–104.

hardware such as hammers, picks, and plows. For children the stores had chunks of solidified sugar. Later there was an abundance of red flannel for homemade underclothing.[14]

With wagon transportation subject to long delays because of bad weather, the supply of coffee, sugar, and other staples would sometimes be exhausted, and until a wagoner could make the long trip to Shreveport or Houston over the crude roads, the settlers did without. The wagoner's long-awaited return was the signal for joyous shouting and for a happy celebration when the wagons were unloaded. Looking for sales, enterprising eastern merchants came to the frontier, as did the Arkansas apple peddler who lashed a supple branch, topped by an apple, to his wagon. Waving in the air, the apple advertised his wares.[15]

Each season wagons were loaded with greasy, acrid wool sheared from the hundreds of sheep which munched grass on the unfenced plain west of Fort Worth. The fleece was taken to the wool markets in Jefferson and Houston to be exchanged for the rare money that the settlers saw.

Money was scarce. Most purchasing was done by barter, when "trading" meant precisely that. For example, Mrs. Elizabeth Teague, a widow, exchanged homespun clothing for the groceries on the rough board shelves of Daggett's store.

The first shoe shop was added about 1858, when Steve, a freedman, began mending and making shoes on a wooden block. Eventually, ready-made shoes became available in the stores. Shoes for boys frequently had shiny brass toes.[16]

By 1860, E. M. Daggett and Charles Turner had founded a store. And M. J. Brinson, with his partner J. A. Slaughter, had built the town's first two-story building, a store on the southwest corner of the square.

The first industry, and still one of the city's greatest, was milling. In 1856, Feild, David Mauck, and R. S. Man built

---

[14] *Research Data,* I, 120.
[15] *Ibid.,* I, 205.
[16] *Ibid.,* I, 120.

a grist-mill a few hundred yards west of the confluence of the Clear and West Forks of the Trinity. Made of cottonwood lumber and painted white, their mill was designed to manufacture flour from the wagonloads of wheat that came in from neighboring farms, but the mill was abandoned when the erratic Trinity's water supply failed. To be nearer the center of the wheat supply, Feild and Man three years later built another mill at what is now Mansfield, named for the two men, although the spelling of Feild was changed in the town name. Famous over the breadth of Texas, their mill filled large government contracts, loading wagon trains that came from as far away as the Río Grande.[17] Other early mills were on the Clear Fork near what is now Botanic Garden and near the E. M. Daggett School on the South Side.

For the young man just out of college and without any school or home ties, the place to go was the open west. Such a man was John Peter Smith. Twenty-two years old, with a new college diploma and no responsibilities, he left his Kentucky home in November, 1853. When he arrived in Dallas, a muddy little village that had grown up as a trading post, Smith was not at all impressed. Moving on, he reached Fort Worth in December, 1853, saying later, "It seemed to me that I had never beheld a more beautiful spot. Here I resolved to make my home."[18]

But to make a home, he had to make a living. He had no particular trade or craft by which he could justify his existence, but he did have a good education. His cousin and guardian, W. H. Garnett, had given him the best that the schools in Owen County, Kentucky, could provide and then had sent him to Franklin College in Indiana and later to Bethany College in Virginia (now West Virginia), where he was graduated in July, 1853, with honors in ancient languages and mathematics.[19]

[17] Julian Feild obituary, *Fort Worth Register*, Sept. 10, 1897.
[18] John Peter Smith in *Research Data*, I, 110.
[19] John Peter Smith obituary, *Fort Worth Register*, April 12, 1901.

Resolving to try his hand at teaching, Smith obtained use of the old army hospital building, which still had a good clapboard roof, and opened the first school in January, 1854, at a time when the surrounding prairie was dotted nightly by the campfires of Caddos, Wacos, and other Indian tribes.

His career as the first school teacher was short, ill health forcing him to give up the confining indoor labor. Furthermore, he had not found the work congenial. Smith then bowed out of the profession. But he had established the first school, helped to make the populace education-conscious, and would in a few years lead in founding a permanent public school system.

For a time after Smith closed his school, children were educated in their homes by wandering tutors, who stayed at first one home and then another. This method was unsatisfactory, finally leading to community action in 1856 for the establishment of the Male and Female schools. By referendum, A. D. Johnson, Brinson, Thomas O. Moody, William Mosely, Feild, and Dr. Peak were named to a board of trustees to supervise the schools. They brought in a Mrs. Mitchell to teach the girls and Professor M. D. Kennedy to teach the boys. The tuition for boys in the primary grades for ten months was sixteen dollars, and for those in the senior grades, twenty-four dollars. Parents paid sixteen dollars for girls in the junior class, twenty-four dollars for higher English, and thirty dollars for seniors.[20]

The early school, a crude structure with rough seats, was heated by a box stove. "Each morning after books were called, the principal would name four students whose duty it was to bring in the wood and water for the day. We had to go down to the Trinity River and break the ice, fill the pail, and climb the steep bluff."[21]

The Male and Female schools were succeeded by those taught by Mrs. Mary Armistead in 1859 and by Professor J. T.

[20] *Research Data*, I, 211–12.
[21] *Ibid.*, I, 52.

Turner, who in 1861 opened a school in a concrete building on West Belknap Street. At that time a Professor Hudson was teaching in the Masonic Institute, on the lower floor of Masonic Hall.

After a mere three years as a completely civilian community, Fort Worth in 1856 had become such an active locality, although still nothing more than a frontier village, that the townsmen felt it should replace Birdville as the seat of justice for Tarrant County. Their feeling crystallized into a determination to have the county seat transferred to their town, which, without the prestige of some institution such as a courthouse, could not be assured of permanency. Since Fort Worth by this time had rivaled and was competing with Birdville, the townspeople thought that Fort Worth was fast becoming the more important of the two.

However, Fort Worth was on the ragged edge of uncertainty. With fortuitous circumstance it probably could develop into one of the important towns of North Texas. Yet without proper impetus it could wither away as just another isolated village. With an attitude of victory at any cost, the men of Fort Worth set out to effect the change.

A delegation from Fort Worth convinced the legislature that a special election should be called to decide the issue of transferring the county seat. The legislature, in which Tarrant County was represented by Isaac Parker of Birdville, set the election for November, 1856. The election meant now or never for each town.

On election day the Fort Worth square was active with excited men. In front of the two mercantile stores stood barrels of whisky, complete with dippers, to attract men to Fort Worth, where they were more likely to vote for Fort Worth. For those who liked their whisky sweetened, a bucket of sugar was considerately provided beside each barrel. A fun-loving Irishman reeled around the square chanting: "Fort Worth water tastes like whisky, Fort Worth salt tastes like sugar. Hurrah for Fort Worth!" Except for the whisky, the activity and scenes were duplicated in Birdville. Birdville leaders had cached their barrel in a live-oak grove. In the darkness of election eve, a band of Fort Worth men had stolen into the grove and siphoned the whisky into their own barrel, leaving Birdville without a lure for voters.

As the voters from the county began straggling to the polls, a counting house was set up in Dr. Peak's office to keep a constant tab on the votes cast at Fort Worth, Birdville, and Johnson Station. When the tally seemed to be unfavorable, riders were sent to hurry friendly voters to the polls. However, Fort Worth trailed badly until Sam Woody rode in from another county. In later years Woody told this story:

> I had until a short time prior been a citizen of Tarrant County, but when the election came off I was living in Wise County. Around me were fourteen other settlers, and on the day of the election I got them together and started down to Fort Worth to help my former fellow citizens get what they wanted.
>
> There were three polling places in the county and each faction had guards stationed to prevent any frauds. Barrels of whisky with heads knocked out stood in front of every building. Buckets of sugar were open for those who did not take their liquor straight. All conditions were favorable for free and frequent drinking. We, from Wise County, did not belong to the "anti" crowd, and under those inviting circumstances we wanted to drink worse than at any time of our lives. But I corralled my lads, and said to them: "Boys, we've got to stay sober til this election is over. I must vote every one of you, so we must hold in til we get home. It is a penitentiary offense, and if they find us defrauding the ballot we will have to leave home for several years."
>
> I knew that would keep them in line, and it did, so that we were the soberest lot in Fort Worth that day. The Birdville people never once suspected that I did not belong to Tarrant County, and supposed that my fourteen companions were neighbors from over in the western part of the county. We never opened our heads about our intentions until late in the afternoon, when I thought it was about time to act.

I led the way to the polls, followed by my supporters, and pretending to be in a great hurry, I pushed forward to the judges, saying, "Come on boys, let's vote, for we've got a long way to go, and must get home before dark." They never challenged one of us, and there were fifteen votes for Fort Worth that came from Wise County.

As Fort Worth won the election by only seven votes, it was due to my help that the courthouse now stands in that city, and Fort Worth certainly owes me a free pass.

Some of my crowd loved whisky awful, and it was the hardest work of my life to keep them away from those tempting barrels that offered refreshment to whomsoever would come and drink.

When the results of the vote gave the courthouse to Fort Worth the Birdville people swore we had voted every man as far west as the Río Grande, and by a careful canvass they were not able to find as many citizens in the entire county as that day had recorded their ballots at the three polling places.[22]

A riotous celebration, the first and biggest that Fort Worth had ever known, took place election night. Huge bonfires were lighted, quantities of whisky were consumed, and jubilant men made jubilant speeches. Escorted by torchbearing merrymakers, a wagon was driven to Birdville and there loaded with record books, antiquated desks, cane-bottom chairs, and yellowed law books, all of which were hauled away in a serpentine torchlight parade while glum Birdville residents watched.[23]

Birdville decayed and her people became embittered as their stores wanted for business, as Court Monday became a mockery. Soon bitterness turned to enmity, and enmity to gunfire. Some time after the election, a barbecue was held at Cold Spring by a "mixed" crowd, which then meant mixed of Fort Worth and Birdville people. At the barbecue, Hiram Calloway and A. Y. Fowler argued, and Calloway pushed

---

[22] Paddock (ed.), *Northern and Western Texas,* I, 205–206.
[23] *Research Data,* I, 222.

Fowler over a cliff. Fowler's arm was broken. Because Sheriff John B. York had befriended Calloway that day, antagonism developed between the sheriff and Fowler. One day York and Fowler met near the wooden courthouse on the square, and, as if by signal, both men drew and fired. Both died. Another time, Jack Brinson, George Slauter, and Tom Johnson, Fort Worth supporters, became involved in an argument with a man named Tucker, who was slain. The three were tried in Fort Worth and acquitted.[24]

A Birdville killing ended the most violent feud, that of the county's first two editors: John J. Courtenay, who established the Birdville *Western Express* in 1855 as the county's first paper, and A. G. Walker, who arrived in 1857 with the Birdville *Union*.[25] Courtenay was a strong Secessionist who also believed that Fort Worth should be the county seat. Walker was a fiery Union man who believed with equal fervor in Birdville. Tempers rose as the two editors campaigned for their beliefs. It was the day of personal journalism when vicious personal attack against competing editors was common. One day the two editors came face to face on the street in Birdville. All of their rancor boiled to the surface. Hands grabbed for pocket pistols. Walker killed Courtenay.

Doggedly refusing to capitulate on the county-seat question, Walker continued the political battle. As state senator in the Seventh and Eighth Legislatures, he sought to invalidate the 1856 election, claiming that the total male population of the county could not be reconciled with the total vote. His surprise move was discovered in Austin by M. T. Johnson, who excitedly reported it to Smith and Terrell, just arrived in the capital to attend a masquerade. Among them the three managed to soften Walker's attack, which was unleashed before a joint committee.[26] As a compromise the committee

[24] *Fort Worth Star-Telegram*, Dec. 15, 1912, Part Five, p. 3.
[25] "A History of the Early Newspapers of Texas," by Anthony Banning Norton, incorporated in F. B. Baillio's *A History of the Texas Press Association*, 352.
[26] Terrell, *Reminiscences of the Early Days of Fort Worth*, 14.

called for another election, this one to choose among Fort Worth, Birdville, and a point in the exact center of the county.

Fort Worth leaders prepared busily for their campaign to retain the courthouse. A determining stroke of strategy was the promise by thirty-eight men to pay, from their own pockets, the cost of building a permanent courthouse if Fort Worth remained the county seat. A bond guaranteeing the cost of construction without expense to the taxpayers was signed by the following citizens: David Mauck, Thomas O. Moody, Lawrence Steele, M. T. Johnson, Julian Feild, E. M. Daggett, M. J. Brinson, A. C. Coleman, John Kidder, Joe Purvis, George Kidder, J. S. Henley, J. W. Chapman, Press Farmer, J. P. Loving, L. J. Edwards, Francis Knaar, W. D. Connor, J. W. Connor, J. N. Petty, W. A. Henderson, B. P. Ayres, Abe Harris, A. G. Davenport, A. D. Johnson, Seabourne Gilmore, William Mosely, W. M. Robinson, A. Gounant, Nathaniel Terry, W. B. Tucker, E. Wilburn, Paul Isbell, G. T. Petty, P. E. Coleman, C. M. Peak, W. L. Brazendine, and Jack Inman.[27]

When at length the election was held, the *Dallas Herald* of April 18, 1860, reported that Fort Worth received 548 votes; the center, 301; and Birdville, 4.[28] With the county-seat controversy finally settled, the backers of the courthouse project made good their word, and Mauck began building the structure, which was to be of stone and roofed with tin, near the main entrance of the present courthouse.

Fort Worth was incontestably the county seat, but in all likelihood it never would have been if the town's leaders had not taken the initiative four years earlier. Probably in no year other than 1856 could Fort Worth have won the election upon the initial presentation of the issue. In 1856, Birdville had a slight advantage in population, and had it remained the county seat, it probably would have attracted in the years ahead the population that made Fort Worth. With the in-

[27] Paddock (ed.), *Fort Worth and the Texas Northwest,* II, 837.
[28] *Ibid.,* I, 192.

creased population it could easily have defeated any efforts to move the courthouse. Birdville, too, in all likelihood would have drawn the county loyalty that supported Fort Worth in 1860.

CHAPTER III

War and Evil Days

S THE eighteen fifties drew to a close, publication of the town's first newspaper was begun by a patrician editor destined for national political fame. He was Anthony Banning Norton, whose chauvinism was looked upon as an eccentricity that caused him to wear shoulder-length hair and a billowing beard.

When he rode into Fort Worth beside an ox-drawn wagon loaded with a three-legged Washington press and boxes of type to establish the *Fort Worth Chief* in 1859, he was recognized as the editor of the *Austin Intelligencer*, a crony of Governor Sam Houston, and a man whose political views were those of a hostile minority. He was known as a Whig and would later be called a Radical.

Because of the pressure of politics and his several publishing ventures elsewhere, he could not remain long in Fort Worth. Returning to Austin where he was corresponding editor of the *Chief*, he left Editor George Smith to run a family newspaper "devoted to agriculture, stock raising, education, politics, literature, art, science, amusement, temperance, internal and social improvement, and general intelligence."[1]

Norton was born in Mount Vernon, Ohio, on May 15, 1821, and was educated at Kenyon College, where he was a classmate of Rutherford B. Hayes, who was to become the nineteenth president of the United States. At nineteen Norton

[1] *Fort Worth Chief,* March 7, 1860, copy from courthouse cornerstone, quoted in *Fort Worth Democrat,* Nov. 3, 1876.

was admitted to the Ohio bar and waded into politics, where suavity and a rich, clear voice made him an advocate worthy of any candidate.

The candidate who drew Norton's loyalty was Henry Clay, to whom he became intensely devoted and in whose behalf he stumped Ohio during a presidential campaign. In the course of that campaign Norton met one day on the platform with Caleb J. McNulty, Democratic candidate for Congress, who also was speaking in behalf of James K. Polk's candidacy for the White House. McNulty was an older man who derided his youthful antagonist by saying, "A smooth-faced youth had better tarry at Jericho and grow a beard before he essays to teach men their political rights." In retaliation, Norton strode to the front of the platform. Before God and man he swore by the beard that wasn't that he would neither shave nor have his hair cut until Clay was elected president.

After Polk defeated Clay in 1844, the disheartened Norton announced that "the country might be going to hell but I'm going to Texas." He arrived in Texas in 1848, proceeding to Austin, where in 1850 he bought part of the *Intelligencer.* Though far removed from the scenes of the Polk-Clay campaign, Norton maintained his allegiance to Clay, for the rest of his life keeping the vow about beard and hair. With Norton when he came to Fort Worth was his cherished possession—an ash walking cane with a silver-dollar head given him by a grateful Clay.

When Houston was elected governor in 1859, Norton was appointed adjutant general, counseling with and helping Houston in the vain battle against the flaming tempers that were taking Texas down the road to renunciation of the federal compact. By then Norton's hair and beard had grown long, giving him a patrician air that was to catapult him into national political attention.

At the Baltimore convention of the Constitutional Union party in 1860, Norton rose to his feet, bellowing Houston's name in nomination for the presidency. All eyes focused on

47

the six-footer with flowing mane who held the ash walking cane aloft as he thundered his arguments. The curiosity led to national attention. Beaten at Baltimore when the convention rejected Houston, Norton returned to Austin, from which place he directed the *Fort Worth Chief* by mail, bringing more and more censure upon himself for his political attitudes. A man with Norton's views could not have picked a more inauspicious time for the publication of a newspaper in Fort Worth—in the light of the mounting tide of sentiment against Northern rule and in favor of states' rights.

The trend of public feeling brought uneasiness to Fort Worth. With construction of a permanent courthouse beginning, good people taking up their homes in the neighborhood, a newspaper publishing weekly, and the Indians friendly, peace and tranquility had been anticipated until the rumblings of civil war disturbed the serene Trinity valley.

Abolition of slavery was not in itself a sufficiently direct threat to anger Fort Worth residents, since the most prominent slaveowner was Terry, and he had but thirty-six blacks on his plantation. But the majority of settlers had come from the slaveowning society of the Southern and Border states.

Already stimulated by the political arguments, Fort Worth was enraged when two Northerners were implicated in an alleged abolitionist effort to incite a slave revolt in the summer of 1860. As strangers who came without recommendation and without a demonstrated intent to settle, Rev. Anthony Buley and a man named Crawford were suspect from the beginning. Their visit coincided with a mysterious fire in the business district and with fires elsewhere in the state. Then Ned, a slave belonging to the Purvis family, told his master that the Northerners had urged the city's few Negroes to revolt. Crawford was hanged forthwith. His gallows was a huge pecan tree, situated about three hundred yards west of the present intersection of White Settlement Road and Northwest Highway, a favorite spot for hangings.

Buley, a Methodist minister, had returned to Springfield,

Missouri, in the meantime. Shortly after Buley had left, Paul Isbell and George Grant found a letter, addressed to Buley, on Grant's farm six miles west of Fort Worth. Signed by one W. A. Bailey, a Republican, and dated Denton County, July 3, 1860, the letter informed Buley that the "Mystic Red" was progressing throughout Texas. The letter was construed to mean abolitionist incendiaries had touched the torch to buildings in Fort Worth and to others in Texas. On a warrant from Fort Worth, Buley was arrested and returned to Texas on a charge of "implication in a nefarious plot to poison wells, fire towns and residences, and in the midst of conflagration and death, to run off with the slaves." When Buley reached Fort Worth, a mob formed on September 13, 1860, and hanged him from the Crawford tree.

The two men were held in such hatred that neither was ever given the dignity of burial. Suspended from rotting ropes, their bodies became skeletons hanging in the breeze. Subsequently, the skeletons were pitched atop a Fort Worth store.[2]

Two days before Buley was hanged, a mass meeting was called to consider the implications of the affair and take counsel on the action to be pursued. With Robert Galaspie in the chair, the letter from Bailey was read, along with Isbell's sworn statement of finding it. In adopting a resolution that blamed incendiarism, murder, and other crimes on Black Republicans, the men present agreed that society must act without law to protect itself, and that every Black Republican in Texas must be "exterminated" by prompt hanging.[3]

The intense feeling turned against Editor Norton, whose hanging was recommended by a grand jury in Weatherford. He quickly disposed of the *Chief* before the month was out, selling it to Captain Hamner, who was commencing publication of a Secessionist paper in Gainesville, *The White Man*. In later years Norton said that "the hostility of the people,

---

[2] Charles Ellis Mitchell in *Research Data*, V, 2000–VI, 2010.
[3] *Austin State Gazette*, Sept. 22, 1860.

growing out of Secession views, compelled [the *Chief's*] discontinuance after the hanging of Rev. Anthony Buley and Crawford."[4]

After the hangings the flames burned low until the results of the 1860 election were known. Texans, who had cast no votes for Lincoln,[5] felt that his election placed the nation at a crossroads. To consider which road to take, a public meeting with unprecedented attendance was held in Fort Worth on November 26, 1860, at a time when the Texas flag had been flying for weeks above a rebellious Birdville.[6] Two resolutions were adopted. One called upon Governor Houston to assemble the legislature at an early date. The other said: "That as a pledge of our fidelity to our state and her institutions and of our prior allegiance to the sovereignty to the State of Texas, we, this day, by public acclaim, hoist in the public square of the town of Fort Worth, the Lone Star Flag as the banner of our liberties." However, the resolutions committee—composed of John Peter Smith, Captain Daggett, A. Y. Fowler, and M. T. Johnson—cautiously amended the minutes to read that the resolution was not an act of revolt or secession.[7]

Aroused by the current of events, Fort Worth citizens listened to debates and speeches four and five nights a week in Masonic Hall.[8] Finally the time for talking was over. The time for action was at hand. Across the state sounded a call for a convention to consider secession, a step that was being blocked by the firm hand and counsel of Governor Houston. Terry, the aristocrat from Alabama, and Josiah Cook, of Birdville, represented Tarrant County at the convention.

On February 1, 1861, the convention in Austin adopted an ordinance of secession, effective March 2, subject to ratification by popular vote. Through the ratification election, the

[4] Norton, *op. cit.,* 352 ff.; *Austin State Gazette,* Sept. 22, 1860.
[5] Paddock (ed.), *Fort Worth and the Texas Northwest,* II, 395.
[6] *Dallas Herald,* Dec. 5, 1860.
[7] *Ibid.*
[8] Charles Ellis Mitchell in *Research Data,* V, 2000–VI, 2010.

Captain E. M. Daggett

A. B. Norton,
the first editor in Fort Worth

issue came to a head in Tarrant County on February 23. By a scant twenty-seven votes out of eight hundred polled, the county favored secession.

Some of the ablest men in the county were opposed to secession, including Smith, Terrell, Dade, and Johnson. But when the die was cast, most of the dissenters honored their allegiance to Texas above all and stood with her in the Confederacy. However, Dade placed his nationalism first, resigned as district attorney, and immediately left Texas. Exodus from the state was accompanied by serious hazard, for men who left were believed to be traitors and sometimes were murdered along the way. But Dade made it safely to Springfield, Missouri, where he lived out his days as a respected jurist.[9]

When the thunderclap of war was heard, men from Fort Worth and Tarrant County donned the gray, marching away to fight. The first county company left on August 20, 1861, raised and commanded by William Quayle, of Grapevine, a former sea captain. It became Company A, Ninth Texas Cavalry, Sul Ross Brigade, fighting in Louisiana and Texas. Next was Company D of the same regiment, commanded by Captain M. J. Brinson, which fought in the Indian Territory, Kansas, Arkansas, and at Corinth. Dr. Peak raised the Tarrant Rifles (Mounted), but could not go with his men because he was injured in a fall from his horse Gray Eagle while drilling troops on the square. The company became Company K, Seventh Texas Cavalry, participating in the recapture of Galveston. Terrell raised Company F, Waller's Battalion, that fought in many battles in the Trans-Mississippi region. Time after time he refused promotion because he wanted to remain with his company. For the rest of his life he was known as Captain Terrell.[10]

While the men were away fighting, the war had a devastating effect upon their homes. County population declined

[9] Terrell, *Reminiscences of the Early Days of Fort Worth*, 5.
[10] *Fort Worth Star-Telegram*, Oct. 30, 1949, Auto. Section, p. 29.

from six thousand to one thousand. Entire families refugeed east. Flour sold for fifteen dollars a hundred pounds, calico for four and five dollars a yard. Lack of scholars and tutors closed the private schools. Mail service was maintained by pony courier reaching Fort Worth at the end of a two-day trip from Waxahachie by way of Johnson Station and Birdville. As the war progressed, merchants could not get goods to sell. Local authorities issued currency signed by the chief justice and clerk of the county. Parched barley and wheat substituted for coffee, which was unobtainable except for a small quantity smuggled from Mexico. Homes were illuminated by tallow candles and sycamore balls soaked in oil.[11]

The High Vigilance Committee superseded the courts, seeking out and liquidating traitors to the Confederacy. During the purge the committee arrested and brought to trial in Gainesville Rev. Mathews, the patriarchal evangelist who traveled by caravan through the wilderness, who was very popular in Fort Worth. Upon being brought before the committee, Mathews was informed that he stood accused of treason, a charge that invariably brought the death penalty.

Hearing of the evangelist's plight, Captain Daggett hurried to Gainesville. In a dramatic appearance before the committee, he pleaded that Mathews' mind might be with the Union, but his heart was with the South. "If that be treason," he said, "then, I, too, am guilty." Reconsidering, the committee decided that Mathews should not die, but stipulated that he remain behind bars for three days more without knowing that his life had been spared. The agony of suspense was to be punishment for even bringing the taint of suspicion upon himself.

Captain Daggett was enraged by the decision. Indignantly he stamped off to Mathews' cell, determined that the injustice should not be carried through. At the jail he was forbidden to see the prisoner alone. A guard who knew of the three-day punishment was to remain in the cell during the

11 *Research Data,* I, 55.

interview and terminate it immediately if Daggett should even hint at the verdict. With the guard, Daggett entered the cell.

Burdened with sorrow and anxiety, Mathews was spending what he thought were his last hours with his Bible. Taking advantage of the circumstance, Daggett began a long biblical discussion. He talked on and on, drawing Mathews ever further into theology. Eventually Daggett noticed the bored guard was ignoring them. That was his chance. Into the conversation he shot the question, "What is your favorite Bible quotation?"

Mathews answered and then put a like question to Daggett. Piously the visitor intoned, "Fret not thy gizzard and frizzle not thy whirligig, thou soul art saved."[12] The guard was unaware that the committee's punishment had been thwarted.

The harshness of law and the austerity of life were accepted as the price that must be paid for freedom from a government controlled by Black Republicans. The men at the front were supported in spirit by those at home who refused to give up faith in the justice and ultimate success of Confederate arms. Never once did Terry, for instance, doubt that Southern manhood would triumph. During the war, when he was growing old, he decided to sell his plantation. The purchaser was David Snow, an antisecessionist who offered twenty thousand dollars in gold. Spurning the Union money, Terry asked for Confederate currency, which he said was better than gold. Financially ruined by the Union victory, he and his wife died soon after Appomattox.[13]

Those who remained at home clung to the vain hope that their men, clothed with victory, would return to push back the undergrowth that was strangling deserted cabins and reestablish families in prosperity. But the bitter years of war gave way to more bitter years, to a peace that was illusory,

[12] Terrell, *Reminiscences of the Early Days of Fort Worth*, 20.
[13] *Research Data*, I, 201.

when the men coming home were tired, depressed, and bewildered in trying to find where they, the conquered, living under the yoke of the conqueror, could pick up their lives.

All over the ravaged Southland, indeed, the men who had followed the Stars and Bars returned to shattered homes that could not, under existing conditions, be restored to anything approximating former comforts. To them it appeared easier to make a completely new start in a new land than to try putting their lives together in hostile surroundings that once had been familiar home ground. The former Confederate soldiers piled families and belongings into wagons and headed west, after scratching GTT—Gone to Texas—on their doors.

These Southern immigrants were the first of six major factors in the development of Fort Worth. To the frontier they brought trained minds, energy, and hope. Among the first to arrive was Major K. M. Van Zandt, son of a onetime Texas minister to Washington, who moved to Fort Worth when he could no longer stomach the galling restrictions of carpetbaggers in East Texas. Van Zandt, who had commanded the Seventh Texas Infantry at Chickamauga, arrived with his family in December, 1865, finding the desolate square ringed by stores long since boarded, the courthouse without a roof. He was a lawyer by profession, but laid aside his law books to open a drygoods store. He built his home at what is now Fifth and Commerce. Three years later he was joined by his brother, Dr. I. L. Van Zandt, who brought the first microscope to Fort Worth.

The former Confederates found only uncertainty and turmoil in the first years of Reconstruction. Serious doubt was cast upon the legality of the county government. Everyone knew a *de facto* government existed, but what of the government *de jure?* Young couples were afraid to marry lest the license issued by the *de facto* government be invalid.

Trying to bring order out of near chaos, Terrell journeyed to the state capital where he conferred with Provisional Governor A. J. Hamilton, late a brigadier general in the Union

Army. Before the war the Governor had practiced law in Austin with Terrell's brother Alexander, who later became a minister to Turkey under President Cleveland. Thus afforded an entree to Hamilton, Terrell submitted a list of names for government offices. Hamilton referred him to Secretary of State James Bell, who made the appointments. On the list was District Clerk Louis H. Brown, whose wife was a sister-in-law of Jerome Bonaparte.[14]

As part of the military occupation of what was regarded as a defeated nation, a company of United States regulars was stationed in the county. Despotic military orders denied franchise to men of the county, a few of whom went underground. They established a branch of the Ku Klux Klan which rode only for a short time, usually terrifying the newly freed Negroes. Their night-riding ceased, however, when they rode upon a farm between Fort Worth and Cleburne one dark night, only to be greeted by a surprise volley fired from a trench. Determined that the hooded figures should not trespass upon their land and harm or even frighten the Negroes living there, the owners of the farm had prepared for the visit. The unexpected opposition halted the bullying.[15]

Complicating the already difficult life in the frontier society, Indians raided more boldly after the Civil War, partly because the white men were killing their game and threatening their existence, partly because military defenses had deteriorated. In the early fifties the Indians had been friendly, riding single file up the bluff to trade. Their first words had been "good morning," "tobacco," and "fire water." But by the end of the fifties they had started making trouble. In 1860 Governor Houston initiated a campaign to quiet the Indians, directing the chief justice of each frontier county to raise a company of twenty-five minutemen. The Tarrant County company was led by M. T. Johnson as far north as Kansas in a fruitless effort to attack the Indians.[16]

[14] Terrell, *Reminiscences of the Early Days of Fort Worth*, 15–16.
[15] *Research Data*, I, 201.
[16] R. N. Richardson, *Texas, Lone Star State*, 206.

55

By the end of the Civil War, Indians were pillaging near Johnson Station. In an engagement near there Corporal Hickey and a detachment from Company H of the Eleventh Infantry killed two Indians in the postwar years. During the same period a group of nine men was driving a herd of horses near Blue Mound, just north of Fort Worth, when they were attacked by thirty Indians and forced to flee. The last Indian raid occurred in 1869 when savages penetrated to Marine Creek, now in the packing house district, where they attempted to trick settlers into an ambush through simulated turkey gobbles. Unsuccessful at making coup, the Indians killed a beef, and then retired toward their sanctuary north of the Red River. On their way home they killed an aged white woman six miles north of Fort Worth.[17]

In spite of the near primitive atmosphere, a pattern of normality was slowly superimposed as Fort Worth struggled through the dreary sixties with business reviving little by little. While business and homes were being rebuilt, Van Zandt, Dr. Peak, Milt Robinson, and W. H. Milwee set out to help build the minds of the coming generation. They pooled seventy-five dollars, bought a load of flour, traded it in East Texas for a wagonload of lumber, and used the lumber to patch the dilapidated Masonic Hall for use as a school. As schoolmaster, they imported Captain John Hanna, a Confederate soldier stranded in Dallas.

Hanna had only a few texts for his classes—Noah Webster's *Blue Back Speller, McGuffey's Reader, Ray's Arithmetic,* and *Monteith's Geography*—but he had a good school which drew pupils from Weatherford, Jacksboro, Mansfield, and Dallas. Within a few months the school was large enough to employ Clara Peak, Flora Robinson, Sue Huffman, and Kitty Andrews to teach the lower grades.[18]

A great occasion every year was the end of school. Clos-

[17] *Research Data,* I, 53, 64, 132.
[18] K. M. Van Zandt in *Fort Worth Star-Telegram,* Sept. 8, 1929; Anne Lenore Goerte, "Some Phases of the Development of the Fort Worth Public School System 1854–1930" (thesis, University of Colorado, 1930), 11.

ing exercises sometimes lasted a week, with the youngsters presenting charades, skits, and plays, demonstrating their learning through recitations and declamations. Often the final examinations were open to the public. For the closing exercises friends and families streamed in from surrounding towns and farm areas. The inadequate hotel was filled, and all homes threw wide their doors to receive and lodge the visitors.

While Hanna was teaching school, he also was studying law at night, and in 1870 forsook teaching for the bar. He was succeeded as teacher by Oscar J. Lawrence and his sister Mary, who opened the Masonic Institute in 1870. Meantime, two ministers of the Disciples of Christ, Addison and Randolph Clark, had arrived with their sister Ida, and in 1869 opened a one-room school for half a dozen children, a school that would in time become the principal university of their denomination—Texas Christian University.

As business slowly returned to normal, money was just as scarce as ever. About 1865, Press Farmer, the former army sutler, sold smoked meat to some cattle drivers, receiving a twenty-dollar gold piece. Farmer rode into town to pay a long overdue medical bill. As he rode out of town later in the day he was hailed by a friend who owed him twenty dollars. The friend paid with the same gold piece Farmer had brought into town in the first place. Checking back, Farmer discovered that the one piece of money had paid over two hundred dollars in debts in a single day.[19]

Stimulated by the incoming Confederates, commerce became more lively. Deadened by neglect in 1865, the square took on some of its former bustle, and even expanded. By 1867 three shuttered business houses had reopened. Each store was a log structure with a rear and front door and a window on either side of the main entrance. There were no streets, only roads around the courthouse. Log residences were scattered here and there east of the square.

In another year or so, the stores of B. Berliner, Van Zandt,

[19] K. M. Van Zandt in *Research Data*, I, 16.

and Medford were augmented by W. I. Ferguson's drugstore and Ambrose Croswell's carpenter shop.[20] As the market expanded, K. D. and W. Q. Bateman came from Jefferson with a grocery, L. N. Brunswig with a drug house, William H. Davis with a general store, William E. Trippett with a hardware store, and B. F. Bamberg with a butcher shop. Bamberg sold meat only once a day, at 5:00 A.M.

By the end of the sixties business was beginning to brighten, schools were open again, men concentrated on the single goal of restoring their personal losses from the war, the Indians were less of a menace, and religion was being revitalized. Some of the stones were being removed from the long road forward.

[20] *Research Data,* I, 156, 385–86.

CHAPTER IV

Thundering Hooves

TILL under the shadow of Reconstruction, Fort Worth in 1870 was on the threshold of a decade that would be the foundation period for a city. For the first few years of the decade, however, it was but a sluggish settlement of not more than three hundred souls, "a dirty, dreary, cold, mean little place."[1]

Nevertheless, it already held a position of prime importance in the Southwest—as the major stop on the cattle trail leading to northern markets.

The trail drives and the subsequent development of the Texas cattle industry comprised the second of the six major factors in the development of a city. Lank, rangy longhorns bawling through the dust trampled the earth of what is now Commerce Street, crossing the Trinity just east of the courthouse bluff. Sometimes they came through on the run, such as the time when Joseph Clark, father of Addison and Randolph Clark, was attending a May Day picnic with some children at Cold Spring. While talking with the youngsters, he heard the unmistakable thunder of a stampede. Rushing the children toward the fenced yard of the only house in the vicinity, he barely pushed them into the protecting enclosure before the wild-eyed beasts swept near. He himself would have been run down had not a cowboy galloped up and pulled the old man up on his horse.[2]

[1] *Fort Worth Star-Telegram*, Oct. 30, 1949, First Section, 8.
[2] Reminiscences of Ida Van Zandt Jarvis, *Research Data*, I, 106.

Hard-faced cowboys coming to town on the trail drives made up for all the lonely, monotonous months on the range. With the abandon of their breed they threw money away on cards and dice, twirled over dance-hall floors with painted women, absorbed quantities of liquor good and bad, fought with men from other ranches, and then galloped out of town, firing their six-shooters as they left. One of their favorite targets while thundering out of town was a large coffeepot that served as a sign for Jim Bradner's tin shop. The metal sign was full of holes left by the slugs from their forty-fives. Nobody minded, for the cowboy was king.[3]

The cattle drive had its inception in the disrupted economy that characterized the years immediately following the Civil War. When the war ended, the people of the North were clamoring for meat. To fill that want, Texas was the only ready source of beef animals in quantity. The only way the cattle could reach the North was by an overland drive that Texas cattlemen were willing to risk in spite of the rigors, the dangers, and the uncertainty. In the first postwar years a few herds had gone north over the Baxter Springs Trail that led to St. Louis, but the distance was too great for the drives to be practical, and the market facilities were unsatisfactory. The cattlemen were still waiting to make the long and dangerous journey, provided there was some place where they could sell their cattle.

Men in the North were working on the same problem. Seeking a means of tapping the Texas beef supply, a northern cattle buyer, Joseph G. McCoy, found his opportunity when the Kansas Pacific Railroad reached Abilene, Kansas, directly north of the Texas cattle country. There he built stockyards, advertising throughout the ranch country that he was in the market for cattle.

Within a few years he succeeded in having all Texas sale herds pointed toward Abilene. Cattle left South Texas on a general trail that picked up feeder trails as it progressed

[3] *Research Data,* I, 215–20.

northward. In later years the trail split north of San Antonio, the Western Trail going to Colorado and Wyoming feeder ranges, the Eastern Trail continuing north with the sale herds. The Eastern Trail was the main branch. Passing through Fort Worth, it led trail herds to the Red River, where it became the Chisholm Trail that snaked across the primeval country of the Canadian and the Cimarron.[4]

The Eastern Trail made Fort Worth important to the cattle kingdom because the village was the last place of any consequence where trail hands could reprovision and take a last fling before striking out for the Indian country to the north. From the trail drives Fort Worth gained its first secure economic footing.

Encouraged by the market at Abilene, Texans drove 300,-000 head of cattle to Kansas in 1870. They found the market even better than before. Demand was at an all-time high, supported by a rate war among railroads fighting one another for the cattle business. When the Texans came home, they spread the word of the fabulous market up north. In anticipation of a huge drive the next year, cowpokes strained to round up every maverick they heard bellow in the thickets. In 1871 about 600,000 head were trailed north.

When the Texans reached Abilene in 1871, the market could not absorb the huge herds. Too, the market was disdupted by superior stock from the corn belt, sleek animals which outclassed the muscular longhorn, whose meat was tough and stringy. Disillusioned ranchmen turned their unsold stock upon Kansas ranges to wait another year. During the hard winter that followed, snow killed thousands of animals. In all, 1871 was a disastrous year for Texas cattlemen.[5]

In 1873 a new chapter was opened in the transportation of cattle to northern markets when the Katy completed a

[4] Old Trail Drivers Association, San Antonio, in *Fort Worth Star-Telegram*, Oct. 30, 1949, Ranch and Farm Section, p. 2.

[5] Paddock (ed.), *Fort Worth and the Texas Northwest*, II, 530.

railroad as far south as Denison, just below the Red River, along the old Baxter Springs trail. To attract business, the Katy offered to ship cattle from Denison to St. Louis for one hundred dollars a carload.[6] To reach Denison, or for that matter Abilene, which still drew goodly herds, the trail drives continued to pass through Fort Worth. Continuously the town grew in importance with cattle more firmly entrenched than ever as the basic economy.

Business opportunities created by the passage of the herds drew many merchants to Fort Worth. Business connections were formed between merchant and ranchman that were to endure for years. West Texas stockmen were coming to think of Fort Worth as their base of supply, and wagon trains laden with merchandise rolled to the west throughout the year.

Prosperity brought money into circulation in appreciable amounts, necessitating a central stabilizing influence in business affairs. Commission merchants and storekeepers acted as clearinghouses for the bulky gold and silver coin that was preferred to the suspect paper currency. But the clearinghouse system was complicated and inadequate. The need for a bank was perceived by a former captain of Confederate cavalry, Martin B. Loyd, of Mississippi. After serving with Rebel horse on the Indian frontier, he came to Fort Worth in 1870 with a capital of forty thousand dollars in gold, opened the first bank, and set up his exchange office in one room of a small house on Main between First and Second streets.

Politically Fort Worth still was in an era marked by turmoil and strife. The lynch law that prevailed during the Civil War carried over into the Reconstruction period when human life was cheap. Courts were functioning, but there was about them an atmosphere that freeborn Democrats did not like. Either carpetbaggers or scalawags sat on the bench. One was Judge Hardin Hart, who couched his rulings in the vernacular of the bar and casino. Once, when J. C. Terrell sought to amend a pleading, Hart replied: "Now, Joe, you

[6] *Fort Worth Democrat,* Feb. 22, 1873.

know you cannot raise at this stage of this game. Gause stands pat on his general denial, and you will have to call or lay down your hand."[7]

Socially the town was showing stability. The need for better quarters for the First Christian Church prompted Van Zandt to pay two hundred dollars for the block just south of the present Westbrook Hotel, where a new church was built. The one-room structure had separate doors for men and women since the sexes were segregated during services. Children who might drop off to sleep were awakened by an usher using a rabbit's foot attached to the end of a long pole.[8]

After the Civil War, French missionary priests began riding from the Gulf to North Texas, holding mass and administering the sacraments to Roman Catholics scattered through the thinly populated land. To Fort Worth these missionary priests first brought Catholicism. The first high mass was held in 1870 by Rev. Vincent Perrier, who made regular spring and fall visits from his San Angelo base. Services were held in the homes of Thomas Carrico, Mrs. Louise Scott, and James Griffin, and in the Lake and Nash hardware store.

The medical community was enlarged. To the aid of Drs. Peak, Van Zandt, and Burts came Dr. Theodore Feild, who is credited with one of the early successful triple amputations. As the first resident dentists, Drs. W. D. Mayfield and N. Wallerich arrived in 1870.

The town's economy also became strong enough for the reestablishment of newspapers. A. B. Norton, the Whig editor who fled Texas in 1860, returned. While the war was raging, he found asylum in the North where he befriended Texans in Federal military prisons, helping them with extra food and medicines. He was repaid by their eternal gratitude, which resulted in a paradox in later years. Texans held him in affectionate esteem personally but despised him politically. As soon as the war was over, he came back to Texas, founding

[7] Paddock (ed.), *Fort Worth and the Texas Northwest,* II, 630.
[8] *Research Data,* I, 106, 138.

63

the *Union Intelligencer* at Jefferson. The strong Republican aroma of his paper offended the sensitive Jeffersonians who stormed his plant, wrecked it, and attempted to mob Norton. Amid the confusion of the nighttime attack, he slipped away in the dark, hiding in the woods of Van Zandt County for several weeks. Eventually he reached Fort Worth again in 1870, re-establishing his newspaper as the *Whig Chief.* During Norton's absence Fort Worth had known the *Chieftain, Times, Epitomist,* and *Exponent.*

Less than a year later he closed the *Whig Chief* and moved to Dallas, where his *Union Intelligencer* was a political testament for the Republican party in Texas. During the Grant and Hayes administrations he served variously as judge for Tarrant and Parker counties, customs collector at Galveston, United States marshal for the northern district, and postmaster at Dallas. He lived out his days in Dallas, dying there on January 31, 1893, his hair and beard yet untrimmed.

Norton's short-lived *Whig Chief* was succeeded in 1871 by the *Enterprise,* founded by J. W. Cleveland. But it, too, fared poorly. All of the old newspapers were published in a concrete building at Weatherford and Throckmorton streets.[9]

Inadequate financial reserves and limited equipment made the early newspaper history of Fort Worth one of start, sputter, and stop. Consequently, a group of businessmen anxious to have a dependable newspaper, with a suitable financial foundation, organized a company to buy the equipment of the *Quitman Herald* from J. J. Jarvis, who had been an accomplished editorialist before coming to Fort Worth to practice law. Backers of the company were Van Zandt, Junius W. Smith, Hanna, W. H. Overton, and Sam Evans.[10] They named their paper the *Democrat* and turned it over to Cleveland as editor. Another of the early *Democrat* editors was John Templeton, later attorney-general of Texas.

On a brisk October day in 1872 a confident young horse-

[9] *Ibid.,* V, 2000–VI, 2010.
[10] *Ibid.,* I, 66.

man rode from the east into Fort Worth, where he eyed every building, every hillock, with a carefulness born of long habit as a captain of scouts. Behind him was a gallant record in the Confederate Army. Ahead was his lifework—Fort Worth—which he was to serve with vision prophetic and faith unlimited. Reining his horse to the square, he dismounted before Van Zandt's store. Entering the store, he introduced himself as B. B. Paddock, saying he intended to make his home in Fort Worth.

"What would you like to do?" Van Zandt inquired.

"I would like to run a newspaper, sir," replied the twenty-eight-year-old veteran.

"Well, we have one here, and we will give it to you if you will operate it," Van Zandt said.[11]

Paddock then took over the *Democrat*, first as editor and later as owner, serving it and his adopted town with the vigor and courage which marked his services to the Confederacy. He was by birth and training a Northerner, but when the Civil War broke out, he left his home in Wisconsin Territory and went to Mississippi. As a stripling of seventeen he enlisted in Colonel Wirt Adams' cavalry in 1861. Daring marked him for promotion in July, 1862, when he became one of the youngest officers in the Confederate Army. To his command were entrusted hand-picked scouts whom he led through engagement after engagement without losing a man or having one wounded until after Appomattox, when the first man of the company was wounded in a skirmish that took place before news of the peace had reached all units.

The war over, Paddock settled in Fayette, Mississippi, where he studied law at night under a private tutor. A few years of law practice made him impatient, and he determined to try newspapering. From Mississippi he came to Fort Worth.

As editor he had no competition, for the *Democrat* was the town's lone newspaper from its first publication in 1871 until the town and the paper entered a more lusty period in 1873.

[11] W. A. Paddock to author, July 28, 1949.

CHAPTER V

Boom Town

IN 1873, Fort Worth rumbled with an excitement, an eagerness that transcended even the natural bumptiousness of the ebullient frontier. Merchants hurried to the town, rushed buildings to completion, flung merchandise on the shelves, and waited for the golden horde. For the railroad was on the way! Sure signs of empire, twin strands of rail were like magnets drawing men by the score from the older states.

The promise of a railroad came from a journey by two men. One was Thomas A. Scott, who had gained control of the Texas and Pacific Railroad. He came through Fort Worth as he moved over Texas looking for a route for his tracks that were to cross the uncharted West. With him was John W. Forney, editor of the *Philadelphia Chronicle*, who wrote voluminous letters during the journey, and later wrote a pamphlet entitled *What I Saw in Texas* in an effort to spur the granting of a subsidy to the T. and P. by Congress.

The hope turned to jubilation when Scott returned from the West Coast and immediately began construction westward from Marshall and Jefferson along a line that would bring the potbellied locomotives and their rickety wooden coaches through Fort Worth. General Grenville M. Dodge, who had been chief engineer of the Union Pacific, directed construction.

Fort Worth boomed, land prices shot skyward, and speculators rushed forward. In the procession of merchants who headed their wagons toward the western town was a young Scotsman, Joseph H. Brown, who saw a tremendous opportunity for wholesale trade in serving outlying regions. He began jobbing groceries through the central and western sections of the state. By 1876 he was the town's leading businessman, as well as the founder of Fort Worth's giant wholesale trade. The "merchant prince of Northwest Texas," as he came to be known, was receiving whole trainloads of groceries at a time in the eighties; in 1883 his annual sales exceeded $1,850,000.

The second major wholesaler was Elliott and Roe Lumber Company, doing business from a yard at Seventh and Taylor, now occupied by the Worth Hotel. Despite the fact that Brown and then Elliott and Roe are known as the trail blazers for wholesaling, a liquor firm was ahead of them as a jobber. Pendery and Wilson "have the credit of establishing the first exclusively wholesale house in Fort Worth."[1]

Those were great years—1872 and 1873—for the business community, with the town filling up fast because of the magic of the railroad announcement. The *Democrat* exultantly announced: "Two more drygoods stores. Two more drugstores. Two more printing offices. Another livery stable. Three brick kilns in progress."[2] In the incoming group were Z. E. B. Nash and B. C. Evans.

Nash and his son Charles sold water-well supplies, operating a tinner's shop on the side for the manufacture of brides' goods such as teapots and kettles. To keep the tinners busy during slack periods, Charles Nash started building a stockpile of household goods that eventually became the Nash Hardware Company, which is still in business.

Evans was a Citadel graduate and a Confederate veteran who came from South Carolina with a capital of five hundred dollars. He opened the first exclusively drygoods store in town, a small shop at First and Houston, where he quickly

[1] *Fort Worth Democrat,* March 8, 1873.
[2] *Ibid.,* Feb. 22, 1873.

gained an outstanding reputation among pioneer businessmen. Within a few years he built a large department store on
First Street, running the block from Houston to Main. But
tragedy was to sever his quick success. In 1889 he returned
from a buying trip to New York to find an employee drunk.
He fired the man, J. W. Davis. Later that day Davis charged
back into the store, found Evans reading the paper, and
fired a bullet through the newspaper, killing Evans instantly.
For the murder Davis was sentenced to die by hanging, a
sentence that was foiled by a conspiracy. For on the eve of
the execution, he committed suicide with poison that had
been smuggled to him.[3]

Optimistic business ventures in 1873 included the manufacture and delivery of ice by the Ladies Ice Cream Parlor.[4]
L. W. Crawford set up shop as a photographer; the first photographer, Abernathy, had come twenty years before but
had stayed only briefly.

Banker Loyd met competition in 1872 when the McKinney firm of G. Van Winkle and Company opened a branch
bank in Fort Worth. About the same time, Loyd went into
partnership with Clyde P. Marklee, Sr., opening the California and Texas Bank of Loyd, Marklee and Company. In
1873 a third bank was formed—Thomas A. Tidball, an experienced banker, teamed with John Wilson, who supplied the
money. A few months afterward, Wilson was called back to
Virginia by the death of his father, and had to remain there
to care for his aged mother. Tidball joined with Van Zandt,
Smith, and Jarvis to organize the bank of Tidball, Van Zandt
and Company, capitalized at thirty thousand dollars; the first
office was at 109 West Weatherford. Later, Tidball, Van
Zandt and Company became the Fort Worth National Bank.

The increased tempo attracted a large number of lawyers,
whose talents were demanded, among other things, by the
many changes of property ownership that were taking place.

---

[3] *Fort Worth Star-Telegram*, Oct. 30, 1949, Commerce Section, p. 42.
[4] *Fort Worth Democrat*, May 3, 1873.

A surprising number were former soldiers from the Southern states. For example, there was R. E. Beckham, a Confederate captain, who came to Fort Worth during the Reconstruction exodus from the South. His opening announcement said: "Mr. R. E. Beckham has his law office in the editorial rooms of the *Democrat* where those in need of an efficient attorney will find him during business hours unless absent on professional business."[5]

Other lawyers who practiced in the early seventies included P. M. Thurmond, C. C. Cummings, E. P. Albritton, W. M. Campbell, Hanna and Hogsett, John J. Good, H. G. Bowen, Junius W. Smith, H. Barksdale, John T. Ault, Dan B. Corley, and John F. Swayne.

Weekly newspaper publishers also jumped into the field in 1873. The first and most conspicuous was J. K. Millican, who came from Homer, Louisiana, in May, 1873, to establish the weekly *Standard*. Other weeklies were founded, but only the *Democrat* and *Standard* had the stamina to last.

The sudden prosperity caused Editor Paddock to publish the following prospectus, intending to attract capital and population, in the *Democrat:*

> The society of Tarrant County is better than is usually found in a new country. The gentlemen are generally well informed, shrewd, and many of them cultivated and refined. The ladies compare well with those of the older states, in point of health, beauty, style, and cultivation; all are social and agreeable. The schools in Tarrant County, about twenty in number, are well-organized and well-supported. Most of them are public free schools, sustained by the state.
>
> Churches are not as numerous as could be desired; but this want will rapidly be supplied. Lands are worth from three to five dollars per acre for unimproved and from ten to forty dollars for improved lands. The price varying with the locality and quality of improvements.
>
> It is impossible to present, by description, a true picture of the beautiful landscape views and natural scenery that are

[5] *Ibid.*, June 27, 1874.

open to view upon the romantic bluffs and grassy plains in and around Fort Worth. The population of Fort Worth is about two thousand, and is increasing daily. Scores of the best men in the country are coming to and locating in Fort Worth, and are going to work with energy and determination to build up the place and make it what it is inevitably destined to be—the city of Northwest Texas. It will be the junction of the Texas & Pacific and the Trans-Continental roads, and probably two others will also form junctions here.

The place is rapidly being built up with good substantial stone, brick and frame buildings. Lumber is scarce and dear. Mechanics of all branches can find constant employment at remunerative wages. All classes of people who are willing to pull off their coats and go to work are in demand. There are two schools and scholars enough for a third. All branches of trade and industry, and all the liberal professions are well and ably represented. Rents at present are high.[6]

The temper of the times encouraged Paddock to publish a drawing of prophetic significance, the Tarantula Map. In the center was a thick black blob representing Fort Worth, with nine lines, like tarantula legs, pushing out to denote the nine railroads which he predicted would fan eventually from the town. Men of other Texas towns scoffed. But in time his vision was fulfilled, even to the ninth railroad.

In 1873 the culture of Fort Worth was entirely materialistic. Men were too busy establishing and preparing themselves for sudden wealth to allow much time for religious or diversional activities. Indeed, the *Democrat* was moved to remark:

It is not unfrequently observed by visitors to our town that while we are rapidly going forward in making improvements, we are sadly deficient in church edifices. Fort Worth has no church building of sufficient dimensions to accomodate its churchgoing people. At every service we have attended since we have been in the place, we have seen persons com-

[6] *Ibid.,* Jan. 25, 1873.

pelled to stand during the entire service. Certainly with as much wealth as there is in Fort Worth, at least two fine churches could be built.[7]

Not only was there insufficient room for church services, but there was a decided lack of any suitable place for decent entertainment. The Odd Fellows used a courtroom for a fancy-dress ball in 1873 where "the ladies all looked as fine as Solomon's lilies and the gents as gallant as hotspurs."[8] Which led the *Democrat* to observe that "among the most urgent needs of a public nature at the present time is a town hall—some place where concerts, shows, and private or public entertainment can be given."[9]

Fort Worth was a pulsative town crowded with flimsily built buildings, as well as a large tent-city population. Since fireplaces and wood stoves were the only sources of heat for warmth and cooking, a constant fire hazard threatened the town that was jammed around the square. Knowing that a good blaze could gut the entire town, Paddock began a ceaseless and vigorous editorial campaign for fire protection. Because a city government was not in existence, he appealed for community action, warning time and again of the danger from fire. Before very long, a serious fire leveled a store building on the square. Disgustedly, Paddock wrote: "The almost miraculous escape from a very destructive fire on Saturday last seems to have produced no effect whatever upon our businessmen. . . . A week has passed and no steps have been taken to prevent a recurrence of the fearful event."[10]

Singlehandedly he then saw to it that Fort Worth should have fire protection. In the columns of his paper he announced that a meeting would be held on the courthouse steps to organize a fire company, and in personal contacts he obtained promises from many men that they would attend. On the ap-

[7] *Ibid.*, Feb. 22, 1873.
[8] *Ibid.*, Feb. 22, 1873.
[9] *Ibid.*, March 15, 1873.
[10] *Ibid.*, Feb. 1, 1873.

pointed night a blue norther struck. Paddock shivered alone on the cold stone steps.

Undaunted, he called a second meeting, also on the court-house steps. Success attended the second effort when on May 2, 1873, the city's first fire-fighting unit, wholly volunteer, was perfected. The membership of sixty men, mostly clerks and mechanics, elected S. P. Greene president, Paddock, secretary, and William T. Field, foreman.

From the members' personal funds came money for the first piece of fire-fighting apparatus—a hand-drawn hook-and-ladder wagon which was shipped by rail to Dallas, the nearest railhead. From Dallas the company members pulled the wagon home.

To raise money, the fire fighters held a popularity contest, charging ten cents a vote, with the winner to name the new company. Miss Sallie Johnson, who received the greatest number of votes, christened the company in memory of her father, who had helped Arnold select the site for the fort. Thenceforward the city's first fire-fighting unit was known as the M. T. Johnson Hook and Ladder Company.[11] The wagon was housed in the first fire station, on the southeast corner of Weatherford and Throckmorton.[12]

When a fire broke out anywhere in town, the nearest man drew his six-shooter and fired into the air. Other shots answered from all sections of the city. Seven-year-old Fred Askew, who lived across the street from the fire station, ran to the station, grabbed the rope attached to an old farm bell on a twenty-five-foot pole, and rang that bell with all the heart a boy can put into something that makes noise.

For fifteen or twenty minutes there was nothing but noise—men shouting, pistol shells exploding, and the furious ringing of the strident bell—while the volunteers hustled to the station. In a frenzy of excitement they grabbed the ropes at-

---

[11] *Fort Worth Gazette,* May 25, 1887; Paddock (ed.), *Fort Worth and the Texas Northwest,* II, 626.

[12] Interview in 1949 with Fred Askew, early day fireman.

tached to the twenty-foot wagon and ran to the fire. At the fire a bucket brigade was formed to pass small leather buckets from the nearest water source to the fire. After the fire each saloon in the vicinity furnished drinks for the firemen. For the first few months the fire company was autonomous, unrelated in any manner to the newly formed city government.

While the town was booming, the men who hoped to keep their homes in Fort Worth realized that a city government must be organized. Nightly through January, 1873, they met and argued and discussed and debated the type of government they would have until agreement was reached on the charter that would be requested of the state legislature. Once agreed upon, a draft of the desired charter was transmitted to Van Zandt, who, as state representative, began piloting the measure through the Thirteenth Legislature.[13]

At home enthusiasm cooled after Van Zandt took the charter draft to Austin. Through the *Democrat*, Paddock fought to keep interest from flagging. Sternly he upbraided the citizenry for their lack of concern. Once he actually accused the public of being "criminally culpable" in neglecting the forthcoming city election.[14]

Efforts of Van Zandt, Paddock, Hogsett, Ball, Daggett, and the others were soon rewarded, for on February 15, 1873, the *Democrat* was able to announce that the legislature had enacted the bill incorporating Fort Worth, effective March 1. That very day the first announcements for office were filed— L. Steele, P. J. Thurmond, and A. Y. Lester for mayor, and Ed Terrell for marshal. Daily more and more candidates entered the field. The first election was held April 3, with Dr. W. P. Burts elected mayor. The aldermen were M. B. Loyd, M. D. McCall, A. Blakeney, W. J. Boaz, and J. P. Alexander. Terrell was elected marshal, N. M. Maben, assessor-collector, W. T. Ferguson, treasurer, and John F. Swayne, secretary.[15]

[13] Paddock (ed.), *Fort Worth and the Texas Northwest*, II, 608.
[14] *Fort Worth Democrat*, Feb. 8, 1873.
[15] *Ibid.*, April 5, 1873.

To govern the town of four square miles, the new mayor and his five aldermen took the oath of office, administered by Presiding Justice Jesse Jones of the county court, at the court-house on Friday, April 4. They held their first meeting there the next day and made city government a reality.

During the first week the council met almost daily. Their first ordinances fixed regular meetings of the council, directed that a corporate seal be designed with the likeness of E. M. Daggett upon it, established fees and salaries, imposed regulations on gambling and gambling houses, regulated shooting galleries, restricted the carrying of deadly weapons, called for construction of sidewalks, directed that shade and ornamental trees be protected, and outlawed mobs.

The first executive agency created was the police department, which came into existence on April 10. On the same day the first policemen were appointed—Henry Shiels, Joe Meyers, Paul W. Keating, and N. K. Ferguson.[16] On April 22 the first police badge, a star, was prescribed by the council, but the policemen hardly had time to buy badges before they were out of jobs. For exactly one month to the day after the department was created, it was abolished for economy reasons, within minutes after the council had awarded a $497 contract for construction of the first jail. The penurious council directed that no more disbursements be allowed until the jail contractor should be paid in full. Marshal Terrell was left as the sole officer.

The freshman council felt an immediate need for accurate knowledge of the town's physical limits. Accordingly, Loyd, McCall, and Boaz were named on April 12 as a committee charged with arranging for a survey of the old city and the "locating of the various streets in the old town and establishing of the boundary lines of the corporation of said city." Execution of the map was detailed to I. C. Terry, who had been appointed the first city engineer.[17]

16 *Minutes* of the Fort Worth City Council, Vol. A, p. 11.
17 *Ibid.*, Vol. A, pp. 12, 18.

A primary problem was water supply. Citizens obtained water from cisterns, shallow wells, and the Trinity, or bought it at twenty-five cents for two barrels from peddlers who hauled water in tarred tank wagons from springs near Birdville. Whether directly from the ground or from tank wagon, the water was used untreated. As the town grew, the question of a water supply became pressing. Frequent editorials in the *Democrat*, advocating a public water works, reflected the public opinion that made water one of the first major issues raised before the council.

Individual citizens frequently advanced schemes needing municipal sanction for creation of water companies. But sometimes their motives were suspect. On April 12, 1873, the council received two petitions for authority to engage in the water business. One was by O. M. Brown and Associates, who wished to lay pipe in various streets. The request was brushed aside. The other was by G. M. Newman and G. Van Winkle, bankers as well as directors of the Fort Worth Water Works Company, who wanted the exclusive privilege of laying water pipe in city streets. Their petition was referred to a committee. One of the two petitions upset the public. Certainly the townspeople wanted a dependable water supply, but they were not willing to compromise on just anything, as was shown by this report in the *Democrat*:

> On Saturday last our little city was thrown into a fever of excitement by the announcement that the City Council had granted to a close corporation, the exclusive privilege of erecting water works and supplying the city with water for 99 years.
>
> The city at once resolved itself into a committee of the whole and expressed its indignation in no measured terms. Towards evening it was discovered that no such extraordinary privilege had been granted, and the city became comparatively quiet.[18]

Constantly the refrain of "Railroad!" drummed through

[18] *Fort Worth Democrat*, April 19, 1873.

men's minds, quickened their pulses, stirred their ambitions, and sharpened their avarice. Everything that was done added to the crescendo. While Fort Worth was building and booming in anticipation of the railroad, Scott went to London to gain additional financial support for the westward expansion of the Texas and Pacific. He had to work fast, for delay could be costly. Texas had agreed to give the railroad large land grants, provided the T. and P. reached Fort Worth by January 1, 1874. Upon the same condition 320 acres in Fort Worth had been offered by Van Zandt, E. B. Daggett, Thomas J. Jennings, and H. G. Hendricks.

Long interested in Texas where their investments were important in developing the cattle industry, the Englishmen were receptive to Scott's prospectus. In jubilation he invited the Londoners to a banquet where all were to celebrate their mutual good fortune. During the meal jubilation turned to despondency.

For while the banquet was in progress, Scott received a cablegram from New York. The stark words: Jay Cooke and Company, one of the world's most potent financial houses, had failed. The words not only rocked Scott, they rocked the world. Jay Cooke and Company had been the fiscal agent of the United States government during the Civil War; through the company's failure the economic structure of America was shaken to its very foundations. Panic seized the country.[19]

When word trickled to isolated Fort Worth, men stared in dismay. The panic struck a body blow to the town because the eagerly awaited railroad was dependent upon loans for completion. Without assurance in a world where such a prominent house as Cooke could not stand, bankers could not or would not make loans. Without financial backing the railroad could go no farther.

The sweating gangs laid aside their sledge hammers at Eagle Ford, a few miles east of Fort Worth, and the rails faded into nothingness on the prairie. Fort Worth's dream vanished.

[19] Paddock (ed.), *Fort Worth and the Texas Northwest,* II, 603–607.

Without the railroad, the investments of scores of business-men were made virtually worthless. Gloom descended on the cow town beside the Trinity.

Bursting of the bubble rained dejection and bitterness on the opportunists who scowled their way out of town like rats leaving a rotting hulk. Behind them remained other men —disappointed, certainly—who thought the hulk was sea-worthy nevertheless. The gloom-crested business district con-sisted of two blocks of stores, including two hotels, three banks, and a score of stores and saloons.

In the absence of brisk business, men turned their atten-tion to politics. Fortunately, changes were taking place that stimulated the interest and participation of the citizens.

For long they had lived in the repressive atmosphere of the carpetbag period when the county judge was Squire B. F. Barkley, a Birdville Republican who found it expedient to be escorted between home and office each day by a bodyguard of Negro soldiery.[20]

Toward the end of Reconstruction, however, Texans were allowed to vote under restraint. To regulate voting, Recon-struction officials divided the state into fifteen districts of six to eleven counties each for voter registration. In each sub-district, ordinarily a county, there was a board of registrars. The Tarrant County board in 1872 was composed of Barkley, Bird Lorantz, and Tony Rucker, a Negro.

After a period of intolerable oppression Texans again were given free rein in the selection of officials. An election called for December 2, 1873, was the first unrestricted opportunity in eight years for Texans to vote for men of their choice. Glee-ful and unintimidated Democrats passed between two files of Negro soldiers when they walked up the courthouse steps to vote out of office the government they had labored under for so long.[21]

[20] *Research Data*, V., 2000–VI., 2010.
[21] *Ibid.;* Paddock (ed.), *Fort Worth and the Texas Northwest,* I, 436–38; III, 713.

Within a year politics of a more normal nature was beginning to be implanted. During 1874 the dominant local organization was the Granger party, composed of leading citizens who met every Saturday in a two-story rock house built in a field that now is lower Houston Street. As the Texas State Grange, the party had been formed in Dallas on October 2, 1873, to improve the social, educational, and material condition of planters who had been harmed economically by the war and to participate in politics when necessary.

After politics was exhausted as a means of continuing diversion, the most thrilling daily event for the several hundred citizens in 1874 was the arrival of the westbound stage at 4:00 P.M. But something more thrilling was about to happen.

The curious crowd gathered at 7:30 A.M. on Saturday, September 12, 1874, at a downtown building where a young man of twenty-two, Max Elser sat at a desk, fingering a queer instrument. A few minutes later, strange noises came from another instrument. Mayor Burts, whose strong face was accented by mustache and beard, was standing at Elser's elbow. To Elser the mayor handed a slip of paper. The young man fingered his instrument again, turned, and nodded. A delighted grin spread over Burts' face.

By Jove! He had just communicated with the mayor of Dallas, and in a twinkling. No longer was the cattle-trail hamlet isolated. Telegraph wires stretching over great distances had enfolded the drab and lonely frontier village to the world's bosom. In joyous celebration of the first telegraph line, spectators dragged out everything that would shoot or otherwise make noise.

Actually the first telegraph communication had reached Fort Worth two days earlier, but that had no effect upon the celebrants. On the very day that is marked as the official completion of the telegraph, the *Democrat* reported:

THE TELEGRAPH HAS ARRIVED.

At last the telegraph has been completed to this place, and the following dispatches were sent over the line on Thursday last:

Dallas, Tex., Sept. 10, 1874.

Capt. Paddock, Democrat—Mr. Millikin, Standard:—Dallas sends a cordial greeting to Fort Worth and congratulates her people upon the near completion of the telegraph line which will place your city in rapid communication with the outer world. We trust this is but a precursor of many ties that shall bind us in social and commercial intercourse; may our hearts respond to the electric current and further increase the kindly feeling between our cities and so unite us that our interests shall seem identical.

J. S. BURTON

Hon. W. L. Cabell, Mayor of Dallas: We respond most heartily to the good feeling expressed by you, and know full well that only by such advantages as in which you so kindly greet us can we be placed on equal standing with other progressive cities. We hail this medium of communication with grateful feelings towards Dallas for a generous interest in our city.

And on the next Saturday, September 19, the *Democrat* reported:

Fort Worth, Tex., Sept. 12, 1874.

Hon. W. L. Cabell, mayor of Dallas:
Today another link has been completed which joins us to your growing and prosperous city. May it increase your happiness as it has ours—and may the prosperity of both be advanced thereby.

W. P. BURTS
Mayor of Fort Worth.

Dallas, Tex., Sept. 14, 1874.
W. P. Burts, mayor of Fort Worth:
Dallas responds to your greetings most heartily and extends
to her sister city Fort Worth its congratulations in at last being
able to tell of her glories in electric words, and trusts that the
near future will bind us with iron bands as well as by the great
electric tongue of thought.

W. L. CABELL,
Mayor of the City of Dallas.

It will be seen from the above telegraphic dispatches, while
they explain themselves, show to our readers that we are in
telegraphic communication with the balance of the world.
Our sister city of Dallas being the nearest station on the east.

One by one our advantages come to us to make up our
future great destiny as a city and country, and this last one
will give to our citizens privileges not heretofore enjoyed
and will add greatly to the convenience of our business men.

Everyone seemed to enjoy the arrival of the company whose
duty it was to put up the wires, on Saturday, and to attest
their joy, every piece of artillery that could be found around
King's Foundry was hauled out on Main Street, and as peal
after peal went up, it aroused in our minds remembrances
of Vicksburgh and Port Hudson.

To the noble and patriotic sentiments expressed by the two
young cities thus happily united, we heartily say Amen! and
Amen! The telegraphic office is located at present in the real
estate office of Messrs. Lawrence, Cetti & Brewer on Main
Street, and is in charge of Mr. Max Elser.

The new telegraph line was privately owned by Elser and
C. L. Frost. For two years they operated it as an independent
venture, until Western Union bought it in 1876.

With contraction of the city's economy in 1873, all municipal officials had agreed to serve without compensation.
So dull became the town that the council did not even meet

for about four months—from November 23, 1873, until March 19, 1874. During that period, too, the town was without police protection, for Terrell had resigned as marshal in October and his successor, T. M. Ewing, was not elected until April.

Nevertheless, the council engendered the ire of at least part of the populace. In the 1874 election the administration of Mayor Burts was criticized for profligacy and neglect, a debt of $4,952, and a delinquent tax list of $19.85. Despite the criticism, the opposition to Dr. Burts was not solidified, and there was but passing interest in the campaign. He was re-elected in April, 1874, only to resign on October 29. In a special election on November 9, G. H. Day became mayor.[22]

Streets were mudholes in rainy weather, dust bowls in dry. Yet a certain amount of work was necessary to keep them passable. City prisoners and delinquent taxpayers were impressed for street work in 1874. The first constructive moves toward street improvement came on February 25 and March 9, 1875, when the council ordered that Main Street be paved from the courthouse fence to Second Street, a distance of two blocks. Pavement was to consist of spreading gravel on the roadbed which was contained by gutter walls made of three-inch lumber.

Despite the general economic lethargy, new industrial horizons were cleared in 1874 when Myron W. Walcott and William T. Blandin built the City Mills on East Bluff Street at the head of Commerce Street. There on June 26, 1875, was ground the first flour in the city's first commercial flour mill. Earlier mills had done only custom grinding.

During the somnolent years of 1873 to 1876 a panther strolled into town, giving rise to a legend that resulted in Fort Worth's nickname as the Panther City. As in the case of all legends, the full truth is difficult to ascertain. At least four versions of the event have been recounted. The first version was that Parson Fitzgerald found a big "Mexican" lion battering his dogs one night. The marauder left a footprint as big

[22] *Minutes* of the Fort Worth City Council, Vol. A, p. 81.

as a man's hand.[23] The second version is that a squatter living near the old fort, at about First and Throckmorton streets, shot and killed a nine-foot panther near his home. The third version came from Terry, the first city engineer, who was awakened one night by two mud-covered drunks. The next morning an "eccentric" old gentleman found four tracks, decided they were made by a panther, and found a spot where it appeared to him the panther had lain down.[24]

But the most accepted version is that in 1875 a Dallas lawyer, Robert E. Cowart, who once had practiced in Fort Worth, wrote an article for the *Dallas Herald* saying Fort Worth was such a drowsy place that a panther had been found asleep in the street.[25]

Perhaps Fort Worth was angered by Cowart's hoax at the time, but capital soon was made of it. Panther City was adopted as a nickname, Paddock placed a panther on the masthead of his newspaper, live panthers became mascots, and the name lives today in many ways—still as the town nickname, in the name of the town's baseball team, and in a number of firm names.

In truth, the town really was not dead enough for Cowart's story to be true, even partially true. What with wagon trains bringing buffalo hides from Fort Griffin, freighters hauling in supplies from the east, and goods being transshipped to the west by jerk-line outfits, Fort Worth at times had a quickened tempo.

The tempo increased lustily toward the end of 1875, because time was about to run out for the railroad of which men still dreamed. For the Texas and Pacific it was now or never. A sympathetic legislature had postponed the January 1, 1874, deadline for construction of the railroad upon several successive occasions. But when the Constitutional Convention

23 J. M. Robbins, who came to Fort Worth in 1872, quoted in *Fort Worth Star-Telegram*, Oct. 4, 1923.

24 J. M. Higgins, early settler, quoted in *Fort Worth Star-Telegram*, Dec. 21, 1938; I. C. Terry in *Fort Worth Star-Telegram*, June 5, 1930.

25 Paddock (ed.), *Fort Worth and the Texas Northwest*, II, 607.

Major K. M. Van Zandt

Captain M. B. Loyd

of 1875 met to draft a new fundamental law, provision was made that the land-grant agreement with the T. and P. be abrogated unless the railroad reached Fort Worth by the adjournment date of the first legislature meeting under the new constitution.

The first legislature convened on the second Tuesday of 1875. A few weeks or months in the future Fort Worth would be without even a glimmer of hope that a railroad would come unless prompt and decisive action was taken. The people of Fort Worth rose to the challenge, determined to build part of the road themselves.

Organizing the Tarrant County Construction Company, they subscribed to its stock with money, labor, material, forage, supplies, or anything else that was marketable or could be used by the company. Van Zandt was elected president, John S. Hirschfield, vice president, Jesse Zane-Cetti, secretary, and W. A. Huffman, treasurer. Van Zandt journeyed to T. and P. headquarters at Marshall and made his proposition—that the Tarrant County Construction Company would prepare the roadbed from Eagle Ford, where the railroad terminated, into Fort Worth if the T. and P. would lay track and place the rolling stock in operation. The bargain was struck. All hands rolled up their sleeves and went to work.

Under a contract from the home-town company, Roche Brothers and Tierney began work on the roadbed. But progress was slow. Confident of their strength, T. and P. officials thought all they had to do to offset slowness of construction was to present their case in Austin. Company lawyers then applied to the legislature for another postponement of the deadline. Coldly the legislature turned the railroad away, insisting that the conditions had been set.

With that, the T. and P. was brought to the brink of a great loss. As a reward for completing the railroad on time, the company was to receive sixteen sections of land for each mile of track completed—too rich a prize to forfeit. Consequently the railroad withdrew the contract from the Tarrant

County Construction Company, dismissed the roadbed contractor, and bent every effort toward building the railroad.

Brawny, cursing section hands began throwing rails in place and driving spikes like fury. Night and day sledges hammered spikes into fresh new ties that were placed in position immediately after each section of roadbed was graded. Yet they were not going fast enough. Hardly was construction really underway when dispatches reported that the Texas Senate was ready to adjourn. Blackness enveloped the men who were pitting themselves against time and distance. Then came word that encouraged and drove them on to frenzied speed.

Yes, the Senate was ready to adjourn. But the House could not. Because the vote over adjournment was so close, the single vote of Tarrant County Representative Nicholas Henry Darnell kept the House in session and thus moved the deadline further away. It was more than the single vote of Darnell, however, that heartened his townsmen. For Darnell was a sick man, and to cast his lone vote, he was carried on a cot to the House chamber each day.[26]

For fifteen days the sick but valiant man bellowed, "Nay!" And for fifteen days his friends at home strained and sweated and prayed. Morgan Jones, the railroad contractor, neither changed clothing nor went to bed regularly during the fifteen-day period. The railroad's vice-president, John C. Brown, of Tennessee, and the chief engineer, D. W. Washburn, drove themselves day and night. Speeding across the fields, the builders soon ran smack into Sycamore Creek, which then was several miles east of Fort Worth. There was no time to build a proper trestle.

To hell with orthodox railroad building. The risk was too great. Rather than build a trestle, they made a crib of lumber and ties to span the creek. Once over Sycamore Creek the builders scampered for home base. Roadbed be damned! They laid their track on a dirt road. Ties were weighted with

26 *Ibid.,* 612–13.

stones. A mile a day they went. Businessmen released employees to work night and day upon the road. Women brought
food and coffee to all the straining workmen. While Darnell
held the legislature in session, the makeshift railroad tracks
finally reached into Fort Worth. Huge crowds gathered to
see the first train come in.

When old No. 20, with its diamond stack sending streams
of pungent wood smoke into the shimmery summer air, rolled
into town at 11:23 A.M. on July 19, 1876, there was an out-
burst of unrestrained joy. The gleeful *Democrat* headlined
the story:

AT LAST.

THE DAY HAS COME.

HOPE ENDS IN FRUITION.

Overjoyed men fired pistols into the air. Some folks were
astounded, others just plain scared by the huffing, puffing
monster that lurched into town over wobbly rails, pulling
several flatcars loaded with construction workers. One of
the persons who saw that first train was a five-year-old boy
who, grown to be Dr. R. F. Line, recalled:

My daddy and mother neither one had ever seen a train.
We made it to Fort Worth that night and camped out there
on the prairie where E. Lancaster is now. There were covered
wagons all over the place, must've been one hundred at least.
It was a little ol' engine. The smokestack was the biggest thing
about it. It had black smoke and a coarse whistle and big
bell that scared me. I'd been threatened all my five and a half
years with boogers. By golly, I thought, there's the booger.
I took off across the prairie like a jackrabbit. I'd never heard
such hollerin' in my life, dogs barking, horses running away.
I wanted to get out of there before the booger got me.[27]

[27] Dr. Line in *Fort Worth Star-Telegram*, July 20, 1949.

All over town people cheered and yelled until their throats were sore. To ease their throats with liquid application, droves of men trooped to saloons. The town was thrown wide open. From the railroad Fort Worth was expecting great riches. Businessmen determined that the first day should bring the first riches. The contractor had planned to pay his workmen at his base office in Dallas. But Mayor Day would have none of that. He persuaded the contractor to pay in Fort Worth, promising there would be no arrests for drunkenness, only for fighting and other serious law violations.[28]

That was Railroad Day—by all odds the greatest day in the history of Fort Worth.

Another occasion for celebration followed a few weeks later. All Fort Worth gathered and sent up more cheers on September 2 when the first railroad station—a frame structure just west of Lancaster and South Main—was dedicated. Paddock walked forward, made a brief speech, and presented a gold-headed cane to the railroad's first agent, L. J. Swingley, who with Cashier Leo F. Hurd represented the company. Paddock then bought the first railroad ticket, one that took him to Dallas. After serving twice as a passenger station and twice as a freight station, the original wooden building became a section house in 1903.[29]

The railroad was the third major factor in the development of a city. But it was more than that. For Fort Worth the railroad was the difference between hope and resignation, between importance and oblivion.

[28] G. H. Day in *Fort Worth Mail-Telegram,* July 18, 1902.
[29] *Fort Worth Telegram,* Aug. 16, 1903.

CHAPTER VI

Blood, Lust, and Gold

Fort worth erupted into the wildest town in western Texas. By the hundreds came men and women who pictured Fort Worth, now the westernmost railhead, as a golden mecca. Throngs of sweaty, desperate men jostled in the narrow streets. In loud, taut voices they screamed their prices for land and buildings at the frantic public auctions which became the best way of buying and selling land. The boom-town crowds gobbled up the scanty housing and multiplied their own numbers so rapidly that by 1877 an estimated one thousand persons lived in tents in and around Fort Worth.

In avaricious quest of gold came cowboys, professional gunmen who made their livings with a quick draw, swaggering buffalo hunters whose dark-bearded faces accentuated their reputation for ferocity and murder, squint-eyed gamblers with pistols bulging under their coats, and saucy dance-hall girls. They came in the wake of the trail herds and behind the pounding blasphemous men who built that wonderful railroad. They made their own rules as they went along.

Fort Worth pulled all stops and threw the gates wide for the entertainment of free-spending adventurers. Through the swinging doors of saloons drifted the banging of poorly played pianos, intermingled with the shrill, coarse laughter of painted women and the yahooing and guffaws of rough men. Into the night from opened second-floor windows came the clink of chips.

Wagons bogged down in the mud of Main Street on the way to the open yard on the square where Tuck Boaz bought cotton. Hogs roamed the streets and had to be chased out of the courthouse. Dead animals littered vacant lots and the spaces underneath the buildings, raising a stench that would turn a tenderfoot's stomach.

Fun was rough and sometimes bloody. Because of the sobriquet "Panther Town," live panthers frequently were mascots, causing a newspaper once to report, "The panther at the Keg Saloon scalped a man yesterday evening."[1] The first theater, the Adelphi, was opened in 1876, with Will G. Burton appearing in *Struck by Lightning.* After a few performances the owners slipped out of town under cover of darkness, leaving eight hundred dollars in debts. Within a month, the Adelphi was reopened as Theater Comique at Third and Main. Lights blazed in front of the theater-saloon to which crowds were attracted by a tight-rope walker performing over the street.[2] One old-timer once recalled that "we all thought we were tough but the toughest guys used to sit in the balcony at the old Theater Comique and for pastime they used to shoot the keys off the piano."[3]

On the second floor of his store B. C. Evans opened the first respectable theater in 1876. From kerosene-lighted Evans Hall came the rough applause of frontiersmen at *Rip Van Winkle, East Lynne, Fate of Captain Frye, On Hand,* minstrels, Josh Billings the humorist, and *Romeo and Juliet.* There, too, Madame Rentz's Female Minstrels introduced "for the first time in this city the Parisian sensation, the cancan" on March 7, 1877.[4]

In the variety houses, usually viewed as disreputable, beefy chorus girls drank and danced and slept with the customers. My Theater, opened January 2, 1880, as a successor

[1] *Fort Worth Democrat,* Jan. 25, 1873.

[2] *Fort Worth Star-Telegram,* Dec. 13, 1914.

[3] Vic Jossenberg, former lamplighter, in *Fort Worth Star-Telegram,* Oct. 23, 1949.

[4] *Fort Worth Standard,* March 8, 1877.

to Theater Comique, was one of the entertainment houses that kept the town lively. John Catchpole and the theater orchestra paraded daily, giving free concerts in front of the theater to attract business for the gas-lighted hall.

Old Fort Town was frisky as a colt and going hell-for-leather. Cowboys galloped through the streets, causing editors to ask querulously: "Is there any absolute necessity for riders to rush their mustangs down the street at break-neck speed? It is done too often."[5] Runaways were common, right down the main streets. Indignant editors also ranted about horsemen leaving their mounts hitched to awning supports, where the animals blocked the pitiful sidewalks. Since, however, the cowboy was still royalty in Fort Worth, no one paid any attention to the editors. As a matter of fact, the Headlight Bar advertised: "Ride right in boys and get bar service in the saddle." Typical cowboy exuberance was shown by the following story which appeared in the *Democrat* of April 10, 1878, under the headline, "The Cowboys' Tear":

A dozen or more of the festive cowboys, imbued with the spirit of pure devilishment, mounted their horses and as is their custom visited the several dance houses, caroused and danced with the "girls," drank when they felt so disposed, and continued their career without much trouble until about 1 o'clock when they all congregated at the Red Light, and after mounting their horses, each drew his six-shooter, and blazing away in the air, fired twenty or thirty shots, at the same time putting spurs to their horses, they made tracks for the depot, and there reloaded and fired another volley.

Subsequently three of the party were arrested at the "Waco Tap" by officers Thomas and Woody with the assistance of George Ware and jailor Elliott. The cowboys resisted efforts to arrest them and made every endeavor to prevent it, and but for the timely appearance of Elliott and Ware, officer Thomas would have been compelled to shoot one of the resisting party who was intent on using his own six shooter.

[5] *Ibid.*, Oct. 31, 1876.

Three of them were calaboosed after much trouble and six shooters taken from them.

Some fears were entertained that an attempt would be made by their comrades to release them during the night. At two o'clock, however, no such break had been attempted. The officers were very much exercised over the treatment they received at their hands.

The cowboys were aided in their carousals by the hours kept by saloons, most of which remained open all night. Indeed, some had no locks on the doors at all.[6] Some were ornate, with long, polished bars and a bar-long mirror behind, serving good food and good whisky. Others were cubbyholes with sawdust on the floor. A favorite was Uncle Bob Winders' Cattle Exchange, self-styled "handsomest saloon in Texas."[7] Herman Kussatz's Tivoli Saloon, complete with variety shows, offered a warm, free lunch every noon, plus German music. Henry Burns' saloon, at Main near Second, had concealed pits in the rear for prize fights, cock fights, and dog fights.[8] The pits were concealed because each type of contest was illegal. Usually the saloon had a big bruiser whom the management offered as the champion. Customers were encouraged to challenge him, with a promise of one hundred dollars should he be defeated. When a challenger came along, customers slipped into the rear, paid their admission, and watched a bloody, knock-down-and-drag-out fight. To avoid paying the challenger if it appeared he might win, a flunky would yell that the police were coming. His warning would send patrons and participants scurrying.

Pendery's Sample Room provided choice cigars and the latest St. Louis, Galveston, New York, and local newspapers. The Lafayette Restaurant, owned by F. Lantery, at Main and First, served meals at any hour for twenty-five cents.

6 *Fort Worth Democrat,* June 27, 1874.
7 *Fort Worth Standard,* Feb. 4, 1877.
8 *Fort Worth Democrat,* Jan. 1, 1877; *Research Data,* I, 48.

Other round-the-clock restaurants were Hunter and Sheridan's Saddle Rock Oyster Saloon and the Delmonico, with board at four dollars a week. The Want and Hartsfield Confectionery offered ice cream, oysters, cakes, custards, and candy.[9] For reading matter, Harry Cobb's newsstand at First and Houston had a selection of seventy-six daily and weekly publications, and eighteen monthly magazines.

Crime was rampant. Even the three courts—district, county, and mayor's—could not keep pace with the shootings, stabbings, thievery, and assaults. Into the rough and tumble, crime-ridden Fort Worth of the seventies stepped "Long Hair" Jim Courtright, an ice-nerved gunman with a capacity for inspiring loyalty. The first city marshal to serve more than one term, he was a tall man with a slightly crippled right hand, who sometimes let his hair grow to his shoulders—an effect common among gunmen and Indian scouts. Around his waist was strapped a belt with two six-shooters, butts forward. But he did not use the cross-body draw. Rather he drew from the right hip with the right hand, claiming it was faster that way. When indoors, he carried his pistols in a sash.[10]

As marshal from 1876 through 1879, his reputation for a fast draw and an accurate shot kept even notorious gunmen in check while they were in Fort Worth. He dealt firmly with flagrant violations of law and conduct, such as the time "Courtright 'snaked in' the rowdy who was shooting in the streets last night."[11] But as marshal he placed little faith in the discipline that would have kept his policemen out of the variety houses when they should have been patrolling.

Murderers, train robbers, and horse thieves he ran down with dauntless persistence. But gambling was something else again—a gentleman's privilege, perhaps. Courtright liked to gamble, and once while marshal he was hailed into court for playing pool. As long as gamblers were not unruly, Courtright

[9] *Fort Worth Standard*, Sept. 21, 1876; Oct. 4, 1876; March 24, 1877.
[10] Interview in 1949 with Dr. Will Woody, who as a boy lived in the same house with Courtright.
[11] *Fort Worth Standard*, March 27, 1877.

seldom bothered them, for they were his friends. Yet, ironically enough, in later years he was to die at the hands of a gambler and a one-time friend—the only man who ever beat him to the draw.

Courtright's jail was a log structure at Second and Commerce. On a busy Saturday night twenty-five to thirty men would be crowded into the two small cells and dungeon that comprised the jail. Two policemen patrolled the city by night and two by day. Usually the two men made their rounds together, covering a stretch of territory from the river bottom to the thinly settled district south of the tracks. Officers did not have badges, helmets, or clubs. They wore black slouch hats and blue uniforms.

Much tact was required in dealing with the unruly element. Cowboy joy parties of twelve to fifteen men frequently came to town to spend in a few riotous days the savings of months. Freighting wagons from Fort Sill and the frontier brought another class of men who sometimes caused trouble. The trail herds coming up from South Texas contributed their share of rough characters. Although the visitors were rough and reckless, they were seldom dangerous. However, they resented any overbearing assumption on the part of an officer. While they usually responded to discipline if treated fairly, they would fight a policeman or anyone else if they believed a friend mistreated.[12]

Besides petty and major crime within the corporate limits, which was bad enough, Fort Worth had another problem in the seventies. Desperadoes terrorized the countryside with train and stagecoach robberies. On January 29, 1878, the mail stage pulled away from the El Paso Hotel, starting west for Weatherford. The halfway stage stand at Mary's Creek was reached on time. Just beyond the creek, masked highwaymen armed with six-shooters and rifles halted the coach, relieving the five passengers of two gold watches and four or five hundred dollars.[13] That specific instance was typical of a wave

[12] Joe Witcher in *Fort Worth Star-Telegram*, Dec. 15, 1912, Part Six, 14.

of stagecoach robberies, not only of the westbound stage but also of stages coming in from the south. One of the robbers' favorite spots was the Mary's Creek crossing west of town. Another was in the Trinity bottom on the Weatherford road, almost within call of the business district. Then there were train robberies:

LAST NIGHT'S MAIL ROBBED!

The mail and express train due here last night at 1:20 and arrived at 1:30 was stopped at Eagle Ford on its arrival there at 12 o'clock, by four masked men armed with shot guns, Winchester rifles, and Navy sixes. They forced conductor Campbell, baggage master Caperton, engineer Smith, and the brakeman to leave the train, and stand on the platform under guard of three, while the fourth, with a six-shooter, got the drop on messenger Hickox, and compelled him to open the safe, from which only a small amount was taken. . . . They were all apparently young men, and seemed to be old hands. They put their plunder in a small bag and threatened, if there was a shot fired on their leaving, to return and raise "merry h——l." They quietly disappeared behind the depot on the north side of the tracks. None of the passengers was molested.[14]

ANOTHER TRAIN ROBBED!

Express Train No. 1, coming west on the Texas & Pacific road last night, due here at 1:30, was boarded at 10:40, immediately after stopping at Mesquite, the first station twelve miles east of Dallas. The first known presence of the robbers was their attack on the station operator who, with the mail bag in his possession, was going toward the express car, when two men approached with cocked six-shooters, and in preemptory tones demanded him to throw up his hands.

Not complying with their demands, they struck him several severe blows over the head with their shooters, flooring him. Eight or ten of the party then boarded the express. Their efforts to force their way inside was disputed by messenger

13 *Fort Worth Democrat,* Jan. 30, 1878.
14 *Ibid.,* April 5, 1878.

Kerley and other occupants who opened fire which was liberally returned by the robbers.

They finally got complete control of the train, and by force of numbers forced their way into the express. In this attempt one of them is reported as being shot dead, and Conductor Jules Alvord was shot in the left arm, while two balls passed through his hat.

Messenger Kerley resisted bravely, but was thrown down and overpowered. He succeeded in hiding about $1,500 before the entrance of the robbers who got away with $150, and all the registered letters.

Among other things, it was the expressed intention of the robbers to release from custody a number of convicted prisoners who were aboard and on their way to Huntsville, but the time occupied in gaining access to the express car was so long that they dared not carry out their intention.[15]

The notorious Sam Bass gang was blamed for both train robberies. Some time later the gang came out of hiding and stole some horses in Denton County. A posse was turned back in a gun battle. The alarm spread through North Texas. Courtright rushed to Denton where he joined a larger posse that was being formed. Bass and his gang eluded the pursuers.

Crime that erupted on darkened street and lonely countryside was seated deep in the nortorious Hell's Half Acre in the vicinity of Twelfth and Commerce, a human cesspool that resisted efforts of law enforcement agencies for years. Information that stagecoach robbers nested there brought a crackdown on Hell's Half Acre. But some quarters of the business community fought the move, with "many citizens and businessmen" paying for this advertisement on April 18, 1879:

> The cattle season beginning, we think more freedom ought to be allowed as everyone is aware of the amount of money spent in this city by the cattlemen and cowboys, thus making every trade and business prosper. We notice especially this year that, contrary to their usual custom, almost all of them

[15] *Ibid.,* April 11, 1878.

remain in their camps a few miles from the city and give as the cause the too stringent enforcement of the law closing all places of amusement that attract them.

The pressure lifted the restrictions on Hell's Half Acre, for the *Democrat* reported on June 15 that "the voice of the cowboy is once again heard in the land," and on June 21 that "the dance halls are in full blast again."

Organized sport made a debut in 1877, when Fort Worth formed a baseball team that was named the Panthers—a name that has remained throughout the years. After a few practice sessions on the prairie, the team donned white shirts, knee pants, and red stockings to entertain a team from Texarkana, which they defeated, on April 5, 1877. On April 18, Fort Worth defeated the arch rival, Dallas. Newspapers gloated at the 17 to 12 result.

On Railroad Day there was nothing but vacant prairie from the tracks to the business district clustered around the square one mile away. But the prairie flowered quickly with activity. New businesses opened so fast that the town had no less than 59 a few weeks after the first train rolled in. Within four years there were 460. The *Democrat* and the *Standard*, which alone of the several weekly papers had survived the depression, began daily publication. A railroad, two daily newspapers, and a population that jumped into uncounted thousands: for any town that signified the approach of prosperity.

The enormous West Texas market became the town's own territory. Regularly wagon caravans loaded at the railhead and rumbled westward, passing from view on the rolling prairies where they faded into the smokelike haze of the western sky. The magnitude of the wagon freight business moved an editor to remark: "Fort Worth gets all the northwestern trade —long streams of wagons roll out every day for the western towns, carrying heavy loads of freight." Teamsters were grasping for the trade of the Texas Panhandle, theretofore the exclusive preserve of Wichita and other Kansas towns, as well as the area from the Trinity to the Pecos and from Fort Worth into Indian Territory.

Incoming caravans were loaded with the skins and bones of buffalo killed on the western plains. In November, 1876, ten thousand hides were brought from Fort Griffin, called the world's buffalo capital, after the biggest hunt ever known at that time. The hides and bones were purchased by the St. Louis Hide Depot, owned by Gurley and Company. The hides were piled ten to fifteen feet high over a ten-acre tract on the T. and P. reservation, where they awaited rail transportation east. Many more acres were covered by horns, hooves, and bones that went east for use in the manufacture of fertilizer. While waiting for westbound consignments, freighters parked their wagons and tethered their animals by the hundreds on a giant commons north of the river.

The coming of the railroad definitely placed the city on a cash basis, supplanting the barter system that had been re-instituted during the depression. Adventurous businessmen hurried in from distant states to invest their money and reap a golden harvest.

One was John Lockwood, who moved in from New Jersey to set up the first artificial-gas plant. He laid this proposition before the businessmen: if they would subscribe ten thousand dollars to the venture, he would match it, erect the gas works, and supply gas at a reasonable price. Shirt-sleeved councilmen met on August 11, 1876, in the Weatherford Street cubbyhole that served as the only municipal office, passing an ordinance that gave Lockwood the go-ahead. To encourage him, the council agreed to pay four hundred dollars a year for each lamp post erected. On the other hand, Lockwood was restricted to a maximum price of five dollars per thousand cubic feet of gas, and was required to furnish an illuminating gas of fourteen candle power.[16]

[16] *Fort Worth Standard*, Oct. 24, 1876; *Minutes* of the Fort Worth City Council, Vol. A, p. 161; *Ordinances* of the City of Fort Worth, Vol. A, p. 81.

At dusk on March 25, 1877, the first street lamp was lighted. Prior to that time, there had been no illumination. Then began the era of the lamplighter. Sometimes he rode a black pony through the muddy streets. Halting at each lamp, he rose in his stirrups and with a stick opened three hood-shaped vents. A pilot light ignited the gas that issued. At dawn the lamplighter made the rounds once more, extinguishing the lights. Sometimes he made his rounds on foot, carrying on his arm a short ladder that he used to reach the lamp.

After a little more than two years of operation, Lockwood passed from the picture. John Peter Smith and associates formed the Fort Worth Gas Light and Coke Company, obtaining an exclusive municipal franchise for ten years. One of the earlier gas plants was on Bluff Street near the foot of Commerce, manufacturing gas from wood and from coal imported from Oklahoma.

Two days after Christmas of 1876, a diminutive mule-drawn car jolted over newly laid tracks on Main Street to inaugurate the first city transportation service. Each windowed car was about seven feet long, with a seat running lengthwise on either side. On December 28, 1876, the *Democrat* reported that two cars, numbered one and two, had gone into service the day before. The fare was five cents.

The line was owned by the Fort Worth Street Railway Company, which was incorporated with a capital of fifty thousand dollars by Van Zandt, W. H. Lawrence, Smith, George W. Newman, W. A. Huffman, and Zane-Cetti. Mule cars traveled over a single track from the courthouse to the depot, a distance of one mile along a Main Street that was seasonally dusty and muddy. While the mule car saved passengers a perhaps unpleasant walk, the rider sometimes would have done better by walking, for frequently the mule bolted, and on occasion the ride turned out like this:

> A bunch of the railroad fellows were loafing on our day off when we saw the car. The man that run the car asked if

we wanted to ride. Of course we got on, to our sorrow. About every block the car jumped the track, and got stuck in the mud. That's what he asked us to ride for—so we could lift the darn thing out of the mud.[17]

The streetcar business was profitable, nevertheless. Superintendent Dan Cary reported in 1878 that the two cars made 160 trips a day, transporting an average of 440 passengers. The annual profit was $7,200.[18]

These advertisements give an idea of what the railroad added to a sleepy village's business community:

WILLINGHAM BROTHERS, wholesale grocers and commission merchants. W. C. Howard, grocer. A. Griffeth & Company, jobbers and retail dealers in hardware, cutlery, iron nails, plows, carpenters, blacksmith and plantation tools, barb wire fence, wagon and carriage material. Builders material a specialty. South Side Square, between Houston and Main. Evans and Martin, dry goods, Houston Street.

MAX ELSER & Co., dealers in books, stationery, wallpaper, curtains, musical instruments, fancy goods, etc., country orders solicited, 25 Houston St. John Solon & Peter Cogley, contractors and builders, Houston St., brick work a specialty. D. M. Williams & Co., manufacturers and dealers in fine jewelry, American and Swiss watches, silver and plated ware, No. 6 Davis' block. Correct time taken from the sun by transit instrument. J. N. Manuel & Co., dealers in hardware, fence wire, iron nails, wagon material, agricultural implements and white-

THE CHEAP CASH STORE of Sanger Bros., the Go-Ahead Dry Goods merchants of Fort Worth, Texas, who will keep ahead of all other merchants in North-West Texas for low price and first class goods. J. B. Wells merchant tailor shop over the Railroad Store in the Peak Block on Houston street. Dodd & Co., wholesale and retail dealer in hardware, stoves

[17] George Walpole in *Research Data,* I, 138.
[18] *Fort Worth Democrat,* January, 1878.

Fort Worth in 1880,
looking south on Main Street from the courthouse

Fort Worth in 1949,
looking south on Main Street from the courthouse

Mule car photographed in 1881
at Boaz and Battle Cotton Yard, Main and Thirteenth streets

and tinware, queensware, wood and willow ware, japanned ware, furniture, lamps, etc., a general assortment of house furnishing goods. Houston Street. W. D. Thomason (late of Cleburne) has in the two-story brick building opposite the postoffice on Houston Street at the sign Here's Whar the Panter Lay Down a complete and good stock of dry goods, boots, shoes, clothing, and notions which he proposes to sell as cheap as anyone in this city or Dallas.

TEXAS CLOTHING HOUSE, A Goldstein & Co., dealers in clothing, hats, boots, shoes, general furnishing goods, trunks, blankets etc. Morris Davis & Walker, receiving, forwarding and commission merchants and lumber dealers, office at Rail Road Depot. R. L. Turner, dealer in staple and fancy groceries, canned goods, plantation and drovers' supplies, and every description of family furnishing goods. Also, candles, crackers &c. West Side of Public Square. The Old Reliable Jewelry Store, West Side Main Street. Call on Sneed & Howard for your watches, clocks and jewelry. E. Kuhn, fashionable boot and shoe-maker. Shop—North side of First between Main and Houston streets. Mitchell & Thurman, carpenters and joiners, Weatherford Street. All kinds of work done on short notice, and in genteel style. Repairs to furniture of any kind neatly executed. We keep coffins on hand all the time, and will attend promptly to all orders in the undertakers line.

MITCHELL will number your house for a nickel. Hofle & Co., dealers in gas fixtures and illuminating oils, gasoline and petroleum at the lowest cash prices, Main Street. Henry Miller, agent for the world-renowned Howe sewing machine, Chickering's, Steck's and Balmer & Weber's pianos, and Geo. Wood's and Peloubet, Pelton & Co. organs. Office:—South Side of Public Square. Henry Jacobs, dealers in Staple and Fancy Groceries, Tobacco and Cigars. Flour and feed a specialty.

ORNAMENTAL WEDDING CAKES at Want and Hartsfield's. All groceries delivered free by William Bros. & Barnes. Fakes & Co. always have all sizes of the celebrated Crone & Breed's Metallic coffins and caskets and rose-wood coffins. Coffins made to order on short notice, in any style. Prices from $3 to any price desired. New York Store, Houston and First Streets. Dry Goods, Ladies Trimmed Hats. J. & S. Brin.[19]

Gentleman of fashion rejoiced in February, 1878, when Dahlman Brothers, a drygoods store, made custom tailoring available. Formerly, gentlemen ordered tailored suits from New York, Louisville, St. Louis, or Chicago. While women could buy ready-made dresses in the small shops, many of them still made their clothing at home. They bought bolts of cloth from the store, and in making dresses they were guided in style by the occasional fashion notes which the *Standard* reprinted from New York papers.

As business reached for big-time levels, businessmen looked to organization as a means of expanding the market to the benefit of all. To this end, they organized the Board of Trade on a temporary basis on October 24, 1876, in the law offices of John Peter Smith and J. J. Jarvis, over the bank of Tidball, Van Zandt and Company. Permanent organization came in the same offices on November 2. But the momentum was not sufficient to keep the organization going. Not until May 31, 1882, was a successful, lasting Board of Trade organized.

In the late seventies insurance began appearing on the business roster. W. E. Kneeland was local agent for the Equitable Life Assurance Society in 1878. Swayne Brothers and Crane was organized, continuing through the years under different names until now it is the George Beggs Agency.

The first telephone was connected in May, 1877, a scant few months after Bell proved the practicality of his instrument in Massachusetts. The first two telephones were single lines. One connected the *Democrat* with the Club Room, a saloon on Main Street, and the other linked the home and drugstore of Dr. W. B. Brooks. Tin cans and tambourines were

[19] *Fort Worth Standard,* Feb. 4, Feb. 28, March 1, 1877.

used at one end to attract attention at the other.[20] On May 31, 1877, the *Democrat* reported:

THE TELEPHONE

A great deal has been said and written about this wonderful invention, but the first real live instrument in the city put in an appearance at the *Democrat* office yesterday. One end was attached to the wall in the Club Room, on Main Street, and the other to the west wall of the Democrat office on Houston street. The cord traversed, including angles, something over two hundred feet and conveyed the sound at this distance with remarkable distinctness. We could sit at our desk and order a lemonade from the Club Room in an ordinary tone of voice and the word would come back, "all right."

The town as a whole, however, was not as anxious for rapid communication as were the newspaper and Dr. Brooks, for by 1879 there were only a few instruments in the city, linking the express office, Waverly Hotel, El Paso Hotel, Leer's Stables, and the First National Bank.

The influx of people made hotels necessary. The Transcontinental, the Virginia House, Peers House, and the Pacific were built downtown, and the frame Clark House near the depot. Competition was strong, each hotel sending drummers to meet every train at the depot, where they fought for the valises of arriving passengers. In 1876 the Peers House daringly used "female waiters" who were said to be ornamental and "exceedingly useful."[21]

In March, 1878, C. K. Fairfax opened the lavish El Paso Hotel. One of the celebrated frequent visitors was the son of the tragic Cynthia Ann Parker, Quanah Parker, who as a chief persuaded the Quahadi Comanches to give up their war against the white man. One of his friends was Burk Burnett, a powerful cattleman whose herds grazed in Indian Territory. When Quanah and Yellow Bear came to Fort Worth

[20] Paddock (ed.), *Fort Worth and the Texas Northwest*, II, 628.
[21] *Fort Worth Standard*, Oct. 5, 1876.

to visit their friend Burnett in 1878, they were ensconced in the gaslighted El Paso, where Yellow Bear merely blew out the flame upon retiring, not knowing the gas must be turned off, too. During the night he was asphyxiated. Quanah, sleeping in the same room, barely escaped death.

On the El Paso site later were the Pickwick and Delaware hotels, both known throughout the ranch country, and the present Westbrook that was built in 1910 by Benjamin T. Tillar. W. H. Dunn built the Mansion of ninety-five rooms in 1876; later it became one of the best hotels in town. Some years afterward it was acquired by Winfield Scott, another wealthy cattleman, who converted it into the Metropolitan, for years the outstanding hotel. The Metropolitan now is the Milner.

The railroad also made Fort Worth a hub for stage lines that fanned north, south, and west. Early in 1877, a new line was opened to Fort Concho (now San Angelo) by way of Granbury, Stephenville, Comanche, Brownwood, Camp Colorado, and Coleman. The coach left Fort Worth at 6:00 A.M. on Monday and Thursday, and left Fort Concho on the return trip at 6:00 P.M. on Wednesday and Saturday. C. Bain and Company operated daily coaches from Fort Worth to Weatherford and thrice-weekly coaches from Weatherford to Jacksboro, Fort Belknap, and Fort Griffin. Dan Taylor ran the United States Mail Line to Cleburne, leaving Fort Worth at "7½ a. m." A daily hack left at 7:00 A.M. for Decatur.[22]

In 1878, Fort Worth became the eastern terminus of the world's longest stage line—the 1,500-mile line to Fort Yuma, Arizona. Opening of the line occasioned Fort Worth's first real parade, "a grand stage coach procession consisting of the coaches and hacks belonging to the eastern division of the 1,560-mile stage route." J. D. Chidester and John D. Adams, partners in the firm which operated the line, participated. In late afternoon the parade pulled away from its starting point at the El Paso Hotel, led by J. P. Alexander, postmaster

[22] *Fort Worth Democrat,* Jan. 1, 1877.

and parade marshal, whose coach was pulled by a team of spirited black horses. Next came the Fort Worth Brass Band in their band wagon. Chidester, referred to as "the old veteran stage king himself," drove one of the coaches. City councilmen, bankers, businessmen, newspapermen, railroad men, and out-of-town guests filled the line of coaches and hacks that stretched for a quarter-mile.[23]

When the Fort Worth–Fort Yuma stage line began operations, a six-horse team galloped out of town with a Concord coach that went as far as Thorp Spring in Hood County. From Thorp Spring a two-horse surrey took the mail and passengers to Brownwood. Thence a buckboard pulled by two bronchos was used for the dash across West Texas, New Mexico, and Arizona—country infested by fierce Comanches, war-maddened Apaches, and white desperadoes.

In later years the line was investigated as the "Star Route Steal" of the Grant administration, but United States marshals could never find Chidester, whose testimony was needed by investigators.[24]

Wagon yard and livery stable were important businesses in Fort Worth. The wagon yard was established to provide a place for immigrants to stop, get water, and reprovision. Sometimes it was enclosed by a fence and sometimes not. For the convenience of itinerants, the yard often had a well and cooking facilities. Some of the more important wagon yards were those of D. T. Copher, 605 Main; H. Dugan, 200 block on West Weatherford; Mitchell Brothers, Throckmorton and Weatherford; Wise and McDonough, Houston at Ninth. The last wagon yard was the Concho, in the 400 block on East Belknap, which ran until 1928. During the eighties, Buffalo Bill Cody reputedly had an interest in the Concho, which frequently sold as much as five hundred dollars' worth of hay and feed weekly.

A companion business was the livery stable, which was a

[23] *Ibid.*, June 16, 1878.
[24] Paddock (ed.), *Fort Worth and the Texas Northwest*, II, 626–27.

meeting place for the whole town. Men gathered for conversation in the shade of the stable in warm weather, and around a potbellied stove in cold. The livery stables performed several services. They boarded horses for fifteen dollars a month for a straight stall or twenty dollars for a box stall that gave the horse room enough to turn around. Rigs were rented for four dollars a day and six on Sunday. Brightly painted buggies of red and green were kept on hand for the dudes. Traveling salesmen were good customers, coming to town on the train and then renting a horse and buggy to call on the trade for miles around. Real estate men received special discounts because of the frequency of their business. For them it was smart business to rent a buggy, because a prospective customer was flattered to ride in a handsome buggy pulled by a spanking horse.

Too, the livery stable always rented hearses—black for adults, white for children—for funeral processions. Thus it was only a step into the funeral-directing business. In that manner George L. Gause started the present Gause-Ware Funeral Home. He came to Fort Worth in 1870 and studied law with his father, Colonel William R. Gause. In 1876 he opened the Missouri Wagon Yard, where a big part of his business consisted of renting hearses. For that reason, he went to the East to study embalming, and upon his return opened an undertaking parlor with Frank Flenner in 1879.

Some of the livery stables were W. T. and J. M. Maddox, "Passengers transported to all points at very reasonable prices"; Kenedy and Scott, who had a cistern in the center of their stable; Wims and Johnson, on the north side of the square; and Kelk Brothers at Fourth and Commerce, with "the finest selection of Missouri horses in northern Texas."[25]

On through the lean years of 1873–75 and into the flush year of 1876, Tidball, Van Zandt and Company and the California and Texas Bank of Loyd, Marklee and Company were

[25] *Fort Worth Standard,* Feb. 4, 1877; *Fort Worth Democrat,* March 8, 1873; Feb. 7, Feb. 15, 1878; *Fort Worth Star-Telegram,* Oct. 30, 1949, p. 14.

the city's two banks. But in 1876, Loyd withdrew from the California and Texas Bank, selling his interest to W. J. Boaz. Then the firm became Boaz, Marklee and Company, lineal descendant of Loyd's Exchange Office, the first bank; later it metamorphosed into the City National that was liquidated during a depression in the nineties. After selling out to Boaz, Loyd incorporated the First National Bank on January 16, 1877, a bank that still is in existence as the oldest national bank in Fort Worth. When the doors opened for business, deposits amounted to $72,000. By the end of the first year they had reached $220,000, and the first city bank dividend, of 12 per cent, was declared. Loyd remained president until 1912.

By the late seventies the legal field was crowded. Lawyers advertised not only their legal talents but also their services as land agents. B. F. Barkley, who had been county judge during Reconstruction, advertised as attorney, United States commissioner, and land agent, with seven thousand acres of choice land for sale in the county. Green and Beall, also land agents, offered their services in state courts of Tarrant and adjoining counties, the Supreme Court at Austin, and the federal District Court at Tyler.[26] Their colleagues included W. S. Pendleton, S. Furman, Henry M. Furman, Jarvis, G. A. Evarts, H. G. Hendricks, and Thomas J. Jennings.

Lawyers took plenty of time in court. Once a chambermaid was tried in the mayor's court on a charge of disorderly conduct. The prosecutor, Henry Fields, and the defense counsel, Byron G. Johnson, argued for two hours each, even in such a relatively minor case. The woman was acquitted.

With the completion of the railroad, Fort Worth assumed a greater stature as the cattleman's town, supplying ranches and serving as a transit point for livestock shipped north. Too, some cattlemen still trailed their herds north, making Fort Worth, as in the past, a major trail stop, because of the traditional Texas cattle with their long, sharp horns made enclosed transportation impractical. Typical of the herds that

[26] *Fort Worth Standard*, Feb. 4, 1877.

came through in 1877 was that of Harvey Brerris of Goliad, who drove 650 head through on April 9, 1877. By mid-May, 75,470 head had passed, including the herds of Ellison and Dewees, Sol West, Kennedy, D. R. Faut, Rachal Brothers, and the Oliver Brothers. In addition, 51,923 head were shipped by rail in 1877. The drives continued in 1878, with a local newspaper estimating that no fewer than 60,000 head had passed within sight of the courthouse cupola during April and May.[27]

Entrepreneurs inquired seriously into the possibility of making Fort Worth a meat-packing center when the newly developed refrigerator car came into use. To try out the idea, cattle were killed and the meat shipped east in a refrigerated car for the first time on May 13, 1877.[28] However, there was little momentum behind the idea. Before Fort Worth could develop as a packing center, a very special set of conditions had to exist. Not until the first years of the twentieth century were those conditions favorable.

During the seventies the two outstanding community influences were the *Democrat* and the *Standard*, which ceaselessly devoted themselves to developing Fort Worth on sound economic, moral, and cultural bases.

The credo of the *Democrat* was that "time or circumstance can never change, alter, amend, or destroy fixed principles of truth, justice, and honor."[29] The paper was active editorially, complaining of poor mail service, urging fire protection, cementing the founding stone of the fire department, and needling citizens into fulfillment of their civic responsibilities. The intensely human nature of the paper was shown by its policy with regard to subscriptions and advertising: "We take all kinds of produce for subscriptions. . . . Corn, wood, oats, butter, eggs, chickens, etc. taken in payment. We take cash only for 'ads.'"

[27] *Fort Worth Standard,* March 8, 1877; May 12 and 22, 1877; *Fort Worth Democrat,* April 10, 1877; January 2, 1878, and May 5, 1878.
[28] *Fort Worth Standard,* May 15, 1877.
[29] *Fort Worth Democrat,* June 21, 1873.

As early as 1873 the farsighted Paddock instituted special agricultural columns to guide and educate farmers. Full of faith in the city's future, the railroad-minded *Democrat* regularly published maps showing railroads radiating from Fort Worth—at first there were nine roads on Paddock's Tarantula Map, later eleven.

With the T. and P. coming nearer each day in 1876, Paddock kept a promise he had been making for three years—to publish a daily paper. From a new plant on the south side of the square, the *Daily Democrat* appeared on July 4, 1876, the city's first daily. Published in tabloid form, the paper had a masthead showing a panther crouched in the foreground of Fort Worth. Almost apologetically Paddock announced: "This morning, July Fourth, 1876, the one hundredth birth day of our young and vigorous nation, we launch upon the unknown seas, our frail and diminutive barque, and commit its destinies to the care and watchfulness of an interested public. We do so with no little trepidation."

His fears were justified, for a town of three thousand could not nourish a daily newspaper, causing the paper to be a "financial failure from start to finish."[30] But it was eminently successful as an institution. Using a candlebox for a desk, Paddock directed the destinies of the daily and weekly *Democrat* with such capability that it served the community with distinction.

The *Daily Democrat* suspended publication on February 4, 1880, for financial reasons, and resumed on July 4, for political reasons. During the period of the daily's eclipse, the weekly appeared regularly. Even with a six-months' suspension the daily outlasted all of its contemporaries, finally merging on December 11, 1881, with the *Advance* to form the *Democrat-Advance*.

Whereas the *Democrat* first was conceived and brought into being in 1871 by businessmen who wanted a journal of some permanence, the *Standard* appeared as the direct result

[30] *Fort Worth Democrat*, Feb. 7, June 27, 1874.

of the railroad boom. Among the men who followed the lure of the railroad was J. K. Millican, who came from Homer, Louisiana, with the intention of founding a newspaper. The equipment and materials arrived on May 2, 1873. Publication began twelve days later. Millican's executives were Editor S. C. McCormick and Publisher W. O. Stillman. From an office near Main and Weatherford, they directed a weekly newspaper that rode the crest of the 1873 boom and bucked the tide to remain alive during the recession that followed.

Under the impetus of the railroad, the *Standard* began daily publication on September 2, 1876, living up to its claim: "Fort Worth Standard, daily and weekly, the largest, best and neatest paper in North-West Texas, excepting Dallas Journals, a Newspaper for the People, Daily, $12 a year by mail, 25 cents per week by carrier."

The *Daily Standard* at first obtained telegraphic dispatches by clipping them several days late from other newspapers, but finally managed to have a telegraphic report of its own. Throughout the time the *Standard* was a daily, Millican employed vigorous editors who made it a crusading newspaper. They hammered at the need for improved fire protection, adequate water works, paved streets, sidewalks, enforcement of the law against fast riding, suppression of rowdies who from time to time shot up the town, for a courthouse and jail, a free bridge across the Trinity, and against local option on saloons. In almost every instance the *Standard's* point was carried.

Elsewhere in the commercial realm changes were taking place. In 1877, when the diminutive police force was clothed in gray coats and hats that resembled Confederate uniforms, E. W. Morton opened the first compress. Houses began to be numbered. The sounds of industry were heard from Myers and Souders Carriage Manufactory and the Fort Worth Wagon and Plow Company.

Along with extensive economic development religion gained a firm foothold. Although complaints had been made in 1873 about the inadequacy of churches, the church column of the *Democrat* in 1874 listed the following services:

Baptist Church every Sabbath at Court Room, Elder Lockett, pastor.

Christian Church, first and fourth Sundays, Elder A. Lark, pastor.

Cumberland Presbyterian Church, first Sunday in each month at Masonic Hall, Rev. W. D. Wear, pastor. Services at 10½ o'clock a. m. and 8 p. m.

Methodist Church every Sunday at the Court House, 11 o'clock a. m. and 7 o'clock p. m. Sabbath School at 9 a. m. R. H. H. Burnett, P. C.

Catholic services, house of Mr. Scott on Main Street, last Sunday in every month, Father Parrier.

Union Sabbath School—at Masonic Hall every Sunday at 9 o'clock a. m. John Hanna, superintendent.[31]

Episcopal services were firmly established in 1874, when Rev. Alexander C. Garrett, as bishop of the Missionary District of North Texas, organized a Fort Worth mission, placing Rev. Edwin Wickens in charge. Garrett traveled far to find money for the financing of his missions and churches. While riding a New Haven and Hartford train, he chanced upon John Henry Smith, senior warden of a small parish in South Norwalk, Connecticut. Garrett's stories of the difficulties encountered in his work in Texas caused Smith to offer five hundred dollars for the construction of a church. Smith said he would be pleased should the church be named St. Andrew's. Garrett returned to Texas with the money. And on December 31, 1877, the cornerstone of St. Andrew's Episcopal Church was laid.

Education was flourishing, too. Under Reconstruction the city had a few free public schools maintained at state expense, but the state stepped out of the picture when federal

31 *Ibid.*, Aug. 8, 1874.

control ceased. From then until the end of the decade, the educational unit was the private or subscription school.

Education was expensive. For example, here are the fees per child levied by Mrs. Leo F. Smith, who opened a school in August, 1874: "Tuition per month in advance: Orthography, $2; defining, reading, and writing, $2.50; English grammar, history, geography, and arithmetic, $3; natural philosophy, algebra, rhetoric, and botany, $4; French, $2; drawing, pencil, $2; oil painting, $3."[32]

In 1878, W. F. Mister opened the first coeducational high school, a departure from the previous system that placed boys and girls in separate schools. Other schools in 1878 were the Weaver Male Institute, operated by Professor W. T. Weaver, whom the *Democrat* credited with building the first high school in town. It also was the only exclusively male high school in North Texas, west of the Central Railroad, where young men could receive a thorough "college course." Another was Mrs. Belle M. Burchill's school of 130 scholars. Other schools were operated by Mrs. E. S. Scribner and Miss Jennie Alford. The Arnold-Walden Institute, one of the best remembered, occupied a building at 614 West Fourth Street.

Because of the stress, strain, and excitement of the West, music was slow to extend beyond the stringed instruments until the seventies, when fast-arriving homesteaders provided a suitable incentive. Early in the decade piano instruction was offered by Clarks' Male and Female Institute. A Silver Cornet Band was organized in 1875. By 1876, H. Miller's Musical Emporium seemed "the resort of all the talent in Fort Worth." Apparently the first music school was the one founded by Professor E. D. Tatum in 1877—the same year that the first operas, *Il Trovatore* and *La Favorita*, were offered at Evans Hall by the Tagliapietra Opera Company.

With wealth came homes, real homes. The trend can be no better exemplified than by the experience of J. J. Jarvis, who brought his family to Fort Worth immediately after the

[32] *Ibid.,* Oct. 30, 1949, Homes Section, 2.

Civil War, settling them in a three-room cottage on the site now occupied by the Westbrook Hotel. Jarvis was an attorney, whose practice in the first lush years gave him an opportunity to participate in several of the corporations that were organized in the seventies. By 1873 he was able to build a better home. Importing lumber by ox wagon from East Texas, he built the first two-story residence. Thenceforward Fort Worth began acquiring the atmosphere that goes with a settled town. Lavish homes were built on Samuels Avenue, stretching along the bluff from the courthouse, and West Seventh Street soon was dotted with elegant houses. The small-windowed log cabins and the simple frame houses with their dogtrots were replaced by homes with leaded-glass windows, high ceilings, elaborately carved mantels, oak and walnut wainscoting, ivory-enameled pillars and panels, many mirrors, spacious drawing rooms, and delicately shaped chandeliers.[33] The homes meant a permanent base for a new town.

CHAPTER VII

Vice and Reform

VICE and lawlessness were virtually unchecked by
1878. Gamblers set up their games on sidewalks.
Because the town was full of prostitutes, respectable women could not walk down the street without the danger of being accosted. Thugs infested dark streets.
Professional men dared not return home from work after dark
unarmed. Reform was imperative.

Municipal government, which had been of slight importance when Fort Worth was only a cattle-trail hamlet, assumed a sudden and dual significance when the town boomed
after Railroad Day. For the unscrupulous politician the city
government became a vehicle for personal gain, while businessmen of a certain stripe knew that their advantage would
best be served by an easygoing city administration. For the
men who wanted to make their homes in Fort Worth and
who hoped to build legitimate careers, the city government
was an instrumentality that must be clear of corruption, graft,
and doubt if law and order were to prevail. A tug-of-war developed between the two forces as the election of 1877 approached, the first election of any importance in the four
years the city government had functioned. With the town
running wide open in the absence of any serious efforts to
check crime and immorality, the entire city government was
brought under fire. Part of the attack was aimed at the form
of government.

The ever critical *Standard* campaigned for a division of

the town into wards, arguing that the practice of electing councilmen at large did not make for the most effective government, whereas the election of aldermen to represent certain wards would assure a more democratic type of government. Swayed by the *Standard's* campaign, the council created the alderman system on February 6, 1877, dividing the town into three wards—the first ward was east of Main and north of Ninth streets; the second, west of Main and north of Ninth; the third, everything south of Ninth.

Because of the importance of the 1877 election, candidates were eager for office, passing out cigars, buying drinks, and chipping in to feed a dog that wandered the streets covered by a blanket on which campaign cards were pinned.[1]

Although Mayor Day and his administration were in disfavor, they were strong. A root-hog campaign developed. Once more the *Standard* stepped into the fray, constantly urging its readers to attend a "monster rally" of municipal candidates on March 24 in the district courtroom, which then was over the Cattle Exchange Saloon, the regular courtroom having been destroyed in the courthouse fire. From the rally echoed the major municipal issues that were rending the city.

With vigor and vituperation J. F. Beall, a candidate for mayor, attacked the city administration, bluntly charging Mayor Day with responsibility for the existence of open gambling and the presence of flourishing brothels in both commercial and residential neighborhoods. Beall campaigned for cessation of public gambling and for laws forcing prostitutes to congregate in one part of the city, for better streets, for a sidewalk on Houston since Main Street had the mule car, and for a water works. Day blandly said that he did not care to attack his opponents personally, and stood on his record. His record must have been good enough for the hell-bent town, because he was re-elected.[2]

Despite the strong warnings contained in the opposition

[1] *Fort Worth Standard*, March 9, 1877.
[2] *Ibid.*, March 26, 1877.

campaign, the administration did little to improve conditions. As a result there were several developments that caused trouble, some of them carried over from pre-election conditions, others new.

While the council made a few feeble efforts that brought about a certain degree of order, the members were subject to pressures that fostered constant turmoil. The area of greatest conflict was in the regulation of certain businesses for the public good. Church pressure forced the first blue law, when the council, on November 28, 1876, passed an ordinance forbidding amusement places and businesses to open on the Sabbath. But the ordinance was repealed less than a month later. An ordinance prohibiting the sale of intoxicants in any place where shows were held reached the council on November 14, 1876, only to be tabled with the notation that it would be enacted unless Joe Lowe, owner of the Centennial Theater, started paying his taxes regularly.

The police department of five men had little to do other than maintain the fine line between anarchy and the turbulent, barely restricted conditions existing in Fort Worth. Police responsibility began and ended with checking violence of the more flagrant sort, like gun fights in the street, and preventing gun bullies from running the town. Certainly there were few ordinances of a civil nature that required police enforcement.

Another source of bitterness was an occupation tax levied in 1877, when the council was trying to find additional revenue to supplement that received from the property tax. When the tax was held illegal under state law, the council was forced, on March 7, 1878, to rescind all occupation taxes and refund the fines that had been assessed for nonpayment. Even though the tax had been erased from the statutes, businessmen continued to hold it against the Day administration.

As the town grew larger between 1877 and 1878, there was a steady worsening of conditions: gambling on the sidewalks to a degree greater than known before; murders, shootings, and beatings in the "bloody third ward" that encompassed the Acre; unrestricted dance houses; neglect of city finances; robberies unpunished; collection of fines that amounted to protection money for some of the lawless elements.

Because there were so many prostitutes in the town, the wife of a prominent man was insulted on the street by a merchant not acquainted with her. Because brothels were scattered all over the city, men unfamiliar with the town sometimes attempted to enter private homes.

Like a slow-burning fuse that hisses long before reaching the charge, public anger waited until mid-March—just a few weeks before the 1878 election—before exploding a political insurrection. Head on, reform and vice collided violently in the first major municipal campaign in the city's history.

Leading the reform forces into the field, R. E. Beckham, a rising attorney, picked Day as his personal target and announced his candidacy for mayor. On March 12, 1878, the first rally of the year was held in the main room of the new courthouse that was then just nearing completion. Like St. George galloping to battle against the dragon, Beckham pummeled Day in a twenty-minute speech, calling the city government a farce. He cited devaluation of the city scrip to twenty-five and thirty cents on the dollar, when a year before it had been good dollar for dollar. During the preceding year, he contended, nineteen thousand dollars was paid into the city treasury; now the city was on the verge of bankruptcy, streets were deplorable, and the city was without credit. He accused Mayor Day of being engrossed with his court, the customary $3.00 fine and the inevitable $9.85 costs. "Why," he demanded vehemently, "are not all city officials paid in greenbacks as are the officers? The city administration is just one little police court."

"Them's my sentiments exactly," chimed in J. M. Peers, hotel owner and another candidate for mayor.

Mayor Day then took the platform, saying, "I come here filled with the milk of human kindness. I love everybody here.

I offer myself as a sacrifice to the dear people for the good of the country."[3]

The dear people took Day at his word, sacrificed him in the election, and placed Beckham with a reform council in office. The young mayor at once ringed gamblers and brothels with toughened laws and reorganized city finances. As the Beckham administration progressively cleaned up municipal affairs, the council, on July 1, 1879, ordered all saloons and beer halls closed on Sunday and the prompt grading of Main Street from the square to a point south of the T. and P. tracks.

Regulatory powers of a municipality began to assume major significance on December 26, 1879, when the council enacted an ordinance regulating the construction of theaters and other public buildings. The intent was to insure sound construction principles for protection of the public.

The Beckham administration also got the hogs off the streets. For years the grunting hogs had been a major nuisance, running loose on the crowded streets and on the sidewalks, where they curdled mudholes into stys. The carcass of an accidentally killed hog would remain on the streets for days, the odor from the decomposing flesh adding to the stench of gutters. But the hogs were important to the larders of many people, making the council loath to do anything about the nuisance. Nor was the Beckham administration ready to rid the city of hogs arbitrarily. Before taking action, the council tested public opinion with a referendum on May 21, 1878. By the narrow margin of 377 to 324, the public favored adoption of an antihog law.

Narrow though it was, the margin was sufficient justification for action by Beckham and his colleagues. On July 16 they enacted an ordinance aimed at all stray animals in general and at hogs in particular. The first poundkeeper, J. P. Alford, was appointed with authority to impound all animals running loose. Everybody was given carte blanche authority to herd hogs into the pound at any time.

[3] *Fort Worth Democrat,* March 13, 1878.

Another nuisance had to be brought under control. Bothersome street salesmen caused the council, on June 6, 1878, to pass an ordinance setting fines of from five to twenty dollars for anyone who stopped, harassed, disturbed, importuned, or grabbed the person or possession of any citizen. Little good was accomplished by the ordinance at first, the council finding it necessary a few months later to adopt a resolution bluntly directing the city marshal to enforce the ordinance.

An inquiry was undertaken by the council to bring police conduct and efficiency under surveillance. The seven-man force was reduced to three. Changes also were made in the fire department. The city had been renting fire horses, which the council thought was a foolish policy. Accordingly, the first city-owned fire team was purchased from Nichols and Monica for $427. At the same time, the first fire department salaries were approved in June, 1878: sixty dollars a month for Engineer G. W. Hill and fifty dollars for H. C. Woody, driver.

By the time Beckham completed his term, he had shored the municipal structure with a stability that John Peter Smith, taking office in 1882, would use as a basis for the first competent response to the challenges of a new town.

Creation of a fire department had been the principal improvement of Beckham's predecessors. The M. T. Johnson Hook and Ladder Company had remained as a volunteer, autonomous group owning its own equipment until May 25, 1875, when the council paid one thousand dollars for the truck, ladders, buckets, rope, grappling hooks, and other apparatus. The hand-drawn wagon remained in service for a total of ten years, and after a period of disuse was sold to Cleburne in 1885 for one hundred dollars.[4]

The weak hook-and-ladder company remained as the sole safeguard against fire, even when population and building mushroomed in 1876. Frame buildings were thrown up more profusely than ever before. Wood fires still were a threat. Harping by the *Democrat* and the *Standard* for better fire

4 *Minutes* of the Fort Worth City Council, Vol. E, p. 346.

protection was to no avail. Then came two disastrous fires. On March 22, 1876, the courthouse burned and with it practically all of the county records. On September 22, the Prairie House, a hotel, burned to the ground, along with the adjoining store of Max Isaacs, the Key Saloon, and a residence.

With the next issue, the *Standard* began a running bombardment of City Hall for a fire engine and several cisterns to supply water. Arguing that the Prairie House fire might be the beginning of a series, the paper urged that a fire engine be purchased and that the money be raised by a special tax if necessary.[5]

At length the council bowed to the *Standard's* insistence, in part, and on October 3 placed an order with the Silsby Manufacturing Company of Seneca Falls, New York, for a horse-drawn pumper costing $6,250—the city's first fire engine. The council balked at the suggestion of cisterns, thinking that they had done enough in spending $6,000 for a shiny fire engine.

To man the new engine, a second fire company was formed on October 17. The twenty-five men present elected Loyd president and E. E. Furman secretary. The company members decided the engine should be named the "Panther" and that their organization should be known as "Panther Company No. 2." For uniforms they selected blue shirts with a red front and a white figure.

Organization of the Panther Company presaged the first true fire department, which was formed on October 21 by merging the new unit with the old volunteer company. John Nichols was elected chief of the new volunteer department. Other officers were Loyd, president; J. P. Woods, vice president; C. McDougal, secretary; and W. T. Maddox, treasurer.[6]

The Silsby engine arrived on November 11. It was tested by J. P. Tiller, an engineer representing the manufacturer, in front of the building occupied by the *Standard,* whose re-

[5] *Fort Worth Standard,* Sept. 22, 1876.
[6] *Ibid.,* Oct. 21, 1876.

porter said that four minutes after fire was ignited in the furnace the whistle blew, indicating steam was ready to work. In another minute and a half, water appeared through a hundred feet of hose. In another fifteen seconds, a stream was thrown one hundred feet.[7]

Because larger quarters were needed, both fire companies were moved into an old store building between Weatherford and First, fronting on an alley immediately east of Main Street —the town's second fire station. In February, 1877, the fire department moved to the newly-built City Hall at Second and Commerce. On the second floor were the city offices. The first floor was occupied by the hook-and-ladder wagon, the fire engine, and Billy, the pet panther. Once Billy broke loose while several firemen were in the station. One terrified man climbed a hot stovepipe, others dived through windows, and some clambered on the wagon.[8]

Finally, the council met the *Standard's* demands for a system of cisterns that would furnish water for fire fighting. On March 6, 1877, W. J. Allen was awarded a $1,025 contract to dig three cisterns—one of fifteen-hundred-barrel capacity on the square, another of five hundred barrels at Commerce and Second, and a third of five hundred barrels near the depot. When Allen was elected to the council a month later, the contract passed to D. O'Flaherty, who finished the cisterns that supplied water until the first mains were laid in 1882.

The vigor of municipal politics was duplicated in state and national politics. In 1876, Fort Worth was a political cauldron, seething with reaction to the despised Republican administration in Washington. Daily the *Standard* thumped for the Democratic presidential ticket—Samuel J. Tilden of New York and Thomas A. Hendricks of Indiana.

The same full support was given Democratic candidates for state and Congressional offices, especially to J. W. Throckmorton, former governor, who was a candidate for Congress

7 *Ibid.*, Nov. 11, 1876.
8 *Ibid.*, Jan. 3, 1877.

from the Third District. His opponent was referred to by the *Standard* in this wise: "J. C. Bigger of Dallas is now the Radical candidate for Congress in this, the third district, against Throckmorton. Put him down in your 'fool's book.'" During the campaign Bigger made a speech in Fort Worth when he was interrupted several times by hecklers. The *Standard* said: "Such men as he is can do but little harm in an intelligent community like this. What they want is to create disturbances for political capital and we ought not to accommodate them, but allow them to pass unnoticed."[9]

County politics that year was something to watch, too. Running for county judge, a post recently created by the 1876 constitution, C. C. Cummings was resented as a newcomer—he had been in town only three years—an astounding attitude in view of the population make-up at that time. In rebuttal he shouted that a combine of all other candidates had ganged up on him. Dubbing them the "courthouse ring," he called their names at every rally. His tactics were successful.

National politics and especially those of the Southern states were watched carefully. Editorially the *Standard* said that the South Carolina elections presaged a "bloody war of races," because Negro voters outnumbered whites, and called the Republican administration "the desperate clique of robbers." During the campaign no innuendo was too sharp, no attack too crude. The *Standard* declared that the bankruptcy of several English ironmasters, a panic in Portugal, and religious riots in China "are only more damning evidences of the incapacity of General Grant and our present Republican administration."[10] Furthermore, the *Standard* said, the Radicals were spreading the tale that Tilden when a boy used to keep one of the two nickels given him for Sunday. In reply the editor wrote that Hayes, when taking collection in church after he was a grown man, put tar in his hat and kept all the money that stuck.[11]

9 *Ibid.*, Oct. 21, 1876.
10 *Ibid.*, Sept. 22, 1876.   11 *Ibid.*, Oct. 3, 1876.

On the day preceding the presidential election of November 7, 1876, the *Standard* took pains to warn readers of certain clauses in election laws—namely, no one could vote more than once, and no one could come within half a mile of a polling place if he were armed with a bowie knife, or six-shooter.

Confident of victory, the Democrats held a special meeting in the *Standard* office to arrange a Tilden-Hendricks demonstration. A committee was named to procure anvils, powder, and "all auxiliaries for a magnificent display, and shoot as much as we blame please." During election day telegraphic reports told of Tilden's victory. That night, crowds gathered on the square, fireworks were exploded, and happy Democrats made speeches. A night or two later Weatherford "had her whiskey and fireworks."[12]

The celebrations were premature. Jubilation soon soured into indignation. The outcome of the balloting in South Carolina had been placed before a returning board that certified all Republican candidates in defiance of a Supreme Court order. The enraged *Standard* screamed, "White livered scoundrels."[13] When the House of Representatives finally decided the election, the *Standard* used this headline on the front page, reflecting the attitude of the community:

WASHINGTON—185 TO 184
R. B. HAYES AND W. A. WHEELER
PRONOUNCED PRESIDENT
AND VICE PRESIDENT.

The Bleak, Wintry Blasts of
Discontent for Four More
Long, Long Years.

*All Honest Men Look Sorrowful
and Ashamed at the
Result.*[14]

---

[12] *Ibid.*, Nov. 8–16, 1876.
[13] *Ibid.*, Nov. 28, 1876.   [14] *Ibid.*, March 3, 1877.

Scattered through the edition were bitter references to Hayes as "His Fraudulency." The editor noted that Hayes had asked for divine guidance, and suggested that "he instead direct his prayers to the devil whose blackness and crimes are more in accordance with the designs of Hayes and his thieves." The one-vote margin in the House of Representatives, which sat as the final appeal body, was described as "palming an infamous falsehood upon the country." There was a dismal prediction that Hayes would be the last president the people ever would have a chance to vote for, and that "to say Hayes will have an opinion of his own is simply preposterous." It was to be a long time before Fort Worth could celebrate a Democratic presidential victory.

Religion was adding one new victory after another as Fort Worth advanced through the founding period of the eighteen seventies. One of the important church additions during the decade was that of the Presbyterians. The earliest contemporary reference to the denomination was the announcement in the *Democrat* of March 1, 1873: "We are informed that Mr. J. R. Knight has very generously donated a lot on which to erect a church building for the Presbyterians."

However, the 1873 panic intervened, and the church was not built until 1874—a frame structure between First and Second streets on Calhoun, later replaced by "the little brown church" at Fourth and Calhoun. Four years later the Taylor Street Cumberland Presbyterian Church was founded at Fifth and Taylor streets. The congregation merged in 1916 with the First Presbyterian Church to form a new First Church.

CHAPTER VIII

"Queen City of the Prairie"

UPON the bruised earth of the seventies, a town of gentility and decorum emerged in the eighties. With the exhaustion of the riotous, blasphemous frontier, there evolved a pattern of life that comes with quieter years. Imperceptibly, subtle changes gradually developed social strata in the heterogeneous community, setting them apart one from another.

To be sure, the new life did not begin abruptly, like the opening of a fresh book with crisp, clean pages. Rather, the metamorphosis was more like opening a book to find the first pages smudged and each succeeding page less soiled than the one preceding, until the middle of the book is reached and one suddenly is aware that all of the pages are clean.

With a population of 6,663, Fort Worth in 1880 was being hailed as the Queen City of the Prairie. But the butcher was a daily reminder that the frontier had not passed altogether, for in his wagon were venison, bear, buffalo, and prairie chicken, all taken from the immediate town area and the plains of West Texas.

Saloons, gamblers, and gunmen—the White Elephant, Luke Short, Ben Thompson—still flourished. Nevertheless, a more civilized atmosphere was developing, as reflected by newspaper advertising. Merchants, who had a few years before advertised only the barest of necessities, now were offering fancy groceries, gloves, stylish hats for men, cloaks, ulsters, carpets, and "gents' underwear."

Happily the *Democrat-Advance* soliloquized on January 1, 1882:

> 1881 was very kind to Fort Worth. It found the city hovering on the ragged edge of uncertainty, as to whether it would remain an overgrown village or develop into a city. It leaves it without a doubt in the minds of any, the most prosperous and progressive city in the state, the admiration of all, and with a future before it full of hope, and which excites the envy of all its rivals.
>
> Railroads have been built into its corporate limits from all directions and there are others yet to come. Factories, foundries, and shops have sprung up and their number will be augmented. Stately business houses and palatial residences have been erected. Thousands have been added to its population and each recurring day brings new faces, more business, more capital, and renewed energies on the part of our people.

Growing commerce, industry, and finance compounded a social mixture that led a correspondent for the *New York Daily Chronicle* to write this impression in 1882:

> The city is cosmopolitan. It has the rush and energy of a frontier town with strange contrasts of nationality. It smacks of Mexico and New York. Broadway and the ranch brush against one another.

Five years later, on May 25, 1887, the transition was marked boldly by the *Gazette* which said:

> Refinement follows wealth according to the law of cause and effect, and social pleasures increase and multiply as refinement ploughs its way into rugged western life. This has been noticeable in the social status of Fort Worth during the last three years. At the beginning of that period, but little attention had been paid to the development or cultivation of social relations among the people.
>
> The previous seven years in the history of the city had been

124

spent with everybody in pursuit of money. Many had scarcely expected to make Fort Worth a permanent home, and their minds occasionally went back to scenes of other days in other states. The border roughness was exhilarating in a business view but depressing in its social aspects.

But the year 1883, with its era of public improvement, caused a revolution in social affairs. Homes were improved. The city began to have a finished appearance. Shrubbery and shade trees were cultivated. Men of wealth built costly residences. Sidewalks sprang into existence in all parts of the city which then was growing very rapidly.

The churches increased in numbers. Their congregations swelled and the social garden budded and blossomed in proportion to the development of business enterprises. The roughness of frontier life was passing away. The city prospered. Everybody prospered, and life in Fort Worth commenced to adorn itself with comforts and delicacies.

A frontier town had blossomed into a cosmopolitan city.

The town's economic structure was basically weak in 1880 because there was only one railroad, the Texas and Pacific, and it was being extended farther westward all the time. Coming through town, the locomotive sounded a moanful whistle, answered at night by the lonely howl of wolf and coyote. Like a mockery, the eerie howls told Paddock, Van Zandt, Daggett, Smith, and the others how insignificant was their town in the vastness of the plains.

They worked with unstinted labors to bring additional railroads. The T. and P. gave Fort Worth an outlet to the east. Now an outlet to the north was needed, along with one to the south that would connect at ship-side with the steamers and the tall-masted schooners that clipped the topaz waters of the Gulf with their cargoes from New York, Manchester, and the Orient.

The northern outlet was provided first, when the Missouri-Kansas-Texas Railroad extended its tracks into Fort Worth. Generally following the old Baxter Springs cattle trail southward through Missouri and the Indian Territory, the Katy reached Denison in 1873, maintaining a southern terminal there as a receiving point for herds trailed from South Texas. In January, 1880, the Katy acquired a line built during the previous year by the Denison and Pacific Railroad from Denison to Whitesboro to Gainesville. By stepping into the east-west trade, the Katy jabbed the T. and P. into activity. For a long time the T. and P.'s Trans-Continental Division, running westward from Texarkana, had terminated at Sherman. Challenged by the Katy's expansion, the T. and P. hurriedly extended a line westward to Whitesboro and then southward to Fort Worth.

Then an arrangement was made whereby Katy trains running westward from Denison to Whitesboro could switch to the T. and P. tracks and come south. Over that line the first Katy train rolled into Fort Worth in May, 1880—the second railroad to reach the town.

Eighteen months later the southern rail outlet was an actuality. The Santa Fe had arrived. A story is told, maybe true and maybe not, about why the Santa Fe built its main line through Fort Worth. The Gulf, Colorado and Santa Fe Railroad was operating regularly between Galveston and Belton in 1881, when officials decided to swing northward. A Santa Fe promoter informed Paddock that the railroad was extending its main line northward from Cleburne and would pass through either Fort Worth or Dallas, depending upon which city placed $75,000 cash money on the line first. Giving Paddock a contract form, the promoter left for Dallas. Through hurried conferences with other businessmen, Paddock assured himself of substantial support. The next morning he was waiting in a Dallas hotel lobby when the Santa Fe man came downstairs. Up stepped the editor, who said in effect, "Here's your contract. We signed. Now you sign." The agent expostulated. He had not had time to make an equal offer to Dallas. "That's too bad," Paddock said in effect, "you told me the town that signed first got the railroad." The agent signed. Fort Worth was assured of the main line, provided it could raise the $75,000.

To get the money, so the story goes, Paddock and Van Zandt called a mass meeting in a theater that very day. When the theater was filled with people, the doors were locked. Not a soul was permitted to leave until the full $75,000 had been subscribed. With that donation the Santa Fe built its main line from Cleburne to Fort Worth. The first train rolled into town on December 2, 1881, to give the prairie city its third railroad.

The next three railroads were home-town undertakings— the Fort Worth and Denver City, the Fort Worth and New Orleans, and the Fort Worth and Rio Grande.

Planning to lay track from Fort Worth to the New Mexico line where a connection would be made with some other line to Denver, the Ft.W. and D.C. was chartered in 1873, but financial conditions prevented construction until the company was sold in 1881 to General Dodge. Grading was begun on November 27, 1881, at Hodge Station, then about five miles north of town. The first track segment, to Decatur, was completed on May 1, 1882. On January 26, 1888, the New Mexico Territory was reached, and a junction made with what now is the Colorado and Southern. In 1890 the Ft.W. and D.C. laid its tracks into the heart of Fort Worth.

Construction of the Ft.W. and N.O. was begun in 1885. But when the tracks had reached only to Waxahachie, 50 miles south, two years later, the line was sold to the Southern Pacific. Construction began in 1886 on the Fort Worth and Rio Grande, directed by Paddock, who wanted to span the 142 miles between Fort Worth and Brownwood. Granbury was reached in 1889, Stephenville and Dublin the next year, and Brownwood on July 16, 1891. Later the line was acquired by the Frisco, and now is part of the Santa Fe. The Cotton Belt ran its lines into Fort Worth in 1887, and the Rock Island in 1893.

It was because of the railroads that Fort Worth first knew

the blood and violence of a bitter strike. As part of the great southwestern strike of 1886, inspired by the Knights of Labor who were trying to crack Jay Gould's stranglehold on the railroads, three hundred employees of the T. and P. and Katy struck on March 1. Their principal tactic was to halt all rail transportation into and out of Fort Worth.

The strikers were supported by their women, who sometimes sat on the tracks to block train movements. One morning twenty-five women with children gathered on the track leading from the yard. Engine after engine was run down the track to frighten them away. Resolutely they refused to budge. Finally one engine rumbled dangerously near a woman with an infant in her arms. To the engineer another woman shouted, "Come on, run her through, but remember when you do, it will be over our dead bodies." No trains left the yard that day.[1]

After a month of strike-imposed restrictions, which permitted only one mail train a day to pass, vexed railroad officials decided in desperation to run the blockade. Comprehensive plans were laid, the federal marshal deputized armed men to ride the train and protect the crew, Jim Courtright— the city marshal of the seventies—was placed in command of the armed guard, and all switches through town were spiked to prevent derailment. With those safeguards a train pulled out of the station on April 3, 1886. No precautions against derailment had been taken beyond the city limits.

When the train reached Buttermilk Junction, then far out in the country but now near the 2200 block of South Main, a group of strikers and sympathizers were waiting. As the train approached, two men stepped from the group and threw the switch. The train slid to a halt, guards clambered down, and a fast, furious gun fight ensued. Strikers were concealed in high grass, from which cover they fired at the guards, who took refuge behind the locomotive and a stack of railroad ties. After one guard was killed, both sides retired.

[1] *Research Data,* I, 136.

News of the clash spread from lip to excited lip in town, transforming Fort Worth into an armed camp, sympathizers of each group fearing that the other would seek reprisals. All gun stores were cleared of Winchesters. Feeling and fear ran high. Governor Ireland dispatched three hundred militiamen to preserve order. With a squad that arrived from Austin several days later was a young scribbler known as Bill Porter, who was to become famous as O. Henry. Twenty federal marshals were on hand. While there was no further eruption of violence before the strike ended as a failure a month later, it left tension and bitterness in its wake.

High feeling spread through the state as a result of the gun battle at Buttermilk Junction. State newspapers caustically criticized the railroad, the governor, and the federal marshal. The presence of Courtright, with his known ability with a gun, was responsible for much of the anger. Indeed, Jim Courtright's record did look black to the people of Texas.

After serving his last term as marshal in 1879, Courtright went to Silver City, New Mexico, where he was a guard for the American Mining Company, along with Jim McIntire, of Wichita Falls. While the two Texans were there, several Mexicans were killed in an attempt to rob a silver train. In another escapade two ranchmen were murdered. Facing implication in both affairs, Courtright and McIntire fled to Texas.

Upon reaching Fort Worth, Courtright opened the T. I. C. Detective Agency (his first name was Tim, but on the frontier it was corrupted to Jim). Although he had placed distance between himself and the New Mexico authorities, he still was in danger.

He was face to face with the danger when three men stepped from a train on Friday, October 17, 1884: Lieutenant Grimes and Corporal Hayes, of the Texas Rangers, and Captain Harry Richmond, Albuquerque chief of police. Careful to allay Courtright's fears, they called on him for a friendly chat and throughout the evening visited with him at various bars, manifesting a great friendliness.

The next morning they invited him to their rooms in the Ginnochio Hotel near the depot to look at pictures of unidentified criminals, saying that they thought he might recognize some of them from his long experience. Courtright, thinking he might be able to gain information of value to him as a private detective and flattered by the request, accompanied the three officers to the Ginnochio. A sixth sense must have warned him to take caution. One of the men was a New Mexico officer, and New Mexico authorities repeatedly had tried to extradite him. Therefore he asked a friend, Deputy Sheriff James Maddox, to accompany him. When the group reached the hotel, however, on some pretext Maddox was persuaded to remain downstairs, and when the others had not returned by 11:00 A.M., he tired of waiting and went home.[2]

Meantime, Courtright had started thumbing through the pictures. Once he looked up—and found three revolvers in his face. He was placed under arrest. Aware of his popularity and fearing that his friends might mob the jail to free him, the officers planned to keep him hidden in the hotel room until time for the 9:00 P.M. train to leave for the west.[3]

But at 8:00 P.M. the Fort Worth and Denver City train rolled in from Wichita Falls. From the train stepped a passenger, Bob Haywood, who reported that the Rangers had arrested McIntire in Wichita Falls and probably had taken Courtright. Within minutes the news was all over town.

Hurried checking by townsmen revealed the events of the morning. At once a mob began forming at the Ginnochio. The outraged mob found that Courtright had indeed been arrested and was at that very moment confined on the second floor of the hotel. Police guarded the stairs. Part of the angry crowd surged into the lobby; the remainder clogged the street between the hotel and the railroad station.

From the start the mob's sympathy was with Courtright. When one man in the lobby shouted that Jim Courtright

[2] *Fort Worth Gazette,* Oct. 19, 1884, p. 1.
[3] *Ibid.*

Captain B. B. Paddock

Long Hair Jim Courtright, frontier marshal

should not leave town, his words were "cheered lustily." The cheering was taken up by the crowd outside. The building "fairly shook with their yells." From the mob came demands that their friend be kept in a Fort Worth jail under guard of local officers to protect him from murder by the Rangers. One man bellowed with rage that Governor Ireland had broken faith by granting this extradition after denying earlier requests.[4]

Several men from the irate crowd were assigned to keep watch and sound the alarm should the officers attempt to take Courtright from the hotel. A Ranger came to the window, appealing to the crowd to disperse, with the assurance that Courtright had not been harmed nor would be so long as he was in their charge. In answer, the crowd demanded that Courtright show himself. Then Courtright stood at the window. Although he was in manacles and chains, the mob yelled in "exquisite abandonment" at the sight of their friend. "Let's turn him loose and give him his gun," came a shout.[5]

William Capps, a lawyer, mounted a shed over the window of the railroad ticket office, across Front Street (now Lancaster Avenue) from the hotel, to address the crowd. He urged them to disband, assuring them that Courtright was guarded by five or six local officers in addition to the rangers. While Capps held the crowd's attention, officers slipped Courtright out the rear of the hotel and into a carriage. As the team galloped away, someone spied the disappearing carriage. "There he goes!" came a shout. In pursuit came the crowd on foot and horse. From their lungs rose a tumultous chant—"Turn him loose!"[6]

Before the mob could catch up with them, the officers had Courtright in the county jail. Unlike a common prisoner, he was not placed in a cell. On the contrary, his captors allowed him the freedom of the sheriff's office—under their watchful

4 *Ibid.*
5 *Ibid.*
6 *Ibid.*

eyes—and permitted his friends to bring him a box of cigars. On Sunday he was allowed to eat breakfast and dinner in a café near the jail. At both morning and noon meals a crowd of his friends lined the street to watch him pass. During the day a *Gazette* reporter went to the jail to interview Courtright and his captors. To the reporter, Richmond seemed nervous, Hayes unable to take his eyes once from the captive, and Courtright "the coolest and most collected man in the room."[7]

The interviewer asked the officers about the rumor that Courtright and McIntire had killed three or four Mexicans who were trying to steal silver ore and that they were wanted on a murder charge. Blandly, Richmond said it was nothing like that at all. Two ranchmen had been murdered, Courtright had seen the shooting, and he was wanted as a material witness against James Casey and Milton Scott, who were charged with the murders.[8]

"That's nonsense," snorted Courtright. "Heavy rewards are not offered for witnesses, and I am wanted on a charge of murder. Knowing the bitter feeling between Americans and Mexicans, I am convinced that I could not have a fair trial. The assertion that I am wanted as a witness is only made to allay the public feeling in this city."[9] Richmond later admitted as much.

That evening, October 19, Courtright was taken again to the Merchants Restaurant near Houston and Second for supper. While eating, he dropped his napkin.

"Do you want to pick it up?" he carefully asked the guard.

"Pick it up yourself!" the guard snapped.

Courtright stooped to retrieve the napkin from beneath the table. When he straightened, he shoved back the chair, and rose to his feet with a pistol in each hand.

"It's my turn now," he told the guards.[10]

Knowing Courtright's accuracy, the guards did not at-

[7] *Ibid.,* Oct. 20, 1884, p. 5.
[8] *Ibid.*
[9] *Ibid.*
[10] *Ibid.; Research Data,* I, 243–44.

tempt to dispute the point. Part of the crowd of men who had jammed into the restaurant stepped between Courtright and his guards to prevent any bloodshed. Backing away, Courtright ran from the Second Street entrance and swung into the saddle of a waiting horse, tethered by his friend Abram Woody. Yelling for the crowd to make way, he fired into the air several times to emphasize his urgency.[11] Through the town echoed the wild cry, "Courtright has escaped!" The electrifying news brought the whole town to its feet. "Every avenue leading to the scene was filled with men and boys hurrying with pale faces and husky breath towards the center of excitement."[12]

Later, County Attorney W. S. Pendleton—outraged by the escape and contemptuous of the officers who had not placed Courtright in a cell—said that the prisoner had been taken freely to a restaurant operated by his friends and served "boiled fish, quail on toast, and pistols under the table for dessert."[13]

Galloping away into the twilight, Courtright ran into trouble. The horse stumbled near the fire station at Second and Commerce, injuring the rider. His friends the firemen helped him remount. The newly made desperado hurried to the Santa Fe yards and to a Galveston-bound train on which Woody—himself a tough hombre, handy with a gun, and one of Grant's cavalrymen before Richmond—was a special agent. Woody hid him in the baggage car for the trip.

At Galveston, Courtright boarded a ship. Soon after he walked up the gangplank, he felt the hot breath of pursuit when two officers came aboard. Tensely eavesdropping from behind a bulkhead, he learned they were hunting a Negro. Not taking a chance, however, he climbed into a bunk, covered up his face, and left only his hand on top of the cover. Seeing the white hand, the officers passed him by. The ship

---

[11] *Fort Worth Gazette,* Oct. 20, 1884, p. 5.
[12] *Ibid.*
[13] *Ibid.,* Oct. 25, 1884, p. 6.

took him to New York, where he spent some time before going west to Canada and Walla Walla, Washington. Throughout his exile he remained in contact with Fort Worth by correspondence, under an assumed name, with Woody's young son Will, who later practiced medicine in Fort Worth.[14]

Eventually tiring of a fugitive's life, Courtright went back to New Mexico, where he was cleared of all charges. Returning to Fort Worth to rejoin his wife and children, he was met at the station by several hundred men who gave him a rousing welcome.[15] He resumed his work as a private detective.

During Courtright's absence, Luke Short had become king of the gamblers. A man whose nerve matched Courtright's, Short had been chased out of Dodge City by vigilantes and had earned a notch for his gun at Tombstone, Arizona, where he coldly and deliberately shot it out with a man who was known as a gun tough. Under his reign in Fort Worth, keno was established as the major game for the nightly fleecing of young men, to the anger of businessmen who reportedly hired Courtright to break it up. Once Courtright was heard to say that he had been treated disrespectfully at the White Elephant, where Short did business, and that Colt's six-gun made all men equal.[16]

The only man who witnessed all that transpired on the night of February 8, 1887, between Courtright and Short was Short's partner, Jake Johnson. He testified in court that he had talked with Courtright outside the White Elephant for several minutes. The conversation led him to summon Short, who was having his shoes blacked in the saloon. Talking, the three men strolled about half a block from the White Elephant, coming to a halt in front of Ella Blackwell's shooting gallery.[17]

"Courtright and Short were three or four feet apart while

[14] Interview in 1949 with Dr. Will Woody.
[15] *Ibid.*
[16] Testimony of W. A. James at examining trial, *Fort Worth Gazette,* Feb. 10, 1887, p. 5.
[17] Testimony of Jake Johnson, *ibid.*

talking," Johnson testified. "Luke had his thumbs in the arm-holes of his vest, then he dropped them in front of him, when Courtright said, 'You needn't be getting out your gun.' Luke said, 'I haven't got any gun here, Jim,' and raised up his vest to show him. Courtright then pulled his pistol. He drew it first, and then Short drew his and commenced to fire."[18]

For the first, last, and only time in his life, Long Hair Jim Courtright was beaten to the trigger. B. F. Herring, testify-ing at the examining trial on the day following the shooting, said that he was standing in the shooting gallery and that Courtright fell near his feet. "The man doing the shooting stepped up to the door, and fired four times after Courtright fell." William Allison, who was also in the shooting gallery, testified that Courtright's pistol did not clear the holster until he was on the floor. "He made no effort to shoot after he fell; he was not able."[19] In their investigation the police found that Courtright's pistol was made useless by a jammed cylin-der, anyway. Represented at the examining trial by Robert McCart and Alex Stedman, Short was released on a two-thousand-dollar bond, and was never convicted.

While the examining trial was in progress, a funeral cor-tege that was described as one of the largest Fort Worth had seen up to that time took Courtright's remains to the ceme-tery. Fire bells had begun tolling early in the afternoon for Courtright, who had been a volunteer fireman. His company, the M. T. Johnson Hook and Ladder, led the cortege, the horses and wagon heavily draped in black.[20]

Courtright's widow and children moved to California, leaving behind them scenes reminiscent of Jim Courtright, the last of a breed.

The Courtright episode was the most spectacular event of its sort in the town's history. And when it was over, a new and more peaceful atmosphere prevailed. Even though organ-

18 *Ibid.*
19 Testimony of William Allison, *ibid.*
20 *Ibid.*

ized society gained the upper hand over Colt individualism, crime certainly was not eradicated.

Hell's Half Acre continued full blast. Courtright's murder brought action because he and Short were popular, but there were other murders as well as robberies which did not reach the punishment stage. One of the more brutal crimes was the crucifixion of Sally. She was a dance-hall girl for whom no other name has come down through the years. One morning she was found dead—nailed to an outhouse behind the dance hall where she worked. There were no clues, nothing but an abiding mystery.

Time, more than anything else, rectified the conditions engendered by crime rampant. As the areas west of Fort Worth developed, many cowboys, frontiersmen, and highwaymen were drained away. In their stead came homeseekers, who helped to make Fort Worth a strong community of 23,076 persons by 1890. With their backing, Mayor H. S. Broiles, another reform mayor, and County Attorney Carlock were able to clean up the Acre between 1887 and 1889, but it was not wiped out until the early years of the twentieth century. Working with the reformers, a stronger judiciary supported the clean-up drive against gamblers, harlots, footpads, holdup men, gunmen, and their ilk. As time progressed, the judiciary became stronger and stronger, and with it society.

Cattle and transportation kept money flowing through Fort Worth. Still there was no substantial industrialization to balance the city's economy, to offer security against particularized conditions that might rock the cattle and transportation business. No one realized that better than Editor Paddock, who, upon taking stock in 1878, had told his readers that the time had come to industrialize. Fort Worth's strength at that time, he reminded the town in an editorial, came from being a railroad terminal. Handwriting on the wall showed that soon the railroad would be extended farther west, causing Fort Worth to suffer when some other town became the railhead. He called in particular for woolen and cotton mills, tanneries, shoe factories, foundries and machine shops.

The wisdom of his counsel became apparent in the conditions that beset the cattle industry in the early eighties. Northern buyers began discriminating against Texas cattle because of ticks. Stockmen lost money. If carcasses instead of live animals could be shipped to eastern markets, ticks would not be a factor. Stockmen could then make money. The result was formation of the Continental Meat Packing Company, which, in 1883 or the year succeeding, built a processing plant in the southeast section of the city. The plant failed, but a snowball had been formed at the top of a hill.

In 1890 the Fort Worth Dressed Meat and Packing Company was established with a capital of $500,000, which bought the Continental site. After a large meat contract was obtained, the company was reorganized as the Texas Dressed Beef and Packing Company, with some of the state's most influential cattlemen as stockholders. A plant was built on the North Side.[21] As the first permanent packing company came into existence, a stockyard was built as an adjunct by John R. Hoxie, A. T. Byers, M. G. Ellis, John Peter Smith, E. M. Daggett, and R. E. Maddox. In 1893 the packing plant was bought by G. W. Simpson, who agreed to pay ranchmen fifty cents more a head than the prevailing Kansas City price.

In return for the wealth and stability attributable to cattle, Fort Worth has contributed to the improvement of the industry. A major contribution has been the annual stock show. Inaugurated in 1896 with only a few animals shown under the trees on the bank of Marine Creek, the show has grown into the present Southwestern Exposition and Fat Stock Show, the purpose of which was in the beginning and is now to encourage better breeding and feeding of animals.

Directed by Victor A. Norgaard of the Bureau of Animal Husbandry, the first successful experiments in dipping cattle

21 *Fort Worth Star-Telegram*, Oct. 30, 1949, Ranch and Farm Section, 16.

to eradicate ticks took place in Fort Worth in 1897. Members of livestock sanitary boards of Texas, Kansas, Illinois, Missouri, Nebraska, Oklahoma, and Colorado came to witness the experiments. While they were in town, the Interstate Association of Livestock Boards was formed.[22]

Meantime, important steps toward industrialization had been taken in other fields. Chief among them, the Fort Worth Brewing Company was founded in 1890, with a capital of $150,000—the city's first large industry. The huge brewery sprawled over a stretch of ground bounded on the north and south by Ninth and Twelfth streets and on the east and west by the Santa Fe tracks and Jones Street. The first products rolled from the production line in 1891. Ten years later the plant was selling ice and beer and making everything it used except bottles. Three thousand freight cars a year were loaded with Fort Worth beer, made close to the wheat supply, that gave the town's economy an annual payroll of $100,000. Prohibition killed the plant in 1918.[23]

Before the brewery was established, the only constantly growing industry was milling. James F. Ellis and W. J. Boaz bought the City Mills in 1880, organizing the City Mill Company with James Swayne in charge. Two years later another man came into the picture, Murray P. Bewley, a former steamboat captain who had come to Fort Worth three years before, after his boat had burned, to set up a feed and grain business. In 1882 he helped rejuvenate the City Mill Company. The capacity of the plant was boosted to two hundred barrels of flour a day—an excellent production rate under the circumstances.

But the good work was for naught. In a few months fire destroyed the mill. With a ten-thousand-dollar loan from the City National Bank in 1883, he bought a block on Lancaster between Cherry and Burnet, constructing a burrstone mill with a capacity of fifty barrels a day. His Anchor Mills was the start of today's Bewley Mills.

[22] *Fort Worth Register,* Aug. 11, Sept. 27, 1897.

Slowly, limited home-market industries came into being. By 1887 there were forty-four establishments, including two ice factories, two flour mills, two foundries and machine shops, two planing mills, brickyards, marble works, and plants making brooms, mattresses, carriages, galvanized iron and tin roofing, boilers, machines, windmills, stationery, feed, crackers, baking powder, ink, bluing, vinegar, mineral waters, soap, buckles, boots, shoes, woodwork, drugs, and clothing. To that list were added two cigar factories near the close of the nineteenth century. J. E. Westland made Westland's Best Perfecto and the Fancy Shape Blue Belle. C. F. Ederle fashioned the Chief Justice and The Raven, advertising the latter as the "best five center in town."[24]

Electricity was added to the industrial complex with a plant that was built only six years after Thomas Alva Edison perfected the incandescent bulb, and only five years after electricity first lighted Broadway. J. H. Andrews, R. E. Maddox, W. H. Little, and Dr. N. Wallerich formed the Fort Worth Electric Light and Power Company as the city's first, obtaining a franchise on October 12, 1885. From their plant at Lancaster and Cherry, they strung lines to magical switches that had been placed in homes.[25] Customer acceptance was spontaneous, making electricity at once a formidable competitor of the Fort Worth Gas Light Company.

Wondering if the streets could not be lighted better by electricity than by gas, the City Council sought competitive bids from the electric and the gas companies, precipitating the first sharp competition between the two forms of power. On May 9, 1889, the electric company offered to illuminate Main and Houston streets for ninety cents a month a light. This angered the gas company, whose manager, W. W. Greene, said that any attempt to light the streets with electricity would interfere with the company's contract. But dur-

[23] *Ibid.*, Aug. 4, 1901.
[24] *Ibid.*, Sept. 4, 1897.
[25] *Minutes* of the Fort Worth City Council, Vol. E, p. 331.

ing the months that the council was pondering what to do, the gas company decided it had better enter the electrical business, too. On July 2, 1889, it received a franchise permitting construction of an electric light system, provided it would furnish three free lights for the city.[26]

In the meantime, the council had turned more and more to the idea of building a municipal plant that would furnish power for lighting the streets. To find out what could be done in the way of a municipal plant, the council sent Aldermen George Neis, A. B. Fraser, and W. J. Bailey to Denver, Dallas, Houston, San Antonio, Austin, and Waco to study their methods of street lighting. But before reaching a decision on the municipal plant, the council, on March 18, 1890, gave the Fort Worth Electric Light and Power Company an interim contract for the lighting of streets, the first time the streets were illuminated by electricity.[27]

Less than a month later the council decided that the course of wisdom would, after all, be the construction and maintenance of a city-owned plant. On April 3, 1890, a contract was awarded to the United Edison Manufacturing Company of New York for the construction of a power plant at the juncture of the Clear and West forks, which was completed June 9, 1891, at a total cost of $32,102.[28]

Wholesale trade had been good in the wagon-train days, reaching a volume of $650,000 a year in 1880, but it became even better after railroad transportation was provided to West Texas, reaching a volume of $8,000,000 in 1888. A typical operator of the eighties was the Fort Worth Grocer Company which pushed wagon trains loaded with staple groceries into the Indian Territory, at the same time serving settled sections of West Texas.

The retail stores that were to endure began appearing. Among the large stores doing business today, the oldest is

26 *Ibid.,* Vol. H, p. 8.
27 *Ibid.,* Vol. H, pp. 198, 307.
28 *Ibid.,* Vol. H, pp. 327–29; I, 380.

Washer Brothers. Yet if Nat Washer had followed his first inclination after stepping into a Main Street mud puddle, the firm would not be what it is. The firm was started in 1882, when Jacob Washer, a twenty-four-year-old Tennessean, moved to Fort Worth and rented a store between Fourth and Fifth streets on Houston, where he sold ten-gallon hats, boots, and bandanas. Because the rent was more than he could afford, he teamed with Leopold August. The town of six thousand persons provided ample business for Washer and August, who soon moved into larger quarters. The firm continued until 1887, when August withdrew to join his brother in the A. and L. August Clothing Store. Nat Washer came to join his brother. Arriving in a driving rain, he stepped into a puddle and concluded that "one year at most would give me my fill of both Fort Worth and Texas." However, he stayed on, and year by year the store grew into a fashion center.

Then in 1889 came Monnig's, which introduced the $1.98 price tag and pennies, of which Fort Worthians were at first suspicious. With a $2,500 assortment of bustles, red flannel, and gaiters, William and George Monnig opened the store on Main Street between Twelfth and Thirteenth streets. During the first years they lived on the second floor. The retail store prospered, and a wholesale house was added in 1901.

In 1890, W. B. Schermerhorn opened a racket store, similar to the present variety store, which in a few years came to be known as The Fair, and it has since been known as a woman's store.

Early in the nineties a young Bowie merchant, W. C. Stripling, was on a buying trip in Baltimore where he encountered William Monnig, there on the same mission. The two young merchants argued over the merits of their respective towns. As a result, Stripling opened a branch store in Fort Worth, using packing cases for counters. Within six years the business volume caused Stripling to move his home to Fort Worth.

The business community was supported by an increasingly strong bank system. In 1884, Tidball, Van Zandt and Company incorporated as the Fort Worth National Bank, capitalized at $125,000, which today is the city's oldest bank. The First National, the oldest national bank, was a potent financial force, too. The third major bank was incorporated in 1889, when John Hoxie, a Chicago financier, organized the Farmers and Mechanics National Bank with a capital of $1,000,000.

Newspapers continued to play a dominant role in the fashioning of a city. In August, 1882, the third of the great pioneer newspapers appeared, the *Gazette.* Formed by fusing the *Democrat-Advance* with George B. Loving's *Livestock Journal,* established a year earlier, the *Gazette* carried on in the tradition of the *Democrat* and the *Standard.* At first, Paddock edited the new paper, with Walter Malone as business manager. Quick shifts of ownership marked the *Gazette's* early years. Financial difficulties forced suspension in 1885, but within a few weeks it was revived by a joint-stock company that made it solvent. Malone became editor, writing an important chapter in Texas journalism. He had learned his trade as a printer's devil on one of A. B. Norton's papers and as editor or publisher of newspapers in Macon, Mississippi, Jackson, Missouri, and Dallas. With Malone at the helm, the *Gazette* became a forceful voice in the West.

The paper added special features in 1885, including short stories, ladies' columns, and a report called "sporting." Departmentalization of the news was effected to a degree. On May 25, 1887, the *Gazette* published the first special edition in Fort Worth history, sixteen pages, claiming the largest bona fide circulation in Texas.

The *Austin Statesman* said on December 26, 1889, that the *Gazette* had done more than any other instrumentality in building Fort Worth into a trade center with a firm grip on the wholesale trade for northern and western Texas. On Christmas Eve grateful businessmen had given Malone a bag of gold in appreciation of his leadership. The City Council once adopted a special resolution saying that the *Gazette* "under his guidance has been largely instrumental in bringing Fort Worth to an enviable position in the list of Texas cities."[29]

After his death in 1893, the *Gazette* ownership passed to a corporation whose officers decided that they did not want their money tied up in a newspaper. Without informing subscribers, the company sold out to the *Dallas Morning News* in 1896, and the next morning subscribers began receiving the Dallas paper. Jobless because of the owners' sudden sale, employees of the *Gazette* pooled their resources to begin publication of the morning *Register* as a co-operative venture. All week the staff scrambled for news and business. On Saturday night they divided the proceeds. Resentful at being otherwise forced to read an out-of-town newspaper, the public liberally patronized the *Register,* making it the first financially successful newspaper in Fort Worth.

All the while the residential area was spreading southward, giving rise to the need for a more extensive street transportation service. Despite the exclusive privileges with which the Fort Worth Street Railway Company originally was cloaked, the council franchised new companies.

The Prairie City Street Railway Company was the second to begin operations. Obtaining a permit from the council on December 7, 1881, the company operated on West Seventh Street between Houston and Taylor, south on Taylor and across the Texas and Pacific reservation to Hemphill. Renamed the Queen City Street Railway Company, the firm in later years made a circle by using the Houston Street tracks of the Rosedale Company to Lancaster.[30]

The next company granted a franchise was the Rosedale Street Railway Company, on April 4, 1884. It operated six miles of track from a railroad hospital south of the city to the driving park north of town, proceeding along Main Street

29 *Ibid.,* Vol. J, p. 43.
30 *Ibid.,* Vol. C, p. 268; *Fort Worth Gazette,* May 25, 1887.

and serving the most thickly populated sections of Fort Worth.

For several years afterward, there was a number of street railways—the North Side, West Fort Worth, Park Street, Fort Worth and Arlington Heights, Hyde Park, Riverside, Polytechnic, and Citizens Railway and Light companies.

Beginning in 1889, the horse- and mule-drawn cars began to disappear as the various companies electrified their routes. However, electrification brought only slight improvements in the cars. They were somewhat larger, but poorly built. Because of inadequate insulation of the cars, passengers often received electrical shocks.

> The car didn't look much different from the street cars of today 'cept it was built mostly of wood and was much bulkier. I remember the car stopped a while at each corner. Once while it was stopped, I dashed off to buy me a cigar. When I started to get back on, I grabbed the iron rail at the door. The street was a sea of mud, and I was standing in an inch or two of water. I got a shock of electricity from that iron bar that sent me sprawling in the mud.[31]

The motormen stood on open platforms, sweltering in summer, freezing in winter. Sometimes an icy motorman would set his car at a slow speed, and trot alongside to warm himself. There was no heat in streetcars until 1909. The motorman's job could be a lonesome one, too. The night man on the Arlington Heights line often heard wolves howl as his car bounced across the prairie between the city and the Lake Como Pavilion, which was built to attract streetcar passengers. Almost every line built such recreation places along its route as business-getters.

The Fort Worth Street Railway Company absorbed competing companies one by one until it monopolized the service, and was in turn acquired by the Bishop and Sherwin Syndicate in 1901, when the name was changed to Northern Texas Traction Company. Later the company came under the control of Stone and Webster.

[31] Uncle Billy Casburn, *Research Data,* I, 139.

With the singing hammers of industry and the hum of commerce, unionization grew. The organized labor movement gained headway in the eighties, fostered by the increasing permanence of commerce and industry. The first labor organization was the Brotherhood of Locomotive Engineers, whose local was chartered in 1881. The printers were close behind, the International Typographical Union's local dating from 1882.

A steady growth of unionism ensued. The American Federation of Labor chartered the Fort Worth Trades Assembly on April 4, 1894. By the end of the century unionism gave meaning to Labor Day, which was a community-wide holiday. Often businessmen marched with their employees in the Labor Day parade, indicating the good feeling that existed.

The Labor Day celebration of 1897 was typical. From early in the morning, people were on the streets, wearing large badges and uniforms indicative of their trades. Festivities started with a long parade led by a squad of policemen. Then came the firemen. Next in line, the mayor and aldermen rode in carriages, followed by Ault and Connor's "full union band." Behind the band marched the Trades Assembly. Plumbers carried their fires. Iron molders rode a float bearing their tools and a sign calling attention to a Dallas strike. Tinners were "handsome in tin hats, with copper ornamentation, and tin canes." Bricklayers, printers, pressmen, carpenters, brewery workers, packing-house employees, cigar makers, and men in other occupations marched down the streets.

The brewers' display occupied a full block of the procession. Hardly less impressive, the Cameron Mill and Elevator Company float contained flour and millfeed, and was followed by thirty employees dressed in white. Grand Marshal Fritz Hardtgen led the parade to the park at the north end of the bridge over the river. There, boys, men, women, and girls competed in foot races, potato races, three-legged races, fat men's race, lean men's race, sack race, high jump, and tug of war, and saw Mrs. E. J. Scott take first prize for entering the prettiest baby in a contest.[32]

Fort Worth's vigorous atmosphere caused it to begin serving as a political storm center for the state. The kick-off came in 1882 when the Greenback party held a state convention in Fort Worth, where the party was well established. Captain Daggett was state chairman at one time, and several successive newspapers—*Greenback Tribune, Tribune,* and *National Texas*—reflected the party views between 1878 and the early eighties. Only 140 persons attended the convention, but they made up with noise what they lacked in numbers. E. W. Morton, of Tarrant County, was their unsuccessful candidate for lieutenant governor, running on a platform that accused the Democrats of doubling the state debt, not righting the wrongs of preceding Republican administrations, granting Chicago capitalists three million acres of domain in exchange for building a statehouse, and exempting cotton and sugar crops of the wealthy from taxation while taxing mechanics' tools.

The bloody rail strike of 1886 had immediate political repercussions. After the strike, a union leader said: "It has been demonstrated that strikes are failures. We must try something else. You may look for us at the ballot box and in the primaries."[33] As an immediate outgrowth of the strike, the Dark Lantern party was formed at a secret convention in Fort Worth. Composed of Knights of Labor, Farmers Alliance men, Greenbackers, and a few Republicans, the party's purpose was to plan a state campaign against the Democrats, with emphasis upon the Tarrant County elections. When the organization of the party became general knowledge, the entire state was alert to the threat, and an Austin newspaper reported: "The Democrats are alarmed and are working hard to organize the party to meet the most powerful foe the party has ever contended with in Texas."[34] The Dark Lantern party

[32] *Fort Worth Register,* Sept. 7, 1897.
[33] Paddock (ed.), *Fort Worth and the Texas Northwest,* I, 463–64.

boasted of a huge parade that was intended to panic the Democrats. But when the day of the parade came, only 352 men marched. "The Democrats of Tarrant County feel greatly relieved."[35]

As election time neared, both the Dark Lantern and the Democratic parties staged torchlight parades that snaked through downtown streets on the same night. In the procession 1,159 Democrats were counted, and only 320 Dark Lanternites. Despite the odds in favor of the Democrats, the fight between the two county tickets was fierce. Blessed by a city majority of nine hundred votes that overpowered a county majority of eight hundred for the Dark Lantern, the Democrats went into office. Not a single Dark Lanternite was elected.[36]

In 1888 there was a new undercover element to fight. The National Order of Videttes was formed in Jack County in 1886, and in Fort Worth a few months later, as a secret military-political organization intended to manipulate local politics through established parties for the good of the laboring classes.[37] The campaign was bitter and intense. Videttes, nonpartisans, union laborites, and all opposition elements combined against the Democrats. Fort Worth attracted statewide attention as the focal point of the opposition. The campaign closed November 5 with a giant Democratic parade. Three thousand men were in line, and the sidewalks were packed with onlookers. An estimated five thousand people crowded the square to hear the last-night speeches.[38] During the campaign, Fort Worth's contests were considered important enough for the Democrats to hold a big barbecue at the Pavilion, at the foot of Samuels Avenue, which was attended by another five thousand spectators. Attorney General James Stephen Hogg and Seth Shepard of Dallas were the speakers.

34 *Austin Daily Statesman*, July 2, 1886.
35 *Ibid.*, Oct. 30, 1886.
36 *Ibid.*, Nov. 2, Nov. 4, 1886.
37 *Ibid.*, Oct. 25, 1888.
38 *Ibid.*, Nov. 6, 1888.

In another arena local politics was eruptive that year, too. Thirty white men bolted the Republican county convention over the issue of Negro voting.[39] That year marked the beginning of the ascendency of a Negro politician, Gooseneck Bill McDonald. McDonald was teaching school in East Texas, where he demonstrated a flair for politics. The way he handled himself attracted the attention of H. R. Green, the son of Hetty Green, mistress of railroads and millions. Green was interested because, as operating executive for his mother's Texas Midland Railroad, he wanted publicity, and he thought politics the best medium. He hired McDonald at $525 a month as his political adviser. His choice was well made, because McDonald's shrewdness placed Green in nominal control of the state party. McDonald picked up his nickname at the St. Louis national convention in 1896, when the correspondent for a Dallas newspaper wired that Hetty Green's son was there in company with a "goosenecked sort of Negro." The nickname stuck with the son of former slaves, who remained dominant in national Republican politics until well into the twentieth century. McDonald made his home in Fort Worth as a prosperous banker from 1900 until his death in 1950.

The most exciting and pivotal gubernatorial campaign before 1900, and one rarely equaled since, was the 1892 contest. Three of the four factions were directed from Fort Worth. The campaign grew out of the riotous "car stable" convention in Houston, which nominated Hogg for governor, while a rump convention nominated George Clark. Hogg wanted railroad regulation, and succeeded in getting the bill passed activating the Railroad Commission. Clark, who had been a railroad attorney, wanted none of it. Added to the Democratic split into two factions, Hogg's progressives and Clark's conservatives, was the Populist party's nomination of Thomas L. Nugent, of Tarrant County.

State headquarters were established in Fort Worth by the Clark or Purified Democrats, the Populists, and the Lily White

39 *Ibid.*, Sept. 14, 1888.

Republicans who were supporting Clark. The Clark Demo-
crats staged their last great rally of the year in Fort Worth.
About 2,800 persons came from Dallas and 1,000 more from
West Texas. Five thousand men paraded.[40] Hogg was elected.

Campaigns were flamboyant, enthusiastic, and bitter,
with candidates ripping one another on the platform. Torchlight parades were the thing. One year a red torch parade
went up Main Street with hundreds in the procession. A steam
engine and caboose were fitted for the street railway tracks.
As the engine tooted its way up the street, it pulled the caboose that was loaded with torch-bearing men as thick as bees
on a hive. Politics consisted more of old-fashioned Southern
oratory than rational vote-getting appeals.

[40] *Ibid.*, Aug. 22, Nov. 6, 1892; Paddock (ed.), *Fort Worth and the Texas
Northwest*, II, 469, 472, 484–86.

CHAPTER IX

Transition

THE municipal government was on solid footing for the first time. The hand-to-mouth days of government by expediency were over. Largely the change came about through reforms and improvements inaugurated successively during the administration of Mayor John Peter Smith, who directed city affairs from 1882 through 1885.

The principal contributions from Smith's administrations were four in number: (1) a municipal water system was provided for the first time; (2) the fire department was reorganized and modernized; (3) the first street-paving program was instituted and carried through; and (4) the first sanitary sewers were built.

Of the four, the creation of a municipal water system was by far the most important. Because there was no adequate water system in the early part of the eighties, at a time when a pattern of urban living was becoming more pronounced with each passing day, the city government had an acute health problem on its hands. Aside from artesian wells, water was supplied by shallow wells and by cisterns, each easily polluted by waste from the outhouses standing in the rear of nearly every building. Overflowing privies, visited rarely by the scavenger, caused much typhoid. Frequently newspapers reminded the public that only artesian well water could be considered safe against the typhoid menace. In support of this thesis it was reported that when Dr. J. R. Feild's artesian well was out of order, forcing the family to use water from a cistern, within twenty days there were three cases of typhoid among the Doctor's children. Too, trash and piles of decomposed garbage harbored swarms of flies that carried filth to food in unscreened homes and restaurants. Mosquitoes rose from dank lots.

To cope with the menacing problems of sanitation, the council was compelled on November 1, 1881, to create the post of health officer—the first time such an official had been necessary, although in the earlier years physicians had been retained to treat paupers. Dr. H. W. Moore was appointed health officer at a monthly salary of forty dollars. Soon he was confronted by a crisis that terrified the town.

Smallpox had struck. An epidemic was feared. Some weeks earlier, the town had been alerted to the threat. Late in 1881 one case of smallpox had been reported in Denison, and a few days later a man with strange eruptions on his face stepped from a train from Denison. An immediate wave of vaccinations succeeded the report of his arrival; the *Democrat-Advance* reported that almost everybody in town had been vaccinated. Nevertheless, men and women were terrified when the dread disease struck. The first suspected case was a Negro living behind the Virginia House, a downtown hotel, on February 8, 1882. The first definite case was a Negro child living on Calhoun between Fifteenth and Sixteenth streets.

Facing the first real emergency since the city government had come into being, the council was slow to act. Anxious citizens, however, finally brought enough pressure upon the councilmen to force them to do something. The Negro girl was moved from her home to a tent on the South Side, and yellow flags were placed on her home. On March 13 the council gave the Board of Health authority to require vaccinations and impose quarantines.

As the scourge cut its way through a small part of the city's population, a regular smallpox colony was established. The city built a pesthouse and erected tents about three miles from town. Weatherford quarantined Fort Worth. Exactly how many cases came under treatment at the peak of the epidemic does not appear in official records, but by May 6, at the tag end of the epidemic, eleven patients still were in isolation in the pesthouse.

Dangerous water supplies were at the root of the city's health problems. Responsible men, both in and out of government, had contended for long that the city should take adequate measures to guarantee a reliable water system. And the council on several occasions timidly had investigated the possibility. Any one of several things may have discouraged definitive action by the council. During the first few years of its corporate existence Fort Worth was in poor financial condition, which automatically militated against the then tremendous investment of fifty or sixty thousand dollars in a public water-supply system. Too, the council certainly would have been under pressure not to enter a field that may have been regarded as the domain of private enterprise. Competitive business interests may have prevented establishment of a water system.

Because the city government would do nothing, Paddock organized a private company to supply water. Forming the Fort Worth Water Works Company, with Loyd, Zane-Cetti, John D. Templeton, and W. D. Wilson, he obtained a franchise on May 23, 1882. Ownership of the company soon passed to Morgan Jones, E. P. Cowan, H. McLaughlin, H. M. Herman, J. S. Drake, M. C. Orton, and M. D. Mather. The plant was completed on April 24, 1883, and Fort Worth at last had an adequate water system. The waterworks, at the juncture of the Clear and West forks of the Trinity, near the present courthouse, consisted of a pump station that drew four million gallons a day from the Trinity and pumped it untreated into six miles of pipe.

The company was doing nicely, but some of the owners wanted to pull out after a time. Drake, whose home was Rock

Island, Illinois, offered to sell one hundred thousand dollars' worth of stock, his entire share and representing one-half of the company, for $32,500. The city happened to be without ready cash at the time, but Mayor Smith was not a man to let a bargain get away from him. The council supported him enthusiastically when he proposed that the city buy the stock if the necessary bonds could be issued sixty days later. Drake agreed to the proposition. On July 22, 1884, the council approved a contract for purchase of one-half interest in the company on sixty-day credit. The city of Fort Worth was in the water business, with a private concern as a partner.

But it was not long before the city became unhappy with the unusual ownership arrangement. On October 7 the council inquired how much it would cost to acquire the remaining stock. Cowan offered to sell for $28,000. His offer was accepted, and the purchase was completed on March 28, 1885. Water thereby became the sole responsibility of the city government. A. W. Scoble was appointed the first water superintendent on June 17.

The system, however, had its limitations, imposed by the not always steady supply of water from the Trinity. To overcome this handicap, the council awarded F. O. Brown a contract on September 6, 1887, to drill ninety wells at the water works to supplement the water supply. The first large expansion of the water-main system radiating from the plant, where capacity had been increased to five million gallons daily, came on May 9, 1890, when a $35,000 contract was awarded to Philbin and Jackson of Nashville.

Yet the plant was still inadequate. Public pressure forced the council to take steps toward providing a larger water works. Contracts were awarded on December 22, 1891, for construction of the present Holly Plant, designed by the Holly Water Works Company which furnished the pumps, the actual construction being done by McArthur Brothers, of Chicago, for $687,000, under the supervision of John B. Hawley. The plant was built just north of Lancaster Avenue on the

Clear Fork, on land purchased from William Capps and Robert McCart for $20,000. Operation began in 1892.

The second major contribution of the Smith administration was modernization of the fire department. Under the leadership of Alderman J. B. Askew, the council reorganized and enlarged the department in a wave of improvements beginning in 1883. The Gamewell electric fire-alarm system, the first in the state, was completed with eleven alarm boxes at a cost of $2,450. The council also bought a three-thousand-pound bell, the largest in Texas, from M. E. Neely and Company, of West Troy, New York, for $700.

The E. M. Daggett, Peter Smith, and John A. Thornton Hose Companies were formed. A horse-drawn hook-and-ladder wagon, replacing the 1873 apparatus, and a hose carriage were purchased from E. B. Preston and Company, of Chicago, for $2,000. Another hose carriage was purchased from the Fire Extinguisher Manufacturing Company, of Chicago, for $750. An ancient four-wheeled cart was acquired in Brooklyn for the Thornton company.

A central fire station was built on Main Street, between Eleventh and Twelfth, a frame building constructed for $1,000. The most marked feature of the hastily built station was a bell tower, graced by the new alarm bell, in which the firemen took great pride. The bell now ornaments the City Hall lawn. In all, the reorganization cost $12,000, giving Fort Worth for the first time a well-rounded fire department, that was further dignified on June 3, 1884, when the post of fire chief became a paid position. R. Matkin was the first paid fire chief.

More improvements came a few years later. The first aerial hook-and-ladder wagon was purchased from the Fire Extinguisher Manufacturing Company, Chicago, in 1891, for $3,350. And the first chemical wagon was placed in service in 1892.

Through the years a volunteer fire department functioned day and night, but the volunteers actually were costing the city an undue amount of money. As an economy measure the council, on November 14, 1893, approved in principle a paid department, but waited until a secret meeting two days later to authorize the new department. The paid department began functioning on December 1, under Chief John Cella, with thirty-four firemen and five companies, plus the aerial hook-and-ladder.

The first professional firemen were Larry Herbert, W. Kinkle, S. Ferguson, G. Oberhoff, Charles Purvis, George Kerr, F. Massengale, E. L. Dunwoody, S. Walker, I. N. Smith, J. H. Burton, P. B. Berry, H. S. Leach, J. M. Jackson, D. Rockett, A. G. Goff, T. N. Blanton, C. McNaught, Harvey Bell, Jeff Wilson, J. M. Harrell, J. O'Brien, W. Bideker, J. R. Shipp, P. McGrath, G. M. Ledford, F. Bishop, W. L. McCart, Fred Askew, C. Sneed, J. E. Haas, J. F. Rufner, J. B. Mayors, and C. A. Trowbridge.

A new central fire station was built, of stone, in 1899, in the triangle formed by Throckmorton and Monroe streets, north of City Hall.

The first real paving program was activated on August 15, 1882, when the council directed that Weatherford, Main, and Houston streets be macadamized, along with stretches between Weatherford and Throckmorton on First, Second, Third, Fourth, and Fourteenth streets.

The first sewer system was installed in 1882. The Fort Worth Water Company, at that time a private concern, had a contract to flush the sewers, many of which were open ditches carrying refuse to the Trinity.

Other modifications were made in municipal affairs. The first board of equalization was appointed on May 17, 1881, to afford a hearing for taxpayers who thought that their property had been assessed wrong. Beginning on August 30, 1887, building permits were required for all construction. On January 1, 1889, fees of office were abolished and salaries set for the attorney, marshal, secretary, engineer, judge, physician, fire chief, electrician, policemen, sanitary police, and scavenger. The post of city auditor was created on August 20, 1889. The first trend toward zoning was discernible when the council, on August 19, 1890, adopted ordinances prohibiting construction of certain types of buildings within prescribed fire limits and forbidding operation of manufacturing plants in specified portions of the city.

All the while the city was growing, and with it the size of the council. From three original wards, the town grew to nine. By 1891 the city was governed by eighteen aldermen. This cumbersome council functioned until 1897, when representation was reduced to nine. And a larger city hall was built at Throckmorton and Tenth in 1893, replacing the one built in 1877 at Second and Commerce.

The city government was having trouble with public utilities. The difficulties were emphasized in the annual message of Mayor Paddock, who said, on April 12, 1898, that the city had been "cursed by the criminal negligence and wanton indifference" of some of the firms to whom electric and street-railway franchises had been granted. He suggested that an ordinance be passed requiring that firms pay for franchises to compensate the city for any losses caused by incompetence or negligence.[1] The council adopted the suggested ordinance immediately, and the attorney was instructed to sue for forfeiture of the franchises held by the City Railway, Fort Worth and Arlington Heights Street Railway, and the Glenwood and Polytechnic Street Railway companies.[2]

As municipal government steadied during the eighties, citizens and councilmen alike recognized the desirability of a permanent police force. Such a force was recommended by the police committee on October 4, 1887, and the council at once put the recommendation into effect. The members of the first permanent police force were Mounted Officers Ben C. Evans and W. L. Rushing; Patrolmen J. W. Pemberton, Ben Bell, A. G. Goff, G. W. Davenport, Richard Kitts, J. W. Coker,

[1] *Minutes* of the Fort Worth City Council, Vol. O, pp. 136, 140, 163.
[2] *Ibid.*

Tom Taylor, and J. J. Turner; Jailer Hill Dearing; and Sanitary Officers G. H. Craig and Will Ashmore. But the force did not remain permanent, as had been intended. Especially under the commission form of government adopted in 1907, politics crept into and ruled the department.

The first patrol wagon came into use when the council, on October 16, 1888, approved the purchase of a wagon and the use of Old Charley, a veteran in city service, to pull it.

The first concrete rules and regulations for the police department were adopted on April 16, 1889. The specified uniform was a navy-blue suit with a double-breasted frock coat, cut high at the neck. Patrolmen wore blue helmets in summer, caps in winter. The chief and his deputies wore slouch hats, the chief's ornamented by two gold cords and the deputies' by silver. Part of the regulations were intended to curb any human frailties that might mark some of the guardians of the law, such as the order forbidding policemen to leave their beats to enter houses of prostitution, variety theaters, or saloons except in line of duty.

The county government went forward during the eighties and nineties, too. A new jail was built for $60,000 in 1884, the same year that the first courthouse telephone was installed. The jail was especially needed. One had been built in 1877 by a local firm, Thomas and Werner, but unfortunately the contract did not call for installation of the firm's newly patented jail lock. The result was that on June 20, 1877, six hardened criminals—murderers, horse thieves, highwaymen, and forgers—escaped.[3] The new jail, with substantial locks, was immediately north of the courthouse.

In 1893, the Commissioners Court voted to spent $500,000 in building the present courthouse. Gunn and Curtiss, of Kansas City, were retained as architects, and the contract was placed with the Probst Construction Company, of Chicago. Work was begun on October 24, 1893, and was completed the next year. Scandalized at the immensity and cost of the

[3] *Fort Worth Standard*, June 21, 1877.

new building, the public voted every member of the court out of office at the next election.

In building roads, the county had the backing of a state law requiring all able-bodied men between eighteen and sixty to "work the road" five days a year, with their own tools and under the supervision of overseers. Taxes paid for the materials used. Regularly, property owners were impressed for road service until about the mid-eighties when convict labor was utilized. Convicts worked on county roads until 1933. The first planned linkage of city and county roads was completed in 1897, when the City Council awarded a four-hundred-dollar contract to Evans Brothers to grade and gravel Maddox and White streets to the Mansfield road, because "we find the greatest country trade comes over the roads mentioned, and that portion of the city is entirely without a graveled thoroughfare and during the wet weather almost impassable."[4]

The county also assumed responsibility for neglected children. Ever since the railroad boom the town had been full of homeless waifs who sold penny newspapers and shined shoes. They lived in packing crates for shelter. Moved by the intolerable condition of the youngsters, sympathetic women prevailed upon Commissioners Court to buy a home for the children. As the first refuge for children, the commissioners bought a large gingerbread house from "Madame" Brown, who had placed it near the race track for the convenience of the sporting gentry. It had been known as the most fashionable establishment of its kind in the region.[5]

The first full-time district court for Tarrant County was created in 1884, the Seventeenth District Court, with R. E. Beckham as judge from the beginning until 1892. The second was the Forty-eighth District Court, established in 1891 with N. A. Stedman on the bench. The Sixty-seventh was created in 1907, with W. T. Simmons as the first judge, and the Ninety-

---

[4] *Minutes* of the Fort Worth City Council, Vol. O, pp. 1–63.
[5] *Fort Worth Star-Telegram*, Oct. 30, 1949, Auto. Section, 23.

sixth in 1923, with Judge Hal S. Lattimore as the first jurist.

When the work load became too heavy for the state Supreme Court, Texas decentralized the appellate work, forming three appeals districts. In the first group of appellate courts was the Second Court of Civil Appeals, established in Fort Worth in 1892. B. D. Tarleton, of Hill County, was the first chief justice.

Two important services of the federal government were expanded. On October 1, 1884, home delivery of mail was made for the first time. Prior to that improvement, which was inaugurated by Mrs. Belle M. Burchill, who always preferred the title of postmaster to that of postmistress, townsmen had gone to the post office for their mail. The first mail service had been organized by Dr. Peak, who had employed a rider to make twice-weekly trips to Dallas for the mail. Peak charged ten cents a letter for bringing the mail into Fort Worth. In 1856, President Franklin Pierce appointed Julian Feild as the first postmaster; on February 28, Feild distributed the first mail from the Fort Worth post office, a shanty on the square. Several years later the post office was moved to a two-story building between Fifth and Sixth on Main. Mrs. Burchill, taking office for the second time in 1889, moved the post office to the new Board of Trade Building at Seventh and Houston. In 1896 it was housed in a brand-new red sandstone, turreted Post Office and Federal Building on Jennings Avenue. Nine acts of Congress had been required before all of the authorizations and appropriations were in order for construction of the building.

On September 1, 1898, the first Weather Bureau station was opened. During the time the army had occupied Fort Worth, regular monthly rain reports had been sent to the government between 1849 and 1853. From 1853 until 1889 weather information was unobtainable. But in the latter year rainfall reports again were collected, continuing until 1892, probably by a civilian agency such as a railroad crop-reporting service that forwarded them to the Army Signal Corps, which had a weather-observing service. The next series of weather reports began in 1894, and has continued without interruption since that time. In 1898 the United States Weather Bureau took over the reports in Fort Worth, when E. M. Ravenscroft set up his barometer, rain gauge, thermometers, and wind-recording instruments on September 1, in the old Federal Building on Jennings Avenue.

Free public schools became a reality in the eighties after nearly a decade of hard, bitter struggle against forces that opposed the creation of a tax-supported school system. The fight was begun in 1874 by Smith, Peak, and Van Zandt. For three years and more, all that they encountered was entrenched opposition. Through dogged determination and their respected places in the community, they were successful in 1877 in having an election called to decide whether the public wanted a public school system. Throughout election day, February 25, 1877, rain fell, causing a light vote. Nevertheless, the light vote was favorable—eighty-five to five.

Not willing to abide by the election outcome, opponents of a tax-supported educational system ferreted out a law which specified that two-thirds of the property owners must have voted in any election that resulted in the establishment of a school system. They contended that two-thirds of the property owners had not voted. Their point carried.

Notwithstanding the soured turn of events, Smith, Van Zandt, and others insisted upon a second election. Again they won at the polls. This time they and the City Council were free to proceed with plans for a public school system. The council rented six schools, theretofore private institutions, in the three wards, opening the doors to children on September 1, 1879. But more trouble lay ahead.

The opposition had gone to Austin and obtained an opinion from the attorney general to the effect that municipal funds could not be diverted to school purposes. The schools were closed.

Once more the progressive element took the issue to the

polls. In the third election they were thoroughly vindicated by an aroused citizenry. The vote was 425 to 45 in favor of the schools. Once more free to proceed with an educational system, the council appointed Jarvis, John Hanna, and W. H. Baldridge as school trustees. Miss Sue Huffman was retained on December 24, 1881, as superintendent of schools—the first person to bear that title in Fort Worth. Under Miss Huffman, who was drawn from the faculty of a local private school, were sixteen teachers. As texts, she chose *McGuffey's Reader, Watson's Speller, Maury's Geography, Ray's Arithmetic,* and *Swinton's Grammar.* From January until June, 1882, the schools operated under her direction.

Again the opposition struck. In their final broadside they claimed that Fort Worth lacked the population of ten thousand that was required for any municipality operating a school system. To bolster their contention, they obtained a court ruling that the city must show a population of ten thousand or forfeit the schools.

Thus a census was required. The City Council was ready to wash its hands of the whole affair, complaining that there was no money for a census. Stepping into the breach, Smith and Van Zandt provided $300 for expenses, and Paddock supervised the count. When the last tally was in, Fort Worth's population stood at 11,136. Having exhausted all possibilities, the opposition withdrew. A one-cent school tax was levied, and free public schools were assured.

The new school board was composed of Peak, Smith, Beckham, J. M. Brown, and S. M. Fry. They decreed that all children between the ages of seven and eighteen should attend school for ten months every year. To find a school superintendent, they advertised in Fort Worth and St. Louis newspapers. From the thirty-three applicants, Alexander Hogg, of Marshall, was chosen on September 5, 1882. His appointment reflected in some measure the gratitude of the public school leaders. When the showdown with the antischool forces came during the summer of 1882, Smith had sent an urgent appeal to Hogg, a widely known educator, who then was working in the Texas and Pacific's land office in Marshall. Hogg responded by making several speeches in behalf of the system of free public schools.

When he became superintendent, the school system owned not even an inkwell. Five private schools and a Negro church were rented as school quarters. Hogg's staff included Mrs. Clara Peak Walden and Miss Huffman as principals. The white teachers were Miss Jennie Oliver, Miss Emma Hildebrand, Miss Pinka Jones, Miss Ida Rich, Mrs. M. L. Pearcy, Miss Bessie Foute, Miss Jennie Howard, J. N. Lacey, R. Madder, Miss Eva Haywood, Miss Clara Burnham, Miss Maud P. Johnson, and Miss Lula Dial. The Negro teachers were I. M. Terrell, J. W. Johnson, H. H. Butler, and T. B. Davis. Butler had been operating a private Negro school since 1875. The African Methodist Church also had conducted a school with a tuition of ten cents a day.

Thus with Hogg and the new teaching staff, Fort Worth's public school system was permanently established in 1882, in the administration of Mayor Smith, who had been the first schoolteacher and who had been a guiding spirit in the enterprise from the beginning.

Until 1890 boys and girls of high-school age attended different schools, the girls receiving instruction from Mrs. Walden in her former private school on Fourth Street, and the boys studying under Will Lipscomb, who was added to the faculty in 1885, at Sixth and Burnet. In 1888 the city bought the First Baptist Church, a one-story building on the site of the present City Hall, as the Girls' High School. Even though the prevailing attitude was that girls needed less academic instruction than boys, Hogg refused to neglect them. He emphasized that girls needed as good an education as their brothers. He stressed, too, that every child should be educated "in entirety—the head, the heart, and the hand."[6] He originated

6 *Fort Worth Star-Telegram*, Nov. 26, 1939; Oct. 30, 1949, Community Life Section, 17.

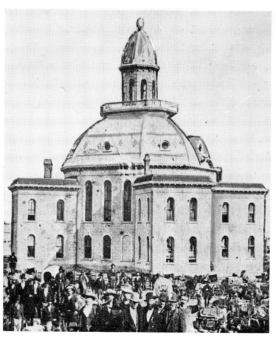

Above:
Tarrant County
Courthouse destroyed
by fire in 1876

Left:
Tarrant County
Courthouse built
in 1876–77
and razed in 1894

Tarrant County Courthouse since 1894

manual training and household arts courses in Fort Worth schools.

Hogg was born in Yorktown, Virginia, in 1830, and was educated at Randolph-Macon College for Men. After serving with Confederate cavalry, he had been school superintendent at Montgomery, Alabama, a mathematics professor at Texas Agricultural and Mechanical College, and a civil engineer for the Houston and Texas Central Railroad. He served as superintendent in Fort Worth until 1889, when he lost his post through politics. He returned in 1891 as principal of the high school, and the next year became superintendent again, serving until 1896. After that he went to Dallas, where he edited the T. and P.'s employee publication. He died in Baltimore in 1911.

Higher education was begun when the Methodist Episcopal church chartered Texas Wesleyan University (not to be confused with the present Texas Wesleyan College) that opened in downtown quarters on September 7, 1881. Eight years later it was renamed Fort Worth University, three years after it had moved to a College Avenue site later occupied by Paschal High School. The intention of the founders was to establish a school that ultimately would be a center in the Southwest where anyone could find instruction in any study and pursue it as far and as long as he chose.

To that end, the school of law was organized in August, 1893. A year later the school of medicine was added, which had quarters at Commerce and Seventh streets. There also was a commercial department. The school carried out its original purpose by offering instruction from kindergarten to the degree of Doctor of Divinity.

Fort Worth University's period of greatest growth was during the twelve-year presidency of Professor O. L. Fisher, who retired in 1903. The university occupied a ten-acre campus, with space for baseball, football, croquet, lawn tennis, and other sports. There were four buildings on the campus—University Hall, Cadet Hall, Science Hall, and the Dining

Hall. A young man could go to school for less than two hundred dollars a year, paying only fifty cents a week for room and three dollars for board in 1903.[7]

With Fort Worth University developing rapidly as an arm of the Methodist Episcopal church, the Methodist Episcopal church, South in 1891 established Polytechnic College on the present T. W. C. campus, then about four miles from Fort Worth. Plans had been made a year earlier by the Northwest Texas Methodist Conference to provide young men and women with a cultural background while equipping them for business and industrial life.

Bishop Joseph S. Key, who had been instrumental in establishing the school, was the first president. In 1911 the church decided to found Southern Methodist University in Dallas and to make Polytechnic College a woman's component. The name was changed in 1913 to Wesley Woman's College, and the next year the school was renamed Texas Woman's College. In 1935 it received the present name—Texas Wesleyan College—and once more became coeducational.

The early colleges established football on the Fort Worth sports scene, following the introduction of a town team in 1890 when Tom Lake and the "Heavyweights" fielded a gridiron machine. Fort Worth University and Polytechnic began playing unorganized football in 1892, and Fort Worth High School had a team around 1900.

The increasing cultural atmosphere typified by the colleges provided an environment in which women began doing their important work in community development through their clubs. The first women's club was the Woman's Wednesday Club, organized on February 11, 1889, in the home of Mrs. John F. Swayne at 503 East First, with seventeen members. The club joined the General Federation of Women's Clubs in 1892 and in 1895 added its voice to the demands for a public library, especially through the activities of Mrs. J. C. Terrell. During the nineties the club began bringing lecturers

[7] *Fort Worth Telegram,* May 17, 1903.

to Fort Worth, including sculptor Lorado Taft among the first. Other early clubs were the '93 Club, the Monday Book Club of 1896, the Symposium (later the Penelope) of 1897, the Sorosis of 1903, and the Shakespeare Club of 1905. By 1923 the many women's clubs established the Woman's Club on Pennsylvania Avenue as a central meeting place for their many and varied programs.

About the same time, the last of the major religious affiliations appeared on an organized basis. The Orthodox Jewish congregation of Ahavath Sholom built its first synagogue in 1893, with W. Goldstein as president of the congregation. Rabbi Charles Blumenthal came in 1908 as the first rabbi. The Reform Jewish congregation of Temple Beth-El was organized in 1902, and reorganized the following year with Rabbi Joseph Jasin. Sam Levy was first president of the congregation.

Educational, civic, and commercial growth was interrupted by the Spanish-American War. When war was declared, two militia companies announced ready. They were the Loyd Rifles, a descendant of the Tarrant Rifles who had fought in the Civil War, and the Forth Worth Fencibles, formed in 1886, absorbing the Light Guards of 1888 and the Trinity Guards of 1878. The Loyd Rifles left on May 3, 1898, for Austin, where they were mustered as Company H, Second Texas Volunteer Infantry. The Fencibles became Company D of the same regiment. At first the two companies were stationed at Mobile, then shifted to Florida, where they lived in an insect-infested land. Their rations were bacon, potatoes, bread, and molasses from an open, fly-covered barrel. The regiment was told to pack for combat, but thirty-six hours later the orders were canceled. The war was over. Another Fort Worth company, Troop F of the First Texas Cavalry, spent the war training at Fort Bliss.

At the end of the nineteenth century, Fort Worth was settling down. All major religious denominations had been established, schools were flourishing, and colleges had been opened. But the town was without a library. The women decided to do something about it. They wanted a good library, one well stocked with books on every subject, housed in an attractive building that would be an important part of the city. To further their ends, they formed the Fort Worth Public Library Association in April,, 1892. For six years they worked hard, trying to get enough money through teas, dances, dinners, cakewalks, and solicitations for their library. They raised twelve thousand dollars—far from enough for the accomplishment envisioned. Then Mrs. D. B. Keeler decided to go after the men. She asked every man in town to donate the price of a good cigar. She even wrote to Andrew Carnegie, asking him to donate the price of a cigar. The great benefactor of libraries throughout the nation responded generously. He gave fifty thousand dollars. The library was assured.

Six-shooter culture had come to an end.

CHAPTER X

A Bold New Century

W HEN the twentieth century opened, Fort Worth was more than ever a blend of Broadway and the range. It was still a cowboy's town, but like any town of Mid-America it also had dignified residential sections where quiet, tree-lined streets were appropriate to the new era.

The Wheat Building Roof Garden was the place to go at the turn of the century. Young men in straw sailors escorted young ladies in white lace to the fashionable roof garden. In one corner, covered by a striped canvas canopy, was a soda fountain, where lemonades and sarsaparilla were mixed for the couples seated at tables among potted palms.

The Hibernians, composed of men whose homes were in Irish Town in the vicinity of Fifteenth and Jones, never let St. Patrick's Day pass without a wearing of the green. With solid German food and beer, the Sons of Hermann spent pleasant Sundays at their own park just north of the river on North Main.

Over the streets paved with vitrified brick clopped carefully groomed carriage horses, which were prided by the men who built spacious homes of imposing charm on Quality Hill, where Lancaster intersects Summit Avenue. Along with the carriage horses thudded tasseled Percherons pulling beer wagons, and the shiny transports of the express company.

But the downtown streets showed that twentieth-century Fort Worth had carried over some of the brashness of the old days. A tangle of electric wires crossed and crisscrossed the streets between dingy brick buildings and crestfallen wooden structures. Raised streetcar tracks scarred the roadways. Noisy trolleys clanged through town. Cattlemen in greasy, dusty hats and high-heeled boots lolled on street corners. Gamblers and toughs frequented the saloons, where floors were covered with sawdust.

The most picturesque saloon was the White Elephant, the same that had figured in the shooting of Jim Courtright. Winfield Scott, a wealthy cattleman, bought the saloon, and built in 1896 an imposing structure to house it at 606 Main Street. Many notables placed their feet on the brass rail at the forty-foot bar. There they drank beer at a nickel a glass and whisky at two slugs for a quarter. Among the notables were "Iron Jawn" McGraw, who brought his New York Giants to Fort Worth for spring training and a visit with his old sandlot chum, Father Malone, who was pastor at All Saints. And there James J. Corbett, John L. Sullivan, and Tex Rickard bent their elbows. Drinkers received telegraphic sports returns from the Turf Exchange that was part of the establishment, and ate a hearty meal in an excellent restaurant. Upstairs were gambling rooms. The White Elephant was a landmark until 1913, when financial misfortunes caused its conversion into a pool hall.

With ordinary bed sheets for screens, the first motion pictures were shown about 1903. One of the first exhibited was *The Great Train Robbery*, shown in Rosen Park by J. S. Phillips, the first movie-house owner, who in 1910 built the Odeon—the first cinema theater designed as such. Admission to the one-reel pictures cost five cents.

Teddy Roosevelt, the first president of the United States to visit Fort Worth, arrived on April 8, 1905, to go on a wolf hunt with Burk Burnett and Tom Waggoner, who had made their fortunes on cattle ranges in North Texas and Oklahoma Territory, and who maintained homes in Fort Worth. Twenty thousand persons were at the T. and P. station to greet the vigorous Mr. Roosevelt. Thousands more lined the streets to cheer him. On the roof of a real-estate building on Ninth Street sat fifty persons, under whose weight the roof collapsed during the parade, but no one was injured.

Flanked by cavalrymen wearing flop hats, the President rode in a carriage to Ninth and Throckmorton, where he alighted and planted an elm tree on the grounds of the Carnegie Library, which had been completed in 1901. The tree died and was replaced, but the second one did not bloom, either, until it was transplanted northeast of Will Rogers Memorial Auditorium when the old library was razed in 1938 to make way for the present building.

Roosevelt came to Fort Worth again in 1911. An audience of five thousand persons in the North Side Coliseum waited and waited for the former President to appear. Roosevelt was delayed because he was in busy conversation outside the hall with a one-legged man who had been a Rough Rider in Cuba. The veteran, Charley Buckholtz, of San Angelo, had been having trouble getting a pension. Hearing that Roosevelt would be in Fort Worth, he came to see the chief himself about it. Buckholtz received the pension.

The men who had played pivotal roles in the development of Fort Worth began passing from the scene. The first to go was John Peter Smith. He had gone to St. Louis on April 5, 1901, to meet with railroad executives. One night he accompanied a friend to a railroad station and started back to the hotel alone. On the way he was attacked and robbed. He died on April 11 in a St. Louis hospital.

At a time when one out of four Fort Worth marriages was ending in divorce, at a time when an odd game called golf was claiming some attention, and at a time when Fort Worth population exceeded 26,000, the automobile appeared. Whether it was in 1902 or 1903, whether it was H. R. Cromer the bicycle man or Billy Kasan the minstrel man who purchased the first one, the date and the owner of the first car are uncertain.

Regardless, there were enough automobiles on the streets by 1904 to warrant municipal regulation. On May 20 the council enacted the first automobile ordinance, with these requirements: Each car must be registered with the city secretary; the motorist was obligated to paint his license number in figures six inches high; and each car must have two lights visible for a quarter-mile at night and a gong or horn audible for at least six hundred feet. Even when traveling at the maximum speed of ten miles an hour, the driver was to begin sounding his horn or gong one hundred feet before reaching a street crossing and to continue sounding it until he had crossed the street.

The first automobile to be registered was Cromer's Rambler. Cromer was the dealer for Rambler bicycles, which he sold for thirty-five dollars each on easy terms. When the bike-maker switched to automobile manufacturing, Cromer took one of the topless, chain-driven vehicles. Some residents have claimed that Cromer's was the first car in town, but in a newspaper interview in 1934, Cromer himself claimed only to have had the first car registration.[1]

At first the automobile was a novelty. People turned out to watch every time one clattered down Main Street. Before long, the novelty turned into a nuisance. Shopkeepers disliked the way their customers' horses were frightened. Farmers were apt to appear with loaded shotguns when cars came out into the country.

Driving in the country was something of an expedition. When Cromer steered his Rambler out of the city, his tool-box included a pick, shovel, and wire cutters; the wire cutter for cutting fences so that he could detour through a field to avoid mudholes in the road, the pick to chop down the high center of the old roads, and the shovel for digging out of sand beds.[2]

City streets were not much better. Although some were

[1] *Fort Worth Star-Telegram,* Aug. 30, 1934.
[2] *Ibid.*

paved with brick and others graveled, many of the principal business streets were disgraceful. In the midst of a street improvement campaign the *Telegram* said:

> By noon today Houston Street had begun to resume its normal condition of muddiness.[3]
>
> Houston Street is in an awful condition. Ruts, holes, and low places can be found along its length at almost any point, and vehicles risk damage wherever they are drawn.[4]

Regardless of road conditions, driving an early car was a chore. Drivers and passengers protected their eyes with goggles, their clothing with long white dusters, their hands with gauntlets, and their heads with special caps. From the beginning to the end of a motor jaunt, mastery over the vehicle meant physical effort.

> On the dash board there was a neat little box holding the matches to light those headlights. Of course you had to stop the car and get out of the breeze to light them, but then you had some headlights when they were lit. And what a picnic we had with the removable side curtains, storm curtains they called them. You had to stop and put them on and by the time they were firmly fastened you were thoroughly wet, or if you put them on while moving you usually got them on upside down and got wet, anyway. If you put them on at the first sign of rain it cleared off.[5]

Those were the conditions that existed when the first automobile speed record between Fort Worth and Dallas was set on August 24, 1903. Establishment of that record was the basis for this newspaper report:

> The fastest time ever made over the dirt road between Dallas and Fort Worth was made yesterday by a party of

[3] *Fort Worth Telegram*, Feb. 17, 1903.
[4] *Ibid.*, Sept. 26, 1903.
[5] Mrs. A. W. Cottar in *Fort Worth Star-Telegram*, Feb. 20, 1940.

prominent Texas men in an automobile. The party consisted of Col. R. Peterson, O. A. Perry and J. J. Pettus. The automobile is the property of Colonel Peterson, and is a large machine, belonging to the "Red Devil" class. It cost $2,600. The trip from Dallas to Fort Worth was made in one hour and thirty-five minutes. Colonel Peterson is a well-known banker and real estate man of Paris. Mr. Perry is from the same place, and Mr. Pettus is a prominent cattleman of Sweetwater. The trip was one of pleasure, the party returning to Paris this morning.[6]

The hit-and-run driver appeared early. On April 30, 1904, George H. Giddings, a Gainesville attorney, was standing at Seventh and Houston, when "a benzine wagon which turned the corner noiselessly and at a rapid speed" struck him and kept going.[7]

Adventuring increased the popularity of the automobile, adventuring of the type that led Roy E. Kamp and A. B. Wharton to make the first car trip between Fort Worth and Denver in 1903. Upon reaching Fort Worth, Wharton opened the first automobile sales agency, the Fort Worth Auto Livery, at 404 Houston. He dealt in Wintons and Franklins, in addition to Indian motorcycles.

By 1910 motoring was quite the thing—959 automobiles were registered. Constantly the *Star-Telegram* boosted the cause of motor vehicles, sponsoring several endurance runs into West Texas. One of the more spectacular was a six-day trip over a route of five hundred miles that extended from Dallas through Fort Worth to Abilene and San Angelo, and back to Fort Worth by way of Brownwood and Stephenville.

The number of motorists necessitated something new on the police force—a motorcycle officer. The first one was Henry Lewis, who went to work on June 1, 1909, as a lad of nineteen. Aboard a skinny-looking, five-horsepower Indian motorcycle, the future police chief began nabbing speeders. He set up a

[6] *Fort Worth Telegram,* Aug. 25, 1903.
[7] *Ibid.,* April 30, 1904.

speed trap in the 1100 block of West Seventh Street, where one-eighth of a mile was measured. He used a stop watch to check the speed of cars over the marked stretch of street. Lewis learned to recognize by the sound of an approaching automobile to whom it belonged and how fast it was traveling.[8]

Because of the automobile, the city began taking better care of the streets, and the state took a new view toward cross-state roads. The need for facilitating construction of trunk-line roads was recognized in 1904, when the state adopted a constitutional amendment that authorized Commissioners Courts and road districts to issue bonds for the construction of graveled, macadamized, or paved roads and turnpikes.

Pioneering and setting a precedent for the Southwest, Tarrant County was the first to take advantage of the road-bond law, approving in 1911 a bond issue of $1,000,000 for paved roads and $600,000 for bridges. J. C. Travilla, St. Louis street commissioner, was retained to supervise construction of primary roads stretching from Fort Worth to Keller, Mansfield, Benbrook, and Grapevine. The following year the county had its first modern road system.[9]

As always, promotional schemes looking toward ultimate substantial gain were thick in the air as the twentieth century opened. This time it was a revival of the packing-house dream, but it was different from the early ventures when Fort Worth men hoped to compete against the moneyed combines. This time Swift and Armour themselves were looking for sites in Texas. Industrial advantages—water, rail, transportation, labor supply, and proximity to cattle ranches—alone were insufficient to determine the plant location. For the packers, like the railroads before them, expected the successful town to subsidize construction of the plant.

Fort Worth bent every effort to raise the subsidy. For sev-

[8] Fort Worth Star-Telegram, Oct. 1949, Auto. Section, 16.
[9] Fort Worth Star-Telegram, Dec. 15, 1912.

eral months during 1901, the fortunes ebbed and flowed as businessmen strained to collect the money. Then one night a final report meeting was held. The next morning the newspaper proclaimed:

> Fort Worth made history for herself and Texas last night.
> Fort Worth today will be on the lips of every man, woman and child who reads.
> Fort Worth, the packing house center of all the South and Southwest.
> Fort Worth, the metropolis of Texas—the metropolis of the South and West.
> Fort Worth started on her road to greatness last night.
> At 11:35 o'clock Monday night, October 7, 1901, the die was cast, and J. W. Springer, of Denver, Col., standing on the rostrum of the city hall auditorium, in front of the packing house soliciting committee and before a vast multitude of Fort Worth citizens, ladies and gentlemen, from all the better walks of life, announced that:
>
> FORT WORTH IS IT,
>
> She having succeeded in raising the $100,000 packing house bonus, with over $600 to spare. Of this amount, $15,669 was raised in the city hall last night. At this announcement, pandemonium took possession of the audience—hats went up, handkerchiefs were waived, handshaking was unanimous, and hundreds rushed forward to grasp the hands of Messrs. Springer and Hall who had so cleverly entertained the vast assemblage during the evening, and the working committees.
> It was midnight when the last of the vast concourse of people passed out of the city hall, just 25 minutes from the time the gavel fell and three cheers reverberated for "Fort Worth, the greatest packing house center of the Southwest."[10]

The prophecy was accurate, for that is exactly what the town became—the packing-house center of the Southwest. The two major packers built their plants on the North Side in 1902, and a year later were processing meat. They drew

[10] *Fort Worth Register*, Oct. 8, 1901, p. 1.

practically all of the West Texas cattle into Fort Worth for either sale or reshipment at the stockyards, or for sale to the packers. When cattlemen came to market, they naturally did their shopping. Their wives came along, and the money spent magnified the boon the packing houses were to the city.

As the first major industry, the packing plants were the fourth great impetus in the development of a city. The impetus was felt immediately, raising the population from 26,688 in 1900 to 73,312 in 1910.

Industrialization was furthered by the advent of natural gas, brought in by the Consumers Heat and Light Company. Owned by George Armstrong and associates, the company was franchised by referendum on September 1, 1905, the first utility whose franchise was made subject to popular vote, under a recently enacted state law.

Natural gas had been discovered at Petrolia, near Wichita Falls, and the Lone Star Gas Company was building a pipe line to bring it east. On September 30, 1900, Armstrong contracted with Lone Star for the gas. And on February 22, 1910, the new pipe line from Petrolia brought gas into Fort Worth, where a flambeau was lighted just west of the packing houses in a special ceremony. There was much interest in natural gas, but there was also much distrust of the mysterious underground fuel. Several years of salesmanship were required before the gas company convinced consumers that the fuel was safe.[11] Within five months after natural gas reached town, Consumers—renamed Fort Worth Gas Company—took over and closed the artificial-gas plant.

The arrival of natural gas was the signal for a realignment of gas and electric companies. Most of the utilities had dual franchises for both artificial gas and electricity. Their officers realized a new approach was needed in view of natural gas. Armstrong's company divested itself of electrical properties, selling them to J. R. Nutt of Cleveland. The electric com-

[11] *Minutes* of the Fort Worth City Council, Vol. R, pp. 189, 416; Records of the Lone Star Gas Company.

panies closed their gas plants. Each utility thereafter concentrated on either gas or electricity.

The electrical field was crowded—Arlington Heights, Stratton and White, and Citizens companies were doing business. Besides, the city still had its municipal electric plant. The various power companies supplied different parts of the city, but sometimes their poles and wires cluttered the same streets, creating unsightly conditions. Nor was there a power standard for the several companies, making it impossible for a customer to buy an electrical appliance for use in one neighborhood with the assurance that he could use it in another. The parade toward centralization began in 1911, when the City Commission decided to cease generating electricity. As a consequence, Nutt was given a contract for lighting city streets by delivering power to the city's River Plant for distribution. A few months later, the Fort Worth Power and Light Company was formed to operate the electric properties of Fort Worth Gas, Fort Worth Light and Power, Citizens Railway and Light, Citizens Light and Power, Fort Worth and Rosen Heights Railway, and Arlington Heights Traction companies. The new company built a steam generating plant on the north bank of the Trinity so that it could provide a standardized source of power for the entire city and thus simplify its electrical problems.

While natural gas had forced the artificial-gas companies out of the field, the Fort Worth Gas Company continued to operate one artificial-gas plant—the Pintsch plant near Lancaster and Cherry, which made gas for use in lighting railway cars.

Keeping pace with the industrial developments, more railroads entered town. In 1902 came the International and Great Northern, which now is part of the Missouri Pacific System, and the Frisco. Misfortune plagued the Frisco's initial operations. After considerable advance fanfare, the Frisco's first through train from Fort Worth to St. Louis left in March, 1902. In the vicinity of Holdenville, Indian Territory, the train was wrecked. The tender and the last four cars—the St. Louis sleeper, two chair cars, and a buffet-observation car —were derailed and all but the sleeper turned over.[12] It was an unfortunate experience for a maiden trip.

To attract railroads, ever since 1876, Fort Worth people had contributed heavily from their own purses. Bonuses raised to entice the railroads, besides the land given the T. and P. and other roads, included $12,000 for the Ft.W. and D.C.; $115,000 for the Santa Fe; $75,000 for the Ft.W. and N.O.; $65,000 for the F.W. and R.G.; $65,600 for the Cotton Belt; and $40,000 for the Fort Worth and Albuquerque.[13] The Fort Worth and Albuquerque was an abortive project begun in 1889. The right of way was graded and an embankment raised for a distance of several miles northwest of Fort Worth, but the railroad was never built.

Meantime, the Northern Texas Traction Company entered the cross-country field. With an interurban service inaugurated in 1902, the company placed noisy Red Limiteds in regular service between Fort Worth and Dallas. Another line linked Fort Worth with Cleburne. The company developed Lake Erie at Handley as a recreation center. The traction company added bus service in the city when it appeared that the automobile was here to stay. In 1917 the company formed the subsidiary Fort Worth Auto Bus Company, which took passengers from the end of the Rosen Heights line to the newly-built Lake Worth Amusement Park. For several years the buses operated during summer seasons, transporting the public to a favorite playground. Later, some of the buses were used on a temporary bus line to Riverside, while the Riverside car line was being built. In 1939, the Fort Worth Transit Company, successor of N.T.T.C., took the last trolley car from the rails and started using buses exclusively.

Heavy industry appeared in 1904, with the establishment of the Bolt Works. A year later, rolling-mill equipment from

12 *Fort Worth Register,* March 25, 1902.
13 *Fort Worth Star-Telegram,* Jan. 10, 1941.

Lyons, Ohio, was added, giving Fort Worth the first rolling mill in the Southwest. Today it is the Texas Steel Company.

Other industrial expansions came in 1904, also with the establishment of Burrus Mills and the Medlin Milling Company. The latter burned in 1910 and was bought by Bewley, as Bewley Mills, an adjunct of Anchor.

Briefly, the Southwestern Bell Telephone Company had competition. The Fort Worth Telephone Company, owned by F. D. McElroy and Martin Casey, began operations in 1903, with about one thousand subscribers; Southwestern had three thousand. The local company, which built the main downtown office now occupied by Southwestern, folded in 1916.

Natural gas, electricity, telephones, automobiles, electric interurbans, big new industries—all were part of the mammoth, grinding progress of the glorious American machine. And in that tradition came the airplane.

For a long time Fort Worth had been hearing about the new flying machines, but had never seen one of them. Then, in 1911, the International Aviators—three Frenchmen and a Swiss—toured the nation. On their itinerary was Dallas, too close for Fort Worth not to attempt to duplicate the event. The idea of bringing those pioneer daredevils of the skyway to Fort Worth is credited to Amon Carter, publisher of the *Star-Telegram.* His idea sent R. E. L. Costan, an aviation enthusiast, to Dallas, where he offered the flying troupe five thousand dollars to appear in Fort Worth. They agreed, and the money was raised by Carter and others through public contributions.

Because cross-country flying jaunts were for the future, the International Aviators and their flimsy crates came by train. They scheduled the town's first flying exhibition for January 12 and 13, 1911, in the old Driving Park between West Seventh and White Settlement Road, near the present Montgomery Ward building.

Word of their coming excited the countryside. An esti-

Aerial view of Fort Worth today

Amon G. Carter

mated fifteen thousand persons were on hand. For hours the crowd waited patiently, a wait dictated by strong winds that the European birdmen dared not brave. After interminable hours, when day was waning, one of the fliers decided that the crowd should not be disappointed. They had come to see a man fly and a man they should see fly, even if he had to risk his life to please them. So he climbed into his "Statue of Liberty" monoplane, and flew 2,100 feet above the earth, traveling ten miles in seven minutes despite a head wind of twenty miles an hour. The following contemporary newspaper account tells the story:

Thursday's throng that was rewarded after four hours of patient waiting by the sight of the reckless Roland G. Garros rocking high above their heads was perhaps one of the largest ever gathered in Fort Worth. After filling the long improvised grandstand and packing themselves around the hangar, the people banked themselves all the way around the track.

Perhaps it was only the anticipation of seeing the world's greatest marvel for the first time that kept the better part of the thousands waiting patiently, although but few of them actually understood the real cause of the delay. The ascension of the first little bright colored kite encouraged the spectators, and when young John Frisbee, Jr., leaped high into the air, supported only by the slender rope that held the five-man-carrying kites to the earth, the crowd applauded enthusiastically. These kites were sent up primarily to test the air currents. By watching the twisting, turning, and diving of the kites the aviators could distinguish the character of the wind. It proved varrying and puffy, as the crowd could tell by the unsteady sailing of the kites. Later the aerometer was sent up by a passenger and the velocity of the wind tested.

The tricks of Frisbee and the others, who were suspended on the rope after him, furnished amusement to the crowd. Hundreds of people in the city, watching from housetops and through field glasses from second story windows, mistook the kites for aeroplanes and kept the distant crowds waiting as patiently as those on the field.

The first actual thrill of the afternoon came when Edmond Audemars in his little yellow Demoiselle leaped into the air, even though the Swiss aviator could not control the little trick machine in the cross currents of air that swept to and fro near the earth. The sputtering of the Demoiselle's engine made the crowd forget its long wait, and there was a buzzing expectancy of seeing for the first time a heavier than air machine leave the ground. The Demoiselle skipped swiftly across the field, and as it neared the judge's stand it made a jerky leap into the air. Audemar's flights, however, were unsuccessful Thursday, and the best exhibition that the Demoiselle could furnish was a series of "hops."

The aviators were aware that the crowd was becoming disappointed and lapsing back into its former restlessness.

"I'm not going to see them disappointed," said Garros, the French aviator, who only two hours before had shaken his head significantly and commented to his fellow birdmen on the peril of attempting a flight in the puffy wind that he knew was in the air.

Rene Simon, the "fool flyer" himself, grasped Garros by the arm almost in fright, and told him he must not try to fly at the risk of his life. Simon and other aviators were still pleading with Garros when the mechanicians started the engine of the "Statue of Liberty" monoplane and Garros mounted the machine.

To the crowd that already had seen the failure of the Demoiselle the whirr of Garros' high power engine gave no unusual thrills. It expected more "hopping." When the engine had attained its highest speed, Garros raised his left hand, the mechanicians released the machine and it sped smoothly across the field.

When it mounted gracefully into the air and moved steadily upward for several hundred feet, the crowd burst into applause. Every head bent upward and not an eye left the machine until it curved gracefully to the left, soared above the grand stand and flew rapidly northward. So high was the monoplane when it passed over the heads of the spectators that the terrific throbbing of its powerful engine could be heard only as a murmur.

Farther into the distance the machine flew and persons on every side were heard explaining to others that Garros was lost, that he already had lost his directions. The bird-like contour of the aeroplane became a blur against the sky and the spectators watched intently at the marvel.[14]

On the next day strong winds delayed flying until 6:00 P.M., when René Simon took his plane into the air. Audemars' "Demoiselle" was damaged in landing. With $6,300 in their pockets, the International Aviators went on to Oklahoma City. They had introduced the flying machine to Fort Worth. But man had yet to fly into and out of Fort Worth, an event that happened later in the same year.

On September 17, C. P. Rodgers—"Daredevil Cal," he was called—left New York on the first transcontinental flight in history, sponsored by the makers of a grape drink called Vin-Fiz. In his "Vin-Fiz Flyer," Rodgers flew from town to town along his route, followed by his family and assistants, who rode in a special train also known as the "Vin-Fiz Flyer." On October 12 the *Star-Telegram* excitedly front-paged a story that the intrepid pilot, whose forebears were Indian-fighting army officers and naval commanders, had placed Fort Worth upon his route.

The word came from Kansas City. Rodgers was due in five days, following the Katy to Fort Worth and then on to San Antonio, where he would pick up the Southern Pacific for the flight to California. The special train which was to carry his family was the fastest the Katy had ever operated.

On the day scheduled for Rodgers' arrival, he left Denison at 9:25 A.M. As he soared away, the word was flashed by a *Star-Telegram* correspondent on the train. When the newspaper relayed the information, whistles from a dozen or more factories began to herald his approach, as did the old fire bell in the Central Fire Hall belfry. Schools were closed to permit the children to witness the great event. Thousands of

[14] *Fort Worth Star-Telegram,* Jan. 13, 1911.

persons flocked to a pasture in Ryan Place Addition, just south of the present Elizabeth Boulevard, to watch the landing of the first man ever to fly into Fort Worth. They scanned the Indian summer sky hour after hour in vain.

They waited in vain because Rodgers had lost his way. Leaving Whitesboro at 11:50 A.M., he followed the wrong railroad track. Friends and supporters discovered what was wrong and frantically tried to reach him. Telegraph and telephone operators were alerted and asked to signal him. Many tried without success. After he had flown his slow crate seventy miles out of the way, he finally was signaled to earth at Bonita, west of Gainesville.

By 3:00 P.M. an estimated eight to ten thousand persons were on hand in the Ryan pasture. In the northwest a speck appeared. It was Rodgers, 2,300 feet above the earth. When he was spotted, whistles screamed again. Because of the excitement, the crowd was too great for the squad of mounted police and patrolmen to handle. Men swarmed over the field, throwing hats and caps into the air and seriously interfering with Rodgers, whose face could be seen as he peered down while slowly circling the field. He could not land because of the multitude.

To get down, Rodgers had to trick the spectators. By pretending to land in one place, he drew the entire crowd over to one side of the field, then sent his biplane higher into the air, sailing over the crowd at not more than seventy-five feet, to land half a block away. He came down at 4:15 P.M. on October 17, 1911—the first man ever to fly an airplane into and out of Fort Worth.[15]

Rodgers was greeted by Amon Carter. To J. M. North, Jr., editor of the *Star-Telegram,* he brought the first piece of air mail delivered into Fort Worth, a letter from Oklahoma. The taciturn Rodgers' only comment to a newspaper interviewer was, "It was pretty cold up there today."[16]

15 *Fort Worth Star-Telegram,* Oct. 17–18, 1911.
16 *Fort Worth Star-Telegram,* Oct. 18, 1911.

For the municipal government it was an age of experimentation and what was regarded as progress. One of the vogues was the commission form of municipal government. In the aftermath of the great storm of 1900, Galveston had placed city government in the hands of commissioners, each responsible for certain functions. Certain advantages over the alderman system were seen in the new method, leading to an election in Fort Worth in 1907, when the citizens adopted the commission form by a vote of 2,177 to 405. Originally there were a mayor and four commissioners; a fifth commissioner was added when North Fort Worth was annexed two years later.

Two other developments were significant during the first two decades of the twentieth century. One was the motorization of the fire and police departments. The other was the initiation of a park system. The first automobile purchased by the city was a Maxwell passenger car bought from the Reid Auto Company for $2,140 on July 9, 1909, for the fire chief. It was a topless, doorless car with a high-set, leather-covered seat. Headlights protruded like grapes popped from their skins. The chief hung a lantern on the left front doorpost and mounted a fire extinguisher on the left running board. A spotlight was in the middle of the area where the windshield would have been, if there had been a windshield.

Less than six months later, on January 18, 1910, the first two fire trucks were purchased. They were combination chemical-hose wagons. One was purchased from Webb Motor Fire Apparatus Company, Vincennes, for $5,000. The other came from American LaFrance for $4,900. Motorization of the fire department was completed in 1919, with eight fire trucks ordered from American LaFrance for $74,050.

The fire trucks increased the department's efficiency, to be sure, but they did not compel the sentimental attachment that an intelligent horse could command. Each fire horse was highly trained, each had a personality, and each was named for something or somebody the firemen admired: Bill, for

Mayor Bill Davis; Casey and Swasey, for a pair of popular saloon keepers; Telegram, for the newspaper; Dewey, for the admiral; Tom and Jerry, for a drink by the same name. The horses knew their jobs about as well as the men knew theirs. When the electric fire alarm sounded, stalls opened automatically, horses stepped quickly to posts in front of the wagons, and the firemen dropped harness, that was suspended from the ceiling, on the horses. Horses that became too old for fire duty were transferred to the street department, with the result that many a street-department wagon was overturned by an old fire horse when the alarm sounded and fire wagons came clattering down the street.

Of all the good horses in the department, the late Chief Standifer Ferguson claimed that Dewey was the smartest of the lot. Dewey learned to unlatch his stall gate. Ears back and tail flying, he would race down the street and out of sight. The only way he could be caught was to ring the fire bell, and back he would gallop to take his place before the wagon.

Fire trucks were in use before the police department was graced by an automobile. Indeed the City Commission agreed to buy one only after Chief O. R. Montgomery told the commissioners that Fort Worth was the only city of its size in the country without a patrol car. The car was ordered immediately, on November 10, 1914. A motor patrol wagon had been in use since 1911, but the Black Maria did not count as a patrol car.

Besides mounted patrolmen, the department also had a bicycle detail from 1913 to 1917. From 9:00 P.M. to 5:00 A.M., fifteen patrolmen on bicycles operated from precinct stations at 1540 North Main, 801 West Maddox, and the 1000 block on Missouri. The bicycle police were more effective in catching burglars than were foot patrolmen or mounted officers, whose approach could be heard.

A start had been made on a park system in 1892, when City Park was created with thirty-one acres that were part of the tract bought from McCart and Capps for the Holly

Water Plant. For years it was the only park, but a beautiful one, with tall and ancient oaks and shaded glades that drew picnickers on Sunday. On summer nights the streetcar company presented free minstrel shows there. As the town grew, interested citizens formed a Park League to press for a larger park system. In 1907 they convinced city officials that a park board should be created.

The men named on the first park board were James Maddox, Glen Walker, A. W. Grant, and R. W. Rogers. George Vinnedge was named superintendent. Two years later, George Kessler, an authority on city planning, was retained for fifteen hundred dollars to draft a master plan for park development. Ever since, the Kessler Plan has been the guidepost for the development of a park system that year by year has grown to 10,750 acres.

Several other municipal advancements were made in the early part of this century. All wooden buildings on Main Street were condemned in 1905. A board of movie censors was named in 1911, and three years later the construction of theaters, as well as safety measures for projection machines, came under city regulation.

Once again the water supply was an irritating public issue. About 1903, thirteen artesian wells at the Holly Plant had ceased flowing, and the Clear Fork supply of untreated water was insufficient. The quality of the water was so poor that the public demanded action. Just before remedial measures were to be taken, a newspaper reported that there was so much mud in the Trinity that water pumped into the mains one morning had the consistency of paste.[17] To remedy the bad water situation, Daniel W. Mead, a Chicago engineer, drilled a large shaft near the Holly Plant and then bored tunnels to each of the thirteen artesian wells, but that did little good. Then the Powell Field of sixteen wells, which supplied water from 1905 to 1914, was drilled near the intersection of University Drive and the T. and P. tracks. By 1911 the de-

[17] *Fort Worth Telegram,* June 29, 1903.

mand for a proper water supply forced the city to begin treating water. For $70,000, the Pittsburgh Filter Manufacturing Company completed the first filtration plant in 1912. And a committee of engineers recommended that a dam be built on the West Fork of the Trinity to provide an abundant water supply. Completed in 1914, the dam impounded a lake since known as Lake Worth. Bridgeport and Eagle Mountain Lakes were added in 1932 and 1934.

The newspaper community in the early part of the twentieth century was young, virile, and ambitious. The *Register*, which had been founded as a co-operative in 1896, had become the first financially successful newspaper Fort Worth had known. Competition in the morning field appeared in 1903, when Clarence Ousley founded the *Record*. Within two years he bought out the *Register*. For a time thereafter the paper was known as the *Record-Register*, then simply as the *Record* again.

D. C. McCaleb, city editor of the *Record*, and A. G. Dawson, Fort Worth correspondent for the *Dallas News*, joined in December, 1905, to form a new publishing company. They imported as editor Louis J. Wortham, then editing a weekly economic paper in Austin. As advertising manager and the sole advertising salesman, they employed an advertising specialty salesman who not many years before had sold sandwiches in Bowie. His name was Amon Carter. From a diminutive shop behind the Senate Bar and beneath the old Eagles Hall, on East Sixth Street, they published the first edition of their afternoon *Fort Worth Star* on February 1, 1906. With that edition they trumpeted their challenge to the *Telegram*, which theretofore had monopolized the afternoon newspaper field.

The *Telegram* was the first modern newspaper, founded upon a long line of antecedents that traced back to the *Mail*, founded in 1882 by Mose Harris, "that brilliant newspaper eccentricity who started more papers and made less out of them than any man in the world."[18] The owners of the morning *Gazette*, becoming envious of the prestige and popularity that surrounded the *Mail*, decided to establish a competitive afternoon paper, the *Telegram*. Eventually the two were merged about 1894, the *Mail-Telegram* continuing publication until 1902.

On July 1, 1902, C. D. Reimers took control of the *Mail-Telegram*, shortened the name to *Telegram*, and produced a good newspaper. On February 17, 1903, he knocked advertising from the front page—the first Fort Worth paper to do so —and announced that the step was taken because "news in a paper is paramount to all else." Prior to that departure, front pages had contained more advertising than news. In 1904 the *Telegram* built its home at Eighth and Throckmorton, the first especially designed newspaper plant in Fort Worth.

The *Telegram* was the primary target for the young giant killers of the *Star*. At the helm of the Star Publishing Company stood Colonel Paul Waples, whose financial backing helped keep the paper alive during thin years. As the months wore on, McCaleb and Dawson withdrew from the enterprise, leaving it in the hands of Waples, Carter, and Wortham.

It was up to Carter, as business manager, to find enough money to meet the daily operating costs of about $150. When receipts failed to meet expenditures, Carter cut his $35 salary to $20 and did the same to Wortham. Still there were weeks when the intake failed to match expenditures. The difference was made up by Carter's prized possession—a 3 and 31/32-carat yellow-diamond ring. He took the ring to the bank when necessary, obtained enough money for bills and payroll, and his left hand was bare. Some of his friends of that era were unaware that he even owned a ring.

Within a short time the *Star* was secure as a newspaper. Subscriptions were mounting. It had earned public respect by being the first to bring news of the San Francisco earthquake and of the appointment of Lon Barkley as postmaster. Therefore it came as a shock to the entire staff when Carter walked

[18] *Fort Worth Gazette*, May 25, 1887; *Fort Worth Telegram*, May 29, 1904.

into the editorial room at 2:00 P.M. on December 31, 1908, and casually handed Editor North a front-page box announcing that the *Star* would suspend publication with that issue. A short time later word was received that the *Telegram* also was suspending publication.

Disconsolately the staffs of the two newspapers, jobless on New Year's Eve, left their offices for a party at the brewery. As the party was breaking up with merrymakers headed for another, backstage at the Majestic, Carter summoned North. He told the editor to assemble a staff and begin publication of the *Star and Telegram* the next day. North followed through on his assignment, with the first issue of the afternoon *Star and Telegram* appearing on January 1, 1909. Thirty-five months after its founding, the *Star* had engulfed its entrenched rival, the *Telegram*.

One of the homes into which that first edition went on New Year's Day was that of Robert L. Hoyt at 1008 Evans Avenue. Hoyt, a grocer, came in from work that evening and wanted two things, supper and the evening paper. The paper was folded at his place at the oval table in the lamp-lighted dining room, where the soft light from a kerosene lamp was reflected from the curved glass front of Mrs. Hoyt's china cabinet. Seating himself in a cane-bottomed chair, he looked at the new paper. Then he held it up for the observation of his seven-year-old son. "Robert," he said, "here is the first issue of the new paper. You will live long enough to see it become a great newspaper."[19] Through the years the *Star-Telegram* has moved forward to fulfill Hoyt's prophecy. It has been the most enduring of the forty-odd newspapers which have been published in Fort Worth since 1859. Editor Wortham, who became vice-president through a reorganization in 1909, retired in 1923, when the publishing company became Carter Publications, Inc.

Higher education made important strides, too. Fort Worth already had two colleges, Fort Worth University and the

[19] Interview in 1949 with Robert L. Hoyt.

present Texas Wesleyan, when an opportunity developed whereby the town could become the home of a third college. Texas Christian University, burned out at Waco, was looking for a new home. When fire destroyed the university buildings at Waco on March 22, 1910, Texas cities began bidding competitively to induce the school to move. Fort Worth was interested especially, because T. C. U. dated from a private school that had originated in Fort Worth.

In 1869 two Disciples ministers, Addison and Randolph Clark, and their sister Ida had founded a one-room school for half a dozen children. But they felt constrained to turn their backs upon Fort Worth in 1873 to get away from "the alluring vices of the city, free from the evils of railroad stations." The railroad had not arrived when they moved, but they wanted to get away just the same. At Thorp Spring in Hood County, they established Add-Ran Male and Female College, named for Addison's infant son, Adran, who had died shortly before. Sixteen years later the financial burden was too great for the two brothers. They appeared before a Christian church state convention in 1889 and turned the school over to the church. It was renamed Add-Ran Christian University, and was moved to Waco in 1895. In 1902 the name was changed to Texas Christian University. To bring the school "home" after the Waco fire, Fort Worth offered fifty-six acres of land, $200,000 in cash, and an assurance that utilities and streetcar lines would be extended to the campus. The bid was better than anything offered by Dallas, McKinney, or Gainesville. The first Fort Worth classes were opened in September, 1910, in a rented building on Weatherford Street opposite the courthouse. A year later buildings on the present campus were occupied. Unable to weather the competition, Fort Worth University closed its doors, later becoming, by a series of mergers, the present Oklahoma City University. T. C. U. continued as an important part of Fort Worth.

Also in 1910, a theological school began offering instruction—Southwestern Baptist Theological Seminary. The school

had begun in the Waco home of Rev. B. H. Carroll, a former
Confederate soldier and Baylor graduate, who had held week-
ly theological classes as early as 1873. As a result of his work,
Baylor formally added a theological department in 1905.
Within two years the school had outgrown its campus. It was
moved to Fort Worth to obtain more space.

Charitable and fraternal organizations were full strength.
The Masons, established since the eighteen fifties, opened the
Masonic Home and School in 1899, when the first two stu-
dents, Emmanuel and Lee Ravey, were taken in by Dr. and
Mrs. Frank P. Rainey, who were living in a tent while the
school that they were to direct was being built. The Eastern
Star had gained much ground since its founding in 1884. The
Knights of Pythias, first organized in 1877, built the first
Castle Hall of their order in the world. The Odd Fellows dated
from 1873; the Elks from about 1900. The Knights of Colum-
bus became active in 1903. The Shriners chartered Moslah
Temple in 1914. The Y. M. C. A. was formed in 1877, withered,
and was revived at a union evangelistic meeting in 1890. The
Y. W. C. A. developed from an inexpensive lunchroom op-
erated for working girls by Mrs. Ralph P. Smith and Mrs.
Q. T. Moreland in 1907. The Boy Scouts were organized in
1919. On July 10, 1898, Rev. George McAdams, pastor of St.
Paul's Methodist Church, met with twelve members of his
congregation, who contributed ten dollars toward a charity
treasury, the first money from which was spent to bury a
woman pauper who had been killed by a runaway horse.
Their informal organization was the beginning of the Red
Cross chapter.

B'nai B'rith in 1878 had been the first organized relief
agency. The first community-wide solicitation of funds came
on December 5, 1880, when churches appointed eight men
to a committee to raise money for the poor. Seven years later
the Fort Worth Benevolent Association was formed. In 1907
it was succeeded by United Charities, that in turn gave way
five years later to the Fort Worth Relief Association. The

latter lasted until it was superseded by the Community Chest in 1923.

The gambler was still on the scene, subject only to local laws that might or might not be enforced, depending upon the vigor of the administration. Finally, however, the gamblers outdid themselves. In March, 1907, County Attorney Jeff McLean was crusading against open gambling. At mid-afternoon on March 21, Sheriff Wood and several deputies raided William Tomlinson's gambling room near Sixth and Main, while faro and poker games were in progress. McLean, who had been for a drive with his wife while the raid was in progress, returned to town while the equipment was being confiscated. Halting his buggy near the corner, he went down to assist in removing the gaming properties. Then he started north on the west side of Main, to rejoin his wife. Near by stood Tomlinson. As McLean passed, the gambler sneered, "There goes the —— who always gets in when he ain't got a chance to get a piece of the pie for himself." McLean turned, walked toward Tomlinson, raising his right hand in a gesture of peace. Without a word, the gambler whipped out a pistol and fired, striking McLean in the throat and breaking his neck. Five minutes later the prosecutor died on the floor of a drugstore. Tomlinson fled, racing through the Stag Saloon at Sixth and Main. He was cornered in the Roe Lumber Yard on the northeast corner of West Seventh and Taylor, where he chose to shoot it out with police. Wounded, he feigned death to escape lynching by a crowd, estimated at three thousand. A few days later, Tomlinson—by some accounts remembered as One-Arm Thompson—died in jail. The murder had occurred at a time when most of the members of the Texas Legislature were in town for the Fat Stock Show, and it shocked the lawmakers into passing a state law against gambling as soon as they returned to Austin.

Until 1917 the district courts held concurrent civil and criminal jurisdiction, with most of the criminal cases tried in the Seventeenth District Court. When a death penalty was imposed, the condemned man was hanged by the sheriff in the old jail that stood immediately north of the courthouse. A tunnel under Belknap Street connected the two buildings. A special criminal district court was formed in 1917 with George Hosey as the first judge. He occupied the bench until 1935. The present Criminal Court building, completed in 1918, was built with a trap door for hangings. The gallows was never used because the state installed the electric chair in the penitentiary at Huntsville and began executing felons there. The last man hanged in Fort Worth had to be transferred to the old jail because the new gallows was not completed in time. He was Rufus Coates, who dangled to his death on November 8, 1918, for the murder of his sweetheart, Zella Faulk, under a tree on the Trinity bottom which he could see from the window of his jail cell.

World War I brought a buzz of activity. Before the United States entered the conflict, Canada established three flying fields—Hicks, Everman, and Benbrook—near Fort Worth to train pilots for the Royal Canadian Flying Corps. As one of the instructors at Benbrook was coming in for a landing one day, he was forced to climb suddenly to avoid colliding with a plane leaving the ground. His motor stalled, and the plane plummeted to earth. His beautiful wife, Irene, was waiting dinner for him at the Westbrook Hotel when word was brought to her that Captain Vernon Castle was dead. Death had severed a world-famous dancing team.

When the United States was drawn into the conflict, Fort Worth leaders made available more than two thousand acres west of the city for a military installation that came to be known as Camp Bowie. One hundred thousand doughboys trained there, including Texas' Thirty-sixth Division, in the area that later became the Arlington Heights residential section.

One of the more tragic stories of World War I came out of Camp Bowie. It centered around a young nurse, Ella Behrens, daughter of German immigrants who had settled near Grapevine many years before. When the camp began receiving troops, a Red Cross representative asked Miss Behrens to help out at the station hospital. She accepted, and later volunteered as an army nurse. Because of a foot ailment, she was not physically able to perform ward duty, but she was capable of supervising diets in the hospital kitchen. There she served her country. About a year later rumors were whispered. She was a German. She had been heard singing a German song. She had been heard conversing in German with another nurse. The terrible influenza epidemic of 1918 struck the country and Camp Bowie, and a new and more hideous rumor was spread. This time the hysterical witch-hunters said that Miss Behrens was slipping flu germs into the food.

With neither warning nor hearing, she was whisked to the city jail, where she was held incommunicado. Eight days later she was released, told by men who identified themselves as government agents to go home and remain quiet or she might suffer serious consequences. In panic she did as she was told. Soon she received a letter from the War Department, informing her that she had been discharged. She wrote to inquire why she had received no pay. Because, the War Department replied, she had been discharged dishonorably. She wrote another letter, asking why she had been discharged dishonorably. Because, the department said, she had been absent without leave for eight days—the eight days she had spent in jail. She attempted to appeal the decision, but there was no machinery for appeals from discharges.

Shame and disgrace settled upon her because of a gross injustice. "Look—there's the German spy," people would say during the long, long years when Miss Behrens was unable to remove the stigma from her name. She began to think she had no friends except her family, whose confidence that the wrong would be righted helped sustain her in her constant fight against bitterness. The strain weakened her health. After many years had passed, a young man from Grapevine was elected to Congress. He was Wingate Lucas, who had known her family most of his life. He began working in 1946 to help Miss Behrens clear her name. Conditions were more favorable after World War II than after the preceding war, because the army had formed a board to review discharges. Miss Behrens called on R. R. Fox, service officer for the Veterans of Foreign Wars in Fort Worth, to supplement the work Lucas was doing. Then she was summoned to Washington to tell her story to the review board—the story of being branded a German and held up as an enemy and subjected to ridicule and disgrace for thirty-one years, without a shred of proof, without a hearing, and without a formal charge.

On January 29, 1949, the review board announced its decision—Miss Behrens had been cleared of all accusations, her discharge changed to honorable. The pall of the years of loneliness and something akin to ostracism, all because of ugly rumor born of hysteria, was lifted from the woman who had reached the age of sixty-seven before her good name was cleared. The blot had been erased. But what had that blot done to the person? "Can you imagine," she said, "how a dog must feel that has had a tin can tied to his tail? Then one day that can is taken off. But the dog still spends the rest of his life looking over his shoulder."[20]

20 *Fort Worth Star-Telegram,* Jan. 30, 31, June 3, 1949.

CHAPTER XI

The Golden Goddess and a Lucky Lady

STRANGE GODS seized the country. The doors of the corner saloon were closed. Greasy underworld bums became minor oracles with wealth from bootlegging. Women strapped their breasts flat, bobbed their hair, smoked cigarets, and drank bathtub gin. Roadsters, hippocket flasks, and the Charleston were in vogue. All of these things were happening amid the fury of a great prosperity, presided over by the beneficent Uncle Andy Mellon and Choosin' Cal Coolidge, who occupied the temples in Washington. And Fort Worth was drunk at the shrine of the Oil Goddess.

Fort Worth had paid little attention to the gamble that led to the oil boom, because the gamble was made by a few men under obscure circumstances. But when that gamble brought a huge wave of wealth cresting over Fort Worth, the town became hilarious. The gamble was made at Ranger in 1917 by W. K. Gordon, superintendent of the Thurber mine of the Texas and Pacific Coal Company, who long had been convinced that there was oil around Ranger. The opportunity to prove his theory came in 1917, when Eastland County was suffering from severe dryness.

Because something had to be done to make money in the face of crop losses, a committee headed by John M. Gholson and Cull Moorman waited upon Gordon, offering him thirty thousand acres of lease in the Ranger vicinity if he would drill a well. Gordon accepted. He moved in a wooden rig with which he began drilling a well on the Nannie Walker farm near Ranger. It came in a gasser. No good. No market. But he was at the same time drilling another wildcat on the John McCleskey farm near by. When the expected pay depth was reached without a sign of oil, the Texas and Pacific Coal Company telegraphed him. "Think we have made a mistake; better quit." Gordon's faith kept him going, giving him persuasion enough to keep the company behind him for a little longer. One October afternoon there came from the well an unaccustomed roar. Oil shot two-thirds of the way up the derrick. Hastily the roustabouts brought the well under control and plugged a ravine for storage. Oil-splattered, Driller Frank Champion walked the mile into Ranger, where he answered excited questions with the calm reply, "The Mc-Clesky is a well." The boom was on.

Champion's quietly-spoken announcement had world-wide impact, coming in the midst of World War I at a time when the Allies were threatened by a critical oil shortage. Operators big and little elbowed their way into the field for a chance at the riches. Jess Willard, the heavyweight champ, had an interest in one well. Billy Sunday came to see for himself if the excitement was as great as reported. After the Armistice, the Ranger field really hit its stride, spreading to Eastland, Cisco, and Breckenridge. Actually the first Breckenridge well had come in a full year ahead of the Mc-Clesky, but it was only a 75-barrel-a-day producer, and the town was without railroad connections, all of which resulted in little interest. But when the big wells started coming in, that was another story. Breckenridge boomed, too, and four railroads raced to the sun-splotched seat of Stephens County.

From Eastland County the oil perimeter spread. In the north of Texas was Burkburnett, with town limits that abutted upon the farm of S. L. Fowler. Fowler was wanting to move and was ready to sell his farm. But Mrs. Fowler thought there might be oil under their land. She refused to budge until a test well could be drilled. To please her, Fowler organized a small company that was capitalized at twelve thousand dollars by him and his friends. When the first load of timber was hauled in, the wagon bogged in sand, fifty yards short of the proposed location. "Oh, well," Fowler said, "unload her here," and that spot was selected for the drilling site. Early on the morning of July 26, 1918, Red McDowell, a driller, awakened Fowler by shouting that the well had come in, that 1,200 barrels of storage had been filled, and "now she's running down the cotton rows." With oil selling at $2.25 a barrel, Burkburnett had a 3,000-barrel well. In less than three months, two hundred wells were being drilled within the town limits.

One after another the wells came in over West Texas. Eighteen miles south of Ranger was Hogtown, more politely known as Desdemona, whose fifty inhabitants clustered their homes around the three stores. Tom Dees of Midlothian came in to drill a well on the Joe Duke farm. The drill bit crunched to one thousand feet when, on the night of September 2, 1918, there was the roar of a gusher and here it came—flame. From the ground shot a column of fire so bright that it is said one could read a newspaper on Desdemona's main street one and one-half miles away. For two days the fire raged before it was brought under control. As a result of the discovery, population zoomed to sixteen thousand, with men and women living in shacks and tents. Five producing wells clogged a one-acre tract. Oil overflowed into roads, forming a lake in which cars became mired.

Those were the three great oil developments: Ranger, Burkburnett, and Desdemona. They were going full blast at the same time, carrying over from World War I into the twenties. And Fort Worth was the town that derived lasting benefits from the booms.

By being a concentration point for oil operators, Fort Worth was a hotbed of oil transactions. Men crowded the streets, clamoring for a chance to invest money that would bring quick, manifold returns. The center of activity was the Westbrook Hotel, where the management was forced to remove all furniture from the lobby to clear space for the oil mart. But even that seemed hardly to lessen the congestion, for the daily crowds overflowed through the big double doors to the sidewalks and into the street. In the lobby was a pedestaled statue that was affectionately dubbed the "Golden Goddess," because she watched over so many oil deals.

The excitement bordering on hysteria was a perfect incubator for shady operators who specialized in bogus stock. Scores of such men hurried into Fort Worth, where the rush and bustle of legitimate oil undertakings gave them both cover and concealment. The shady operator had a batch of fictitious stock printed and peddled it on street corners. Men were only too anxious to place their money in an oil well, sight unseen, operator unknown. In front of the bogus operator standing on the street corner, long queues of men formed. They waited patiently in line to hand over good money for worthless paper. Not infrequently an impatient speculator far down the line could be heard to shout," Save some for me!"

Like the men they duped, the fraudulent operators became too eager. Not content with their street-corner harvest, they turned to the United States mail. That was their blunder, for it was a signal for the government to step in. The result was the sensational oil-fraud trials of 1922. Thirteen men went to trial in the federal District Court. Federal Judge Killits was imported from Toledo to preside. Joe Weldon Bailey, former United States senator from Texas, was a defense counsel. One of the men tried, and convicted, was Frederick A. Cook from Casper, Wyoming, who, as Dr. Cook, several years earlier had stirred up quite a sensation by claiming to be the discoverer of the North Pole. The triumphant prosecutor was Henry Zweifel, who used two hundred witnesses and nine hundred exhibits.

The oil fraud was but an incident. The oil era was the thing—a substantial, motivating, and lasting factor that took its place as the fifth great impetus in the development of a city.

Fort Worth became the gateway to the West Texas oil fields. Companies in need of a major supply base, yet not wanting the inconvenience of a boom town, made Fort Worth their headquarters. Oil-rich ranchmen and farmers moved to Fort Worth, where they lived in luxury. With oil, the skyscraper era arrived. Oil earnings were responsible for the Life of America, Sinclair, and W. T. Waggoner buildings. Oil meant refineries—nine were operating in 1922 as an important addition to the city's industries. Refineries meant increased activity in transportation, pipe line and rail. Fort Worth gained tremendously in payrolls and population, and administration—all motivated by the discovery well at Ranger that touched off a great new day for Texas. Fort Worth's population reached 106,482 in 1920, and 163,477 a decade later. Even this long after the boom of the twenties, Fort Worth has two refineries, ten oil companies employing eighteen hundred persons who earn $7,000,000 a year, and scores of independent oil operators.[1]

The oil boom drew two large newspaper chains into Fort Worth. In 1921, Scripps-McRae, now Scripps-Howard, founded the *Press;* and in 1923, William Randolph Hearst bought the *Record,* sending in one of his crack executives, Publisher Dan D. Moore, to direct the paper. Two years later Hearst sold out to Amon Carter, who established the *Record-Telegram* as the morning edition of the *Star-Telegram.* In 1930 it became the morning *Star-Telegram.*

Besides oil there were other activities encouraging prosperity in the twenties. For $5,000,000 the government built the world's only helium plant in 1921, later transferring it to Amarillo. In the same year Universal Mills was established, expanding the already sizable milling industry.

The banking field still was dominated by the "Strong Three," the Fort Worth National, the First National, and the Farmers and Mechanics National, all dating from the nineteenth century. Other bankers had fought the economic

[1] *Fort Worth Star-Telegram,* Oct. 30, 1949, Oil and Gas Section.

storms of the years as Fort Worth progressed from village to metropolis, but had either expired or had been absorbed by one of the three stronger banks. In 1927 the powerful Farmers and Mechanics National, which had built the city's tallest building (twenty-four stories) at Seventh and Main, was taken over by the Fort Worth National. In 1903, J. G. Wilkinson had established the Continental Bank and Trust Company, which merged in 1921 with the National Bank of Commerce, founded two years earlier. In 1923 the Morris Plan Bank was formed, becoming the Trinity State in 1944. Dan Lydick incorporated the Union Bank and Trust Company in 1928. Thus the three big banks gave way to five—Fort Worth National, First National, Continental National, Trinity State, and Union.

Several smaller banks also came into the field. The First State Bank of Handley, formed in 1913, was nationalized in 1925. The North Fort Worth State was founded in 1941, the Riverside State in 1946, West Side State and South Fort Worth State in 1947, and University State in 1951.

Wealth and a steadily increasing population, both permanent and transient, called for new hotels. The first big hotel had been the Worth, built in 1894 at Seventh and Main by John Scharbauer and W. C. Stonestreet. Later the Metropolitan, now the Milner at Ninth and Main, had been the plush hotel. By the twenties both were aging. The Citizens Hotel Company, headed by William Monnig, raised $2,000,000 by public subscription, bought and razed the Worth, and replaced it with the Texas, which opened in 1921 at Eighth and Main. Six years later the present Worth Hotel was opened at Seventh and Taylor, controlled by the Jesse Jones interests of Houston. In 1929 the twenty-two-story Blackstone was constructed.

In the merchandising community, the early stores of Stripling's The Fair, and Monnig's were still pre-eminent. But others were rising. Meacham's, a fashionable ladies' store, had come far since 1904, when H. C. Meacham established a small-town drygoods store. The newest comers to the ranks of important merchants were the Leonard Brothers. In 1918, Marvin and O. P. Leonard opened a 25-by-60-foot grocery store at 111 Houston, vowing that their store would never be completed. Their first sale was a nickel can of condensed milk. Two years later they had added automobile tires and accessories. Four years later they had taken in all the property in their block fronting on Houston Street. By 1953 a customer could buy anything from a can of beans to a television set. Cox's was added in 1933, when R. E. Cox and Company chose Fort Worth as the location for its fourth store. R. E. Cox first went into business with a drugstore in Stephenville in 1907, which he sold in 1915 to open the R. E. Cox Drygoods Store, also in Stephenville. In 1922 he established a second store, in Waco, and in 1924 a third store, in Marlin. The first Fort Worth location was on Main, at Fifth and Houston streets, where the store remained until 1946 when it was moved to the first five floors of the Fort Worth Club Building on Seventh at Throckmorton and Sixth streets.

Business activity was aided by a strong Chamber of Commerce that had succeeded the Board of Trade in 1912. Men who have served as president of the chamber through 1949 are Amon Carter, William Monnig, Ben E. Keith, George H. Clifford, William Massie, C. A. Wheeler, S. S. Lard, Morris E. Berney, R. E. Harding, Walter B. Scott, R. O. Dulaney, W. Lee O'Daniel, John B. Collier, Jr., Lionel W. Bevan, Gaylord Stone, W. L. Pier, B. B. Stone, A. A. Lund, R. Mayo Bowen, Homer Covey, Melvin J. Miller, and Web Maddox.

Hospital facilities, too, were more extensive than ever before. Pennsylvania Hospital in 1920, Harris in 1923, and Cook in 1929 were added to St. Joseph's, which was founded in 1889, to All Saints, which had opened in 1895, and to City-County, which was established in 1907.

And the radio was catching on in 1921, as amateurs tinkered with crystal-set receivers at home and flooded every frequency with greetings, records, and news. One of the amateurs was Harold Hough, circulation manager of the *Star-Telegram*, whose crystal set picked up the voices that were floating through the ether. The voices gave him an idea. He suggested to Carter that the *Star-Telegram* enter the radio business. Not at all sure of the venture, Carter agreed to invest three hundred dollars in radio, telling Hough that when that much was spent the paper was out of the radio business.

Hough went to Washington to obtain federal approval. Herbert Hoover, then secretary of commerce and head of the Federal Radio Commission, personally named the station W B A P, telling Hough the letters stood for "We Bring a Program." The first station in Fort Worth, W B A P went on the air in 1921, broadcasting from a two-room suite on the second floor of the *Star-Telegram* Building. The furnishings included a shiny grand piano and heavy drapes, the standard acoustical treatment of the time. In 1922 it was the first in the nation to broadcast regular reports from cotton and grain exchanges and to schedule church services. It was one of the first in the country to establish a regular newscast.

Mindful of Hoover's admonition, Hough also was working under Carter's single instruction: Perform a service. Sometimes, though, he might have preferred to forget, because every once in a while someone would fail to arrive in time for a regular program and Hough would have to fill in by ad libbing. In the custom of the day he signed off with his initials. H. H. Once an announcer jokingly asked what the initials stood for. "Hired Hand," Hough grumped. Then was born one of the most famous radio personalities of the twenties. He opened and closed programs by jangling a cowbell, conforming with the radio custom of having a memory signal. Thirty years later, W B A P still uses the cowbell signal.

W B A P closed the communication gap for West Texas stockmen. Many times the station warned of impending blizzards. The warnings enabled ranchmen to protect their stock in time to avoid heavy financial loss. For that service, W B A P received national recognition.

By 1927, W B A P was a 10,000-watt station affiliated with the National Broadcasting Company. Eleven years later, a second station, K G K O, was added. When N. B. C., because of its size, split into the Red and Blue networks, W B A P took Red and K G K O took Blue. When the Federal Communications Commission put a stop to the dual operation, K G K O became part of the American Broadcasting Company. In April, 1947, the F. C. C. directed W B A P to surrender the companion station's call letters. Thus, K G K O because W B A P–570 and the regular W B A P became W B A P–820. Each station divides time with W F A A, Dallas.

During the years W B A P moved from the *Star-Telegram* Building to the Blackstone Hotel, to the top two floors of the Medical Arts Building, and, in 1948, to its own extensive plant on the east side of the city, where, in September, 1948, it became the first television station in Texas.

In 1924, Rev. J. Frank Norris, pastor of the First Baptist Church, recognized the advantages of radio for spreading the gospel, installing K F Q B, which he sold two years later to J. M. Gilliam and which eventually was absorbed by K F J Z, established in 1926. The other radio stations active in Fort Worth are K W B C, owned by Worth Broadcasting Company, founded in December, 1946; K C N C, owned by J. H. Speck, 1947; K X O L, Fort Worth Broadcasting Company, 1947; and K C U L, East-West Broadcasting Company, 1949.

Labor violence marred the rosy picture of prosperity in the twenties. In 1921 the International Butcher Workers Union called a strike in the packing plants, resulting in a riot. Fred Rouse, a Negro strikebreaker, fired into a crowd of pickets. The sullen crowd turned into a ferocious mob that attacked the Negro, beating him into insensibility and cracking his skull. He was thrown into a wagon for dead as the mob milled. An ambulance picked him up and was en route to a mortuary when Rouse raised up, startling the drivers. He was taken to a hospital. Five nights later a group of masked men walked into the hospital and, over the protests of a nurse, took Rouse from his bed. He was hanged on Samuels Avenue.

Otherwise the labor-management picture in Fort Worth has been peaceful. By 1953 there were approximately sixty unions, including twenty-eight in the A. F. of L. and fourteen in the C. I. O. From 1919 to 1948, the Oil Workers International Union maintained its headquarters in Fort Worth, the only major international union that ever had its principal office in Texas. The O. W. I. U. moved to Denver because the officials did not like what they considered Texas' stringent antilabor laws.

Commercial activity so expanded the metropolitan area in the twenties that Fort Worth proper was only an island surrounded by a large area of residential suburbs. The town had started with an area of four square miles, roughly in the center of the present business district. Because the river formed a natural northern boundary, the town grew to the south. Minor annexations extended the corporate area only slightly between 1876 and 1909, when the area was doubled through the annexation of North Fort Worth.

Between then and the nineteen twenties, large sections were developed to the west, south, and east, all on the outskirts of Fort Worth. To make the corporate boundaries coincide with the physical limits of the true Fort Worth, city officials decided to take in all of the principal adjacent sections. Their decisions resulted in the annexation in 1922 of Arlington Heights, Riverside, Polytechnic, and Niles City— an annexation that again doubled the size of the town. Through that expansion, the more important divisions of the city were the South Side, North Side, Arlington Heights, T. C. U., Polytechnic, Riverside, Mistletoe Heights, Cheltenham, Berkley, and Park Hill.

The South Side was developed earlier than the other sections. The residential area naturally spread to the south, because the river on the north formed a natural boundary.

Homesteading was encouraged there during the early years, when Captain Daggett and Colonel Johnson gave land to newcomers as an inducement to settle in Fort Worth. J. B. Alford, a real-estate promoter from Dallas, had been prominent in the early development of the South Side, which came to have a greater value than was envisioned, when Press Farmer, the one-time army sutler, traded forty acres in the heart of the South Side for a black pony. Expansion to the south was steady if not rapid. In the nineties, Mrs. T. O. Hubbard, whose home was a farm in the vicinity of the present Southwestern Baptist Theological Seminary, used field glasses to watch for her husband coming home from work in town. When he topped the hill just south of Lancaster and Jennings, she had time enough to put the biscuits in the oven and have them ready when he reached home.

Development of the North Side had begun about 1888, when A. T. Byers bought a large tract of land north of the river and began planning a city. Around 1890 he sold the land to the Fort Worth City Company, which platted North Side, devoting much attention to Buena Vista Heights near the present Technical High School. A town did arise in the area, centered about the packing plants and stockyards. When the major packers built plants in 1902, North Fort Worth was incorporated, with J. D. Farmer as the first mayor. It remained an independent city until annexed, by act of the legislature, in 1909.

The T. C. U. section had been open prairie until the university was established in Fort Worth in 1910. Land for the college was donated, a streetcar line was built, and a residential community developed around the college. It grew by stages until it reached the bounds of Mistletoe Heights. Mistletoe Heights had been developed about 1890 by Robert Harrison, an attorney, just west of Eighth Avenue and north of Forest Park, as a projection of the Summit Avenue neighborhood, which once was called Quality Hill. In the same general area, C. L. Mobley and Floyd Delaney converted the

Rogers dairy farm into Cheltenham in 1919. Wilkes and Barber platted the Berkley Addition in 1924.

Arlington Heights had been a speculator's dream, portions of it purchased by persons in the far corners of the earth from a globe-trotting promoter. The promoter was H. B. Chamberlain, a wealthy Denver suburban real-estate man, who bought two thousand acres from Tom Hurley, a Chicago financier who built the town's first tall building, the eight-story Hurley Building. As president of the world Y. M. C. A., Chamberlain was a world traveler who sold many of his lots abroad. Before he was killed in a collision while riding a bicycle in a London fog, he had accomplished some constructive work with Arlington Heights. Principally, he brought visitors in to Lake Como and Arlington Inn, which achieved some renown as a resort. In 1906, Arlington Heights lots were selling for three hundred dollars each. In the next four years other promoters and adjacent subdivisions appeared—Alfred Crebbins with parts of Hillcrest and Rivercrest, John P. King with an area east of Montgomery, William Bryce and Duff Purvis with the remainder of Hillcrest, and W. J. Bailey with the Bailey Addition. Everything was in readiness for a rush of home builders. But the home builders did not rush. The residential trend continued to be on the South Side. Purchasers of Arlington Heights property were dismayed. One disillusioned speculator traded his lot for a set of tires; another traded his for a typewriter. Arlington Heights remained dormant until World War I. Within its environs was built Camp Bowie, which, when the war was over, left a network of utility lines and roads. Those necessities were ready for use when the oil boom sent population skyrocketing. Arlington Heights at last had come into its own as a residential area.

Niles City was a chesty little place known as the richest per capita in the United States. Deriving its wealth from the investments in packing plants and stockyards, Niles City was incorporated in 1911, because the packing plants wished to be free of Fort Worth jurisdiction. It was named for L. V. Niles, who operated the old Fort Worth Packing Company. Everything was lovely for Niles City until 1922, when the legislature passed a bill, written by Fort Worth's Representative Wallace Malone, that empowered a city of 100,000 population to annex a neighboring community of less than 2,000. Horrified, Niles City rushed to expand its corporate limits, bringing its population to 2,600. But Fort Worth went ahead with the annexation on July 22, 1922. A court fight followed, but Niles City conceded defeat a year later.

Riverside once boasted the plushest streetcar line in the South, but it was lack of streetcar facilities that brought it into the city in 1922. The section was known as Sylvania Addition until 1891, when it was platted by the East Fort Worth Town Company and given its present name. Ed Chase, a Boston financier, built the famous car line that operated Pullman-type cars, said to have been the largest and most comfortable ever used in the South. However, the cars were too long to negotiate the sharp curves without frequent derailments. For that reason Chase suspended streetcar operations. To be sure of adequate streetcar service, Riverside was willing to be annexed in 1922.

Polytechnic grew up as a town around the old Polytechnic College, the Methodist institution that is now Texas Wesleyan. When the section began developing in 1892, one streetcar pulled by a tired donkey linked Polytechnic with Fort Worth. Sometimes passengers had to get out and push the streetcar up the hills of Vickery Boulevard.

Through the annexations, the city gained a corporate area of almost sixty square miles. The many problems involved—representation, streets, water, sewers, taxation, fire and police protection, and utility regulation—in such a large area quickly revealed the deficiencies of the commission form of government. The added burden accentuated the fissures and shortcomings that had existed from the beginning in the commission—principally too much politics and too much sectional representation.

Businessmen took a strong interest in the city government and decided that the city needed a more centralized municipal authority, with a council representing the entire city, rather than a governing body composed of individuals who represented certain sections. Accordingly, a city-manager form of government was proposed.

Good government advocates drafted a new charter—the first complete home-rule charter Fort Worth had voted on since 1912, when the legislature had made home rule possible. On December 11, 1924, voters went to the polls, where they adopted by a vote of 6,946 to 5,549 the council-manager form of government—the council composed of nine members elected from the city at large, a mayor elected by the councilmen from among their number, and a manager appointed by the council. The first mayor elected under the new plan was H. C. Meacham; the first city manager, O. E. Carr.

To bring better order to the politics-ridden police and fire departments, the first civil service board was appointed on June 25, 1925. Civil service regulations then were drawn up for those two departments, but civil service has not yet been extended to the other municipal departments.

Under the city-manager system, extensions and improvements were made in municipal recreation facilities. Until 1915 there had been no public playground, but in that year part of the T. and P. reservation was donated for use as a playground. Public subscription furnished the funds needed for equipment. A regular playground program was instituted the next year, and seven years later the city charter was amended to create the recreation department. Worth Hills was opened in 1923 as the first municipal golf course; the Forest Park swimming pool had been built two years earlier as the city's first municipal pool. In 1927 the Recreation Department Building was constructed on Vickery Boulevard for $67,000. Since that time the department has grown to encompass thirty-three playgrounds, six swimming pools, three golf courses, and two recreation buildings.

One of the first important programs undertaken by the new council was aviation. In this the city was encouraged by the Army Air Corps, which then was experimenting with every spare dollar it could find. In 1925, Colonel Harvey Burwell and Sergeant William G. Fuller came from San Antonio —then the very nerve center of the army's visionary air service—and recommended that the city provide an airport. If the city had an airport, they said, it would figure in the transcontinental flights that were then firing the imagination of daring men. The two soldiers recommended as the site a plot of one hundred acres north of town, which the city purchased on July 3, 1925, for one hundred dollars an acre.

Sergeant Fuller then came to Fort Worth as resident in charge of the airport—a pasture ornamented by Fuller's small frame house and a water tower. Once a week the army flew a plane from San Antonio to Fort Worth en route to St. Louis and Chicago, testing the feasibility of regular plane service. When the practicability of such service was proved, the Air Corps stepped out of the picture, National Air Transport took over the route, and the city assumed full control of the airport, retaining Fuller, by then a civilian, as the first airport manager.

Soon thereafter National Air Transport extended day airmail service from Chicago to Fort Worth. The canvas and spruce planes landed on the spot of open prairie that was called an airport. At first there was no hangar for the plane, but growth and expansions were implicit in aviation. The field was improved, a hangar was built, and on July 26, 1927, the airport was formally opened with an air show that included forty-six army and twenty commercial planes. Charles A. Lindbergh, conqueror of the Atlantic, landed on September 27. And in the same year the first air passenger emplaned at Fort Worth when Mrs. Fuller rode an N. A. T. mailplane to Oklahoma City.

The next year air passenger business was established in and out of Fort Worth. N. A. T. began regular passenger service. Mrs. Temple Bowen bought the first ticket on her husband's new Texas Air Transport. The Bowen line in 1929 became part of Southern Air Transport, which grew by stages into the present American Airlines.

Air traffic grew magically. The six-passenger planes operating from the field transported 5,446 passengers in 1929, a year in which 4,511 flights were made into and out of the airport—representing a mighty stride in the space of four years. But aviation faced a setback. The stock market crashed that year, and business began to melt.

For Fort Worth as a whole, the immediate impact of the depression was cushioned by a large-scale building program that delayed the day of hungry men. When finally it struck with full fury, men raked leaves in downtown parks as part of a make-work program. By the time the New Deal, with Roosevelt's revolutionary innovations, began rolling, part of the slack was taken up by the alphabet agencies, especially P W A and W P A.

Part of the depression attitude was an antagonism toward utilities and monopolies. This antagonism was manifested on January 27, 1931, when the city voted almost two to one—8,075 to 4,511—in favor of a municipally owned gas company. Again, on July 21, the people voted 8,460 to 6,177 for the city government to acquire facilities for gas distribution through purchase or condemnation. Businessmen on the council held firm, however, until the depression fears became less of a motivating force. A similar effort was made four years later, when a different council sought to build a municipal light plant, which would have displaced Texas Electric Service Company (this name had been adopted in 1929 by the former Fort Worth Power and Light Company). The move was thwarted on April 10, 1935, when the P W A denied a request for $2,228,000 needed for construction of the plant.

Conditions were so bad by 1932 that on November 30 the council appropriated one hundred dollars a month for the operation of a soup kitchen. On February 22, 1933, City Manager George Fairtrace was ordered to make no extensions or improvements in any department unless absolutely necessary. When the federal government, under the New Deal's pump-priming efforts, began giving away money to build public structures that would give men jobs, the city asked for its first helping hand from Washington. On October 11, 1933, the council applied for federal money to build the Ballinger Street overpass, the Daggett Street overpass, improve Rosedale, and install a lighting system at the Municipal Airport, at a total cost of $544,700. In the years that followed, the federal government spent about $15,000,000 in Fort Worth, which, with approximately $5,000,000 in local funds, added a variety of improvements, chief among them being a new City Hall, the Will Rogers Memorial Auditorium and Coliseum, and the library.

When business revived in the late thirties, the council voted, on December 3, 1937, to restore all salaries to the levels existing before the general pay reduction of 1931. At that time, salaries had been slashed as much as 25 to 35 per cent. On April 15, 1936, the City Council approved the first parking meters.

The only recall of an elected city official occurred in 1938, when a majority of the City Council were ousted. Several movements had been made in the direction of public ownership of public utilities, leading to suspicion of the councilmen's motives in some quarters. On May 26, 1938, a citizens' committee presented a petition for an election to recall six councilmen. A council committee attacked the legality of the petition, referring it to the legal department for further investigation. On July 13 the council adopted a resolution stating that the electric and transit companies, along with other corporations, were rumored to be behind the recall petition. The resolution stated further that the recall movement was directed against five men who had voted for municipal power and five-cent bus fares. Following the publication of the resolution, the citizens' committee appealed to District Judge

A. J. Powell, who directed that the recall election be held on July 23. By tremendous majorities, the six were ousted and a new council constituted.

Meantime, municipal services had been improved through inauguration of the first police radio system. The system went into operation in 1933, with equipment purchased from R. C. A. Victor for $3,460. At first, patrol cars could only receive calls. To communicate with headquarters, officers had to leave their automobiles and telephone. The first radio call went out from Police Station W 5 X B at 7:18 P.M. on October 31—boys were stoning a house at 3454 Lovell as a Halloween prank. Two-way radios were installed in 1939.

By the late thirties an economic renaissance had set in. With it came hope and fun. For Fort Worth, two of the greatest events were the Frontier Centennial and T. C. U. football.

The greatest phase of the town's entertainment history was the Frontier Centennial and its famous *Casa Mañana.* At 3:30 P.M. on July 18, 1936, President Roosevelt, who was fishing off the coast of Maine, pressed a button aboard his yacht, sending out an electrical impulse that cut a lariat in Fort Worth. The lariat fell, and the big show was on, commemorating Texas' centenary. *Casa Mañana,* good enough to be repeated for three successive years, was a glittering musical staged by Billy Rose and John Murray Anderson. Their singing star was Everett Marshall. Sally Rand and her bubbles enticed the crowd. Paul Whiteman's band set feet to tapping. Their show was on the world's largest revolving stage.

Slingin' Sammy Baugh and Davey O'Brien were by-words in Fort Worth. Each sparked T. C. U.'s razzle-dazzle football teams, and each made All-American. During the period from 1935 to 1941, T. C. U. won the Southwest Conference title once, took the mythical national championship once, produced at least one All-American for each of four consecutive seasons, and earned the right to play in three postseason games.

About the same time, Fort Worth was taking prideful note

of another figure in sport—Bantam Ben Hogan, one of the most remarkable figures ever to appear upon the American sports scene. Hogan moved from Dublin, Texas, to Fort Worth when he was eleven years old, after the death of his father. As a boy he began learning to play golf while a caddy at Glen Garden Country Club. In 1932 he turned pro and went to Los Angeles with seventy-five dollars. A month later he returned, broke. For the next five years he worked at various jobs while perfecting his game, in the meantime marrying Valerie Fox, whom he had known in school. By 1937 they had saved some money, which they used for their first big professional swing, from Canada to Nassau to Florida to California. By 1938 their money had about run out, and they were almost living on oranges. In a round at Oakland, Hogan tied for sixth-place money, $285.

From then on, Hogan—whose studied calm earned him the titles of "Texas Iceman" and "Little Iceman"—kept climbing. By 1940 he was the leading professional money winner and held the Harry Varden Memorial Trophy. In 1941 he earned $18,000, and again won the trophy. After serving as a lieutenant in the army during World War II, he returned to tournament play in 1945. In 1948 he became the first and only golfer to win the P. G. A., the United States Open, and the Western Open in the same year.

On February 2, 1949, he was severely injured in a highway accident in West Texas, and for a time his life was despaired of. An Air Force plane flew a New Orleans specialist to El Paso so that he might perform a critical operation on Hogan. By November, having recovered from a crushed pelvis, a fractured left leg, a crushed shoulder, and a broken ankle, Hogan was hitting golf balls again. In January, 1950, he entered the Los Angeles Open Tournament, wearing tight athletic bandages on both legs and resting on a polo seat between shots. He lost, but only in a final round play-off, to Sam Snead. That summer he won the National Open, and in October he was voted the golfer of the year for 1950, the man who had made perhaps the greatest comeback American sports have ever known.

During the late thirties and early forties, Fort Worth felt fairly well acquainted with the President of the United States, for F. D. R. visited the city no less than five times during his record occupancy of the White House, traveling to Fort Worth to see his son Elliott, who had radio interests there. The President's first visit was on June 12, 1936; his open car was drenched by a rain that struck just as the motorcade crossed the county line en route from Dallas. He came again on May 11, 1937, July 9, 1938, and September 27, 1942. His last visit, April 18, 1943, was during the dark days of war. His heavily guarded train, secret of movement, stopped for only thirty minutes to allow a visit with Elliott and his family. F. D. R.'s distant cousin, Theodore Roosevelt, had been the first president to visit Fort Worth. Former President Taft spoke there twice, in 1919 and 1920, and President Truman stopped for a campaign speech in 1948.

In 1937, Rev. J. Frank Norris, pastor of the First Baptist Church, formed the Fundamental Baptist Bible Institute with the English Bible as its only textbook, growing in a few years from a handful of students to more than 3,000, studying theology, music, and religious education.

In 1938, Fort Worth supplied its first governor of Texas. W. Lee O'Daniel was associated with Burrus Mills, whose products he advertised in a noontime radio program featuring a hillbilly band. One day he announced that some of his listeners had sent him one-dollar bills as contributions toward his campaign if he would run for governor. His daily mail bag became heavy with contributions, and O'Daniel took to the sawdust trail. One of his campaign appeals was for more assistance for the old folks. With his hillbilly music, attacks upon the "professional politicians," and quotations from the Bible, he put a field of experienced campaigners to rout. The people loved his campaign, placing him in office with a strong plurality. O'Daniel was re-elected in 1940, and went to the

United States Senate the next year, where he served until 1948. Upon leaving public office, he established an insurance company in Dallas.

Almost as if they were the same problem, the economic crisis of the thirties blended into the military crisis of the forties. With a new war coming on, the council on September 24, 1941, bought 526 acres from Mrs. Genevieve Tillar for $99,750, and turned the land over to the United States Army for a bomber-plant site.

On the site was built a government plant operated by Consolidated-Vultee Aircraft Corporation in anticipation of a war that German aggression made imminent. On the afternoon of the ground-breaking ceremony—Fort Worth loves ground-breakings, has one at the drop of a hat—Major General Harry C. Brant grasped a silver spade and told the audience, "We're starting to dig Hitler's grave this afternoon."

One year later, in April, 1942, the huge plant was completed, two months ahead of schedule. And in the same month the first B-24 bomber rolled from the assembly line. One of the men present that day was Lord Halifax, the beloved British ambassador, who called the construction and production feat "nothing short of a miracle." More than three thousand bomber and transport planes were produced by November 27, 1944, when the last B-24 was assembled. From then until the end of the war, Convair built B-32's. At the peak, Convair employed 35,000 persons—the largest industry in the city's history.

Adjacent to the Convair plant, the army in 1941 built Tarrant Field, where crews were trained to fly the B-24's being made next door. Four thousand bomber pilots were trained there during the war.

All over Fort Worth large and small manufacturing plants were retooled for war work. At the beginning of the war the town had a respectable, though not commanding, industrial position. Manufacturing had tripled between 1920 and 1940. At the end of the war Fort Worth industry was sizable

—between 1939 and 1947 the number of manufacturing establishments increased from 284 to 382, the number of production workers increased 257 per cent, and payrolls jumped 708 per cent.

Fearful that the end of the war would bring a recession with a sudden drop in war-boom population, the city government obtained referendum authority for a $20,000,000 bond issue. The money was to be used for public works that would keep men in jobs. The money was needed, as it turned out, but for totally different reasons. For Fort Worth not only retained its heavy war increase in population, but gained more month by month. The city had to use the $20,000,000, and still more, to expand municipal services for the thousands of new residents, many of whom came into the city when Fort Worth in 1946 annexed approximately forty square miles, bringing the corporate area to just under one hundred square miles. Two subdivisions were added—J. E. Foster's Kellis Park and the Luther Construction Company's Ridglea, two of the largest ever undertaken in the Southwest.

Several factors were responsible for the postwar growth, which Fort Worth shared in common with the rest of the Southwest. Decentralization of war industry had given the region a much-needed stimulus. With the end of the war, every effort was made to keep and to expand industrial activity. The jobs and the constantly opening opportunity for individual initiative kept new faces coming into the town. Too, many servicemen who had been stationed in the Southwest returned to make their homes after the war. West Texas oil fields continued to be dominant in the town's economy, as did record wheat crops and high livestock yields in the Fort Worth trade territory.

It thus developed that the war and postwar increases in population, manufacturing, and general business activity accounted for the sixth major impetus in the city's growth. In summary, the six phases, occurring over a period of three-quarters of a century, were these:

1. Influx of Confederate veterans
2. Cattle drives and development of the cattle industry
3. The railroad
4. Establishment of the packing houses in 1902
5. West Texas oil
6. War and postwar industrial and population growth.

The following tabulation shows the census figures for each decade of the past century for Fort Worth and Tarrant County:

	Fort Worth	Tarrant County
1850	- - -	664
1860	- - -	6,020
1870	- - -	5,788
1880	6,663	24,671
1890	23,076	41,142
1900	26,688	52,376
1910	73,312	108,572
1920	106,482	152,800
1930	163,477	197,553
1940	177,662	225,521
1950	278,778	361,253

Two of the most important reasons for the postwar growth were the Convair plant and Tarrant Field. Employment was drastically reduced at Convair when warplane production was curtailed, but several thousand persons remained on the payroll, working on a secret project begun during the war.

In June, 1948, that secret project roared into the sky above Fort Worth, to the astonishment of the world. It was a huge six-motored bomber called the B-36, that could fly ten thousand miles without stopping to refuel and was capable of delivering an atomic bomb almost any place in the world from a continental base. As more and more of the aerial monsters were placed on order, employment at the plant increased steadily.

As the army had done during the war, the newly separated air force after the war maintained the air base next door to the Convair plant. On February 28, 1948, Tarrant Field was renamed Carswell Air Force Base in memory of Major Horace S. Carswell, a Fort Worth man killed in China and a holder of the Congressional Medal of Honor.

At the time the first B-36 came from the line, Carswell Air Base was occupied by the Eighth Air Force, which had amassed a long and glorious record in the air war over Europe. The Eighth had been sent to Carswell in November, 1946, with orders to be ready to fly anywhere in the world at any time. As America's atomic bomb force, Major General Roger Ramey and his men began training in B-29's for their global mission. Their orders came during a period of tension. Russia, once an ally, had become antagonistic. War and the threat of war was always near. America could not feel secure in a world where a mightier armed strength represented a dia-metrically opposed ideology. In that atmosphere, the Eighth Air Force regularly sent training flights to distant corners of the earth—Japan, England, Alaska, the Caribbean, Panama, Arabia, and the Arctic Circle.

When the B-36 came from the Convair line, it was added to the Eighth Air Force. As more and more of the aerial giants, later equipped with four jet engines for a total of ten power plants, entered service, the B-36 became standard equipment for the Eighth. With the bigger plane it was easier to fly global missions, ranging from England to far over the Pacific.

Civil aviation was making strides, too. Air lines were using larger planes, four-engined planes that were too large for the municipal airport. Fort Worth decided to build a new airport.

Plans were made for the Greater Fort Worth International Airport on the eastern edge of Tarrant County, a project that evoked a spectacular conflict with Dallas, a conflict that was not settled until both cities took their fight to the very halls of Congress. Once before the two towns had tried to develop an airport jointly, but plans fell through when Dallas officials objected to the location of the terminal building. In 1947, Fort Worth decided to undertake the project alone. An application was filed with the C. A. A. for funds to help build the field that was to cost $11,000,000.

The action was like jabbing Dallas with a hot needle. When the C. A. A. approved the request and asked Congress for the money, Dallas was upset, fearing a conspiracy between Fort Worth, the air lines, and the government, which would make Love Field nothing but a dust bowl, for the projected field would be large enough to serve both Fort Worth and Dallas. Congressman Frank Wilson, of Dallas, battled the appropriation on the floor, and won. Fort Worth's sole hope was the Senate.

When the appropriation bill reached the upper house, an amendment restoring the full amount to Fort Worth was introduced. The opening of committee hearings found a determined Fort Worth delegation on hand to battle for the airport. Forty businessmen paid their own way to Washington. They argued their case before the committees, buttonholing senators until they finally won. Ground was broken for the airport in November, 1948.

The City of Fort Worth and its civic leaders were ready to name the Greater Fort Worth International Airport for Amon Carter, but were stymied by a government rule which forbids the naming of airports for living men. However, it was possible to name the administration building and the airfield for him, and the City Council did so in 1950. The council's action was taken upon the presentation of a petition signed by a large number of citizens. In presenting the petition, Marvin Leonard said:

> Amon G. Carter brought the first aviation to Fort Worth and for forty years he has tirelessly and unselfishly devoted his boundless energy, and his own money, to the purpose of building here a great aviation center. His exceptional effort

has brought to Fort Worth a cash flow of several billion dollars for payrolls, material and supplies, and it has brought more than twenty thousand happy and prosperous neighbors to our midst.

Mr. Carter's contributions to the development of Fort Worth have gone far beyond his activities in aviation as mentioned by Leonard, for he has been the most forceful figure in the city's history.

Amon G. Carter was born in an unchinked log cabin at Crafton, Wise County, Texas, on December 11, 1879. His blacksmith father had just finished building the cabin of oak logs when the baby and a norther arrived about the same time. But he had not been able yet to chink the large gaps between the logs. To keep Mrs. Carter and the baby warm, a neighboring farmer wrapped them in quilts, placed them in a rocking chair, and he and the new father carried them down the road to his home.

Like most boys in the rural West of that period, young Carter had no formal schooling past the eighth grade. His mother died in Montague, Texas, and from there he went to Bowie, when about thirteen years old, where he took a job in the Jarrott boardinghouse. There he waited on tables and was "chamber maid" in the eleven rooms of the boardinghouse (which had its plumbing in the back yard), at $1.50 a week. In his office today, Mr. Carter has a platter, which was called the big steak plate, that he used to carry to and from the table. In it he keeps baseballs from World Series games going back to the period of World War I, each ball autographed by baseball greats like Connie Mack, John McGraw, Hughey Jennings, Ty Cobb, and Tris Speaker. He also has a pewter caster, still with the bell that called him to service, which sat in the middle of the dining table. Later he sold sandwiches at the railroad station to passengers on trains passing through Bowie—business was good because there was no dining-car service at that time. He once re-enacted those days by selling a sandwich to President Franklin D. Roosevelt, who was passing through Bowie on a train.

Along in the nineties, Amon Carter moved to Norman, Oklahoma, where Michael McGinley, his cousin's husband, had a grocery store. There he worked in the Davis Confectionery, regularly grinding the crank of a five-gallon ice cream freezer and selling sweets. While in Norman—working for thirty dollars a month, paying fifteen of that for board and room at the Grand Central Hotel, and working from seven in the morning until midnight—he heard in the Davis Barbershop that a man was in town trying to hire a tourist.

"What's a tourist?" Carter asked.

"That's a man who travels around the country."

"You mean they pay him for it?" he asked incredulously.

He investigated, and the result was that he went on the road selling enlarged portraits—sepia, black and white, and water-color pictures. He and a friend, Bill Ince, would go into a town, make arrangements with a merchant, and canvass from house to house. The deal was that the housewife got the picture if she bought ten dollars' worth of goods from the merchant. When she came in for the groceries, she naturally wanted to buy a frame for her new picture. The frame was there waiting for her, at a price that covered the cost of both frame and picture. No other frame would do because the picture was an outsize, seventeen by nineteen inches.

After traveling in every state in the Union, Carter left the company as general sales manager, winding up in San Francisco, where he worked with an advertising agency. Then in 1905 he went to Fort Worth, where he joined Colonel Wortham in starting the old *Fort Worth Star*. Amon Carter was the one-man advertising staff, and he and Wortham each earned thirty-five dollars a week. But when he saw where the paper's finances were heading, he cut his salary and Wortham's to twenty dollars a week after the first three months.

During the first two or three years, he and Wortham, J. M. North, Jr., B. N. Honea, and James R. Record had a tough time making the *Star* go, and many times he was offered more money by other concerns, even by the *Star's* archrival, the *Telegram*. Mr. Carter might have been tempted to quit, but he was angered by some of the competitive practices of the *Telegram*, and, as he once said, just "bowed my neck" and helped bring the *Star* to the point where it bought out the *Telegram* in 1908. He acquired control of the *Star-Telegram* in 1923 through purchase of Colonel Wortham's stock, later adding the *Record* through purchase from William Randolph Hearst, which he turned into the morning edition of the *Star-Telegram*, as was related earlier.

During the years that he has directed the *Star-Telegram*, Amon Carter has helped lead the business community in one expansion after another, frequently involving the location in Fort Worth of factories, stores, branch plants, and warehouses of important national corporations.

He was able to do these things through salesmanship and through his contacts with bankers and industrialists. The contacts were established by a standing policy of his newspaper to represent itself in national advertising, in contrast to the usual newspaper practice of having offices in New York and Chicago with national representatives. This system has continued to prevail since 1910.

Once when he was in the office of E. W. Sinclair in New York, he noticed a wall map on which pins showed the many operations of the Sinclair Oil Company, and asked if the pin at Dallas meant that Sinclair had bought the Pierce Oil Company. When Sinclair replied that, confidentially, it did, Mr. Carter simply moved the pin half an inch to the left, placing it at Fort Worth. Sinclair laughed and rearranged his business by establishing the southwest regional office in Fort Worth.

A number of other major oil companies established offices in Fort Worth through Carter's efforts. He was instrumental in bringing the American Petroleum Institute's fifth annual convention to Fort Worth in 1924, the first time that the A. P. I. had held an annual meeting in any town smaller than, or west of, St. Louis. While oil executives from all over the world were in town, he saw to it that they were sold on Fort Worth. Establishment of several offices followed.

Mr. Carter also was instrumental in bringing to Fort Worth the United States Public Health Service Hospital and the Consolidated-Vultee Aircraft Corporation plant which makes the globe-girdling B-36 bombers, and was a leader in the construction of the Will Rogers Memorial Auditorium and Coliseum, the Texas Hotel, the Fort Worth Club, the Harris Memorial Methodist Hospital, and the Amon Carter– Y. M. C. A. Summer Camp for Boys. He organized the T. C. U. Stadium Association in 1930 and helped sponsor the construction of the stadium, which was named for him in 1951. He also was chairman of the first board of Texas Technological College in Lubbock, for whose founding he campaigned actively. In appreciation of his efforts in behalf of the local public schools, a high school in the Riverside section of Fort Worth was named for him. He frequently attends graduation exercises at Amon G. Carter Riverside High School.

Tom Connally, who represented Texas in the United States Senate for many years, once remarked, "The gates open when he comes to Washington and the Treasury Department puts on extra guards because they know he will take back some money for a civic improvement in West Texas."

Amon Carter disclaims any specific philosophy or pattern in bringing new businesses to town, other than "merely my enthusiasm for Texas, more particularly West Texas, its great opportunities, and pride in Fort Worth."

As a matter of fact, his activities on behalf of the state— he always travels as Amon G. Carter of Texas—led the Texas House of Representatives in 1941 to name him "Ambassador of Good Will" because of his willingness "at all times to sacrifice his own pleasure, business, finances in order to help some worthy cause of Texas."

John Nance Garner, former vice-president of the United States, remarked one time, "That man wants the whole government of the United States to be run for the exclusive benefit of Fort Worth."

Mr. Carter has always figured prominently in Fort Worth's competition with Dallas and other cities. The story is often told, though not true, that he took his own lunch to Dallas so he would not have to spend money there. Right after World War II, he and Sid Richardson, a Fort Worth oilman, bought the Texas Hotel on one hour's notice when they heard that interests in a certain near-by city planned to buy it. In spite of the ofttimes bitter rivalry between the two towns, Dallas made him an honorary citizen because the competition was healthy and beneficial to both, and the *Dallas Morning News* said "he punched Dallas like cowboys are wont to do slow steers in a shipping chute."

But he also works closely with Dallas men in projects for the benefit of North Texas, such as trying to obtain the Air Force Academy, and the multimillion dollar improvement of flood control on the Trinity River and its upper tributaries, looking toward the day when the Trinity will be navigable from the Gulf to Fort Worth and Dallas.

An avid world traveler, Mr. Carter made all of the first Clipper flights except the one to Bermuda. He is an intimate of the great and near great around the world. In the foyer of his office hangs an oil painting bearing the legend: "Painted especially for Amon G. Carter by his friend Ike Eisenhower 1949."

The late O. O. McIntyre once wrote in his column: "There are few out-of-towners so well known in New York as the Texas newspaper publisher, Amon G. Carter. And in turn no visitor is so keen in three-sheeting his own town as Carter. In festive moments he is likely to loose three cheers for West Texas with a special yipee for Fort Worth. Wherever Carter goes he is usually recognized. Comedians banter with him from the stage, masters of ceremony make him stand for a bow. . . . He is surtouted up to the minute, save his hat, which is pure Stetson Texas."

Not only is Amon Carter's narrow-brimmed Stetson his trade-mark; it has become an identifying mark for his cronies and the dignitaries who come to Fort Worth. For every important guest is asked to leave his old hat behind and wear a brand-new hat presented by Carter—a Shady Oak hat of Stetson manufacture. The old hats left behind, many of them military caps, are those of Franklin D. Roosevelt; Harry S. Truman; Charles Lindbergh; John Garner; Otto Kahn; Robert Lovett; W. S. Knudsen, former president of General Motors; Walter McLucas, outstanding Detroit banker; Generals Eisenhower, H. H. Arnold, James Doolittle, "Tooy" Spaatz, and Jonathan Wainwright; and Admirals Stark, Halsey, and Nimitz.

The Shady Oak hat takes its name from his farm at Lake Worth, constructed to entertain more than one thousand guests at a time, in the wide-open style of western hosts. His popping six-shooters, fired while he is mounted on a golden Palomino given to him by his friends, have called thousands of guests to gather in the chow line. Shelves in the house hold hats of his celebrated friends, but on a peg out in front of all the others is a battered ten-gallon hat once worn by Will Rogers.

The great humorist was a close personal friend. He and Carter flew around the country together, making Carter incidentally famous at the time as Rogers' flying companion. His devotion to Rogers' memory resulted in the naming of the Fort Worth auditorium and coliseum and the placing there of a bronze equestrian statue of Rogers mounted on his horse Soapsuds. Electra Waggoner Biggs of Vernon did the bronze, and it was unveiled by General Eisenhower on November 4, 1947. Mr. Carter placed similar statues at the Will Rogers memorials in Claremore, Oklahoma, and on the Texas Tech campus at Lubbock, Texas. He also commissioned Seymour Stone to do a sixteen-by-twenty-foot portrait of Will Rogers on Soapsuds, which was presented to the city of Fort Worth and unveiled in the foyer of the Will Rogers Coliseum by

General Eisenhower at the same time that the equestrian statue was unveiled. Today Rogers' picture is on Carter's desk —and above it burns a light that is never turned off.

Amon Carter personally is a forceful man, soft-spoken, but direct. His drive obtained for him the Frank M. Hawks Memorial Award in aviation and a special citation from the Secretary of Air, Stuart Symington.

His hobby is a collection of western paintings and bronzes by Charles M. Russell and Frederic Remington—one of the world's largest collections. Mr. Carter recently acquired the William Luther Lewis collection of fifteen hundred volumes, of which nine hundred are first editions, and many other literary rarities, which will be made available for the benefit of Texas Christian University of Fort Worth.

Also he has acquired a library of Western Americana consisting of some twenty-four hundred volumes, including first editions, rare and fine books, complete histories of the Texas counties, and many illustrated books and original drawings by James Santee, Frederic Remington, Charles M. Russell, and others, which will be housed in a western museum he plans to construct in Fort Worth.

Fort Worth ended its first century with one of the most exciting exploits in world history. The event was centered at Carswell Air Force Base, where tension and excitement gripped all officers and men who knew what was happening high in the air.

On February 28, 1949, a B-50 bomber had risen into the air above Fort Worth with its silvery nose pointed eastward. It kept on flying. At various points around the world it was met by other air force planes. From each rendezvous plane dangled a hose, which in mid-air was attached to the B-50. Through the hose flowed gasoline that took the plane on to the next rendezvous. On March 2, ninety-four hours after leaving Fort Worth, the throbbing motors of the plane— dubbed "Lucky Lady II"—brought it to Fort Worth again.

The United States Air Force had made the first nonstop flight around the world—Fort Worth to Fort Worth.

Appendices

A   Military Orders and Correspondence
Relating to the Establishment
and Occupation of Fort Worth

B   County Officers Since 1849

C   Congressmen Since 1849

D   State Legislators Since 1853

E   City Officials Since 1853

Military Orders

and Correspondence Pertaining to
the Establishment and Occupation
of Fort Worth

ORDER No. 2
Headquarters, 8th Military Dept.
Galveston, Texas, Nov. 7, 1848.

The following points now occupied by companies of volunteer service, will be occupied as follows by the four companies of the 2d Dragoons now in the Department:

One company at Conner's Station, on Richland Creek, east of the Brazos.

One company at Ross' Station, on the Boscha River, west of the Brazos.

One company at McCulloch's Station, six miles east of the Colorado, and about fifty miles above Austin.

One company on the Medina River, at a point ten or fifteen miles above Castroville.

I. The Headquarters of the Regiment will be established at either of the above points to be selected by the commanding officer. Lt. Col. Fauntleroy will proceed with as little delay as possible with the four companies, from which point they will be detached to their different stations.

II. Capt. Eastman, with his company 1st Infantry, will proceed to, and take post at the German town of Fredericksburg, on the Pierdenales, a branch of the Colorado, and about eight miles northeast of San Antonio.

The two companies, 1st Infantry, Beubanks and Scotts, now en route for San Antonio, will proceed to Austin and there await further orders.

III. Every effort will be made by the different commanding officers to cultivate a friendly understanding with the different tribes of Indians near their respective posts. Great discretion and vigilance must be used in preventing any depredations by either the inhabitants or Indians upon each other.

The Indians will be required to remain north and west of a line connecting the different posts above established—except on friendly visits to the posts for the purpose of trade.

IV. Capt. Blake will muster out of service the different companies of volunteers without delay, going if necessary to their different posts.

By order of Maj. Gen. Twiggs:

W. T. H. BROOKS, A. A. A. Gen.

ORDER NO. 9

Head Quarters 8th & 9th Departments
San Antonio, Texas, February 8, 1849

1. Company F, 2nd Dragoons, and Company I, of the same regiment, the former now at Ross's Station the latter at Conner's Station, will, as soon as practicable, be concentrated, and establish a post, at the point called Towash Village on, or near the Brazos River. The site for the new post will be selected by the senior officer of the command, with a view to the supply of wood and water, and, if possible, for timber for building purposes. All the public stores, and subsistence, will be transported from Conner's and Ross's stations, to the new post.

2 . . . . .
3. . . . . .
4. . . . . .
5. . . . . .

By order of Major General Worth:
GEORGE DEAS
Asst. Adj. Genl.

ORDER NO. 13

Head Quarters 8th & 9th Departments
San Antonio, Texas, February 14, 1849.

1. Companies A, B and F, 1st Infantry, will march to Presidio Rio Grande, and establish a post at, or near, the crossing at that point.

2. Companies D and I, 1st Infantry, will move to, and establish a post, at, or near, the point on the Leona, where it is crossed by Woll's route, from San Antonio to Presidio Rio Grande.

3. The Commanding officer of the 8th Infantry, will designate four companies of that regiment to relieve the command at Fredericksburg. As soon as relieved, Captain Eastman will march with his command, as indicated in par. 2.

4. The Quarter Master's Department will furnish the necessary transportation, in execution of the movements directed.

5. The Senior Officer on the Rio Grande (at present Brevet Lieut. Colonel Morris, 1st Infantry) will command the "Rio Grande District, 8th Department," including the posts on that river, from Fort Polk to Laredo, Head Quarters at Fort Brown. The Senior Officer on the North Western frontier (at present Brevet Brig. General Harney, 2nd Dragoons) will command the "Frontier District 8th Department," extending from Presidio on the left, including the posts of the Leona, Fredericksburg, San Antonio and Towash Village on the right, Head Quarters at present at Austin.

6. Brig. General Harney, will, as soon as practicable, make personal inspection of, and give the necessary orders for, the construction of such partial defense arrangements as may be sufficient to guard against surprise, and for the security of the public stores, animals &c. No permanent construction of quarters &c. will be made, until the disposition herein ordered, shall be sanctioned by the Superior authority. General Harney is desired, at an early date, to ascertain and report upon, the expediency of placing a post, intermediate between the post at Towash, and Fort Washita, suggesting the mode of supplying said post, &c.

7. The first and highest duties of the troops throughout the line of posts along the northwestern frontier, and the line of the Rio Grande, Department No. 8, is to afford security in person and property to citizens residing within, or near, such lines—next, to prevent, as far as practicable, hostile incursions, of Indians residing within the limits of the United States, upon the border of the neighboring Mexican states, as our Country has bound itself to do, by treaty stipulations, and finally, by kindness, and all proper forbearance, to conciliate the Indian tribes—protect them from violence and injustice, and make them to understand their

233

true interests and their obligations. In the fulfilment of these duties, the intelligence of officers and zeal of soldiers will supply deficiency of numbers.

8. Returns, Reports &c. will be sent direct to Dept. Head Quarters, Commanders of Districts being furnished with duplicates.

By order of Major General Worth.

GEO. DEAS.

Asst. Adj. Genl.

Head Quarters 8th Department
San Antonio, June 4th, 1849

Sir:

I have the honor to forward, herewith enclosed, a report made by me, when in command of the "Frontier District 8th Dept.," in reference to the frontier defense, position of posts, mode of supply &c.

The recommendations therein made, and the views expressed, I have not been able (since coming into the comd. of this dept) to carry out immediately, owing partly to the want of the necessary disposable force, and on account of the multiplicity of duties which have called my particular attention in other directions.

These, and other subjects of importance, will, in a subsequent communication, be laid before the Genl. Comdg. the Divn. I may, however, here state that I have occupied a point between Jose Maria's village (Ft. Graham) and Fort Washita, on the West Fork of the Trinity, with Compy. F, 2nd Dragoons.

I am, very respectfully,
Your obt. servt.
WM. S. HARNEY
Bvt. Brig. Genl. Comdg 8th Dept.

Asst Adj Genl.
Head Quarters Western Div.
    Cincinnati
       Ohio

        Head Quarters, Frontier District, 8th Mily. Dept.
              Austin, Texas, May 1, 1849.

Sir:

    In obedience to instructions conveyed in Dept. Orders No. 13 (Par 6) I left this post on the 1st of March for the Towash village, and a personal inspection of the Northern Frontier, with a view to the establishment of a post intermediate between the Towash and Fort Washita. I was detained at the former station by sickness, which will account for any delay in making my report. Temporary buildings for the protection of the public stores were in progress of erection at the Towash on my arrival; but considering the site chosen as objectionable, I ordered the building to be discontinued, and after an examination of the country in the neighborhood, I directed the post to be moved to Jose Maria Village, six miles north of the Towash, near the banks of the Brazos. The objections to the Towash village as a site for a military post are, its being on a narrow sandy ridge, surrounded with post and scrub oak, and affording no grazing within sight of the post, besides having an extensive swamp circumjacent, which in the summer season must render it unhealthy, and the owner of the land would not come to terms with the Government; nor did I consider it necessary to locate the post at the precise spot indicated, but supposed that any point in the vicinity or neighborhood would carry out the intentions of the order—due regard being had to the necessary requisites for a Dragoon post, all of which are to be had at the Jose Maria village, but in some of which as already mentioned the Towash is deficient. I have called the new post Fort Graham. With regard to the expediency of erecting a new post between Fort Graham and Fort Washita, I would recommend that a post which shall be the northern extremity of this chain, be established on the Red River, at the upper or western edge of the lower cross timbers, and a little north of Lat. 33° 30'. The western edge of the lower cross timbers runs in almost a direct line from the point suggested for the new post to Jose Maria

Village, and not as laid down in Cordova's Map, in a southwesterly direction—the map being entirely defective in this respect; the western or upper edge of the lower cross timbers does not extend further than three miles from Camp Thornton, Towash Village. Between the western edge of the lower and the eastern edge of the upper cross timbers there is an extensive prairie, about forty miles in width, which I would suggest as a boundary to the Indians. I deem it appropriate to state here that my convictions—strengthened by two years experience, and also from a personal knowledge of the localities, to be that the interests of the service would be far better secured by giving a more southern locality to the troops now stationed at Fort Washita, and who, if removed, as I would suggest to the above mentioned point on the river, would insure a direct communication between scouting parties from that point and the more northern and western posts in this department. The settlers along this line have lost almost all their horses, and up to this time I have restrained with difficulty from retaliating. In continuation of the chain of posts which I hold it necessary to establish, I would recommend that a post be established on the West Fork of the Trinity at or near the 33rd degree of latitude, while a third post should be placed at some point between Fort Graham and Hamilton's Creek. Besides the addition of this third post to the two already occupied at Hamilton's Creek and Fort Graham, I would recommend that Fredericksburg be converted into a dragoon instead of an infantry post. The supplies for the post on the Red river could for the present with . . . . convenience and economy be drawn from Fort Towson, or some other point above the Red river, and those required for the post on the Trinity and Fort Graham could be drawn from Buffallo, to which point boats can ascend with Government stores. The river is navigable in most seasons of the year to within one hundred miles of the positions designated for the new posts. The facilities for supplying the two posts above named are fully equal to those now in existence for the supply of Forts Gibson or Towson. These are the best arrangements which can be made; but with the improvements that are being made in the navigation of some of the streams in Texas it is probable greater facilities will be afforded the transportation of supplies in a short time. For the intermediate post between Fort Graham and Hamilton's Creek, and for Hamilton's Creek and Fredericksburg I would advise that supplies be drawn from Lavaca, via Austin; and for San Antonio and the posts west of San Antonio as far as the Leona from Lavaca, via San Antonio. After the present year, I am fully satisfied that the supplies to be drawn from the coast will be so few, that it will be of little consequence from what point they may be brought. In view of the increased security that would be afforded to settlers by establishing a chain of posts as herein recommended, and the increased immigration induced thereby, it may safely be asserted that in one year such supplies as pork, flour, beans, and sugar, will be furnished cheaper by the pioneers of the country, the people who have explored and settled in the neighborhood of the posts, and who are even now rapidly filling up the country, than could possibly be done by procuring them from New Orleans, and, with perhaps the exception of sugar, of a better quality than has usually been furnished to frontier posts; of this I have been fully assured by commanders who have been stationed here formerly. The suggestions made herein as to the establishment of three new posts are communicated as the results of a close examination into the wants of the frontier settlements, and with a view also to the best interests of the service; should they find favor at Genl. Head Quarters, I am prepared to insure an efficient protection to the Frontier District, excluding the posts on the Rio Grande, where I should require assistance from other corps, provided I am allowed my entire regiment, increased to an organization of 100 men in companies, and armed as I daily expect it will be with Colt's pistols. Looking to the possibility of a general war, I would suggest, that the infantry companies—both for economy and convenience of supplies, and that they may be in a position to render prompt assistance in case of need, be stationed at the following points, viz: two companies at Buffalo, four at Austin, four at San Antonio, and as many on the Rio Grande as the interests of the public service will permit. In conclusion I cannot refrain from urging on the Department, as calculated to repress the predatory incursions of the Indians, a temporary increase in the number of Indian Agents, to be stationed on this frontier, until such time as a general council or treaty can be had to settle the respective rights and limits between the Government and the numerous bands of Indians who have long disturbed the

infant settlements on the Texas frontier, and who will continue
to retard the filling up of the country by their depredations, unless
deprived of all excuses for aggressive movements by a treaty
definitive of rights and limits.

I have the honor, sir, to be
respectfully your
obedient servant,
W. S. HARNEY,
Bvt. Brig. Genl. Comdg.
Frontier Dist.

Major Geo Deas,
Asst. Adj. Genl U. S. A.
8th Mily. Dept.
San Antonio
      Texas

Fort Graham, Texas,
June 2nd 1849.

Genl:

    I have the honor to acknowledge the receipt this day of a
letter from your office, requiring the Returns of F Compy 2nd
Drags. for the months of February and March 1847. I have succeeded in finding them (one without a signature) and having
had copies made of them for the Company Desk, I herewith forward the original.

	Very Respectfully General
Maj. Genl. Roger Jones	I have the honor to be Yr. obt. svt.
Adj Genl U. S. Army	R. A. ARNOLD
Washington D. C.	Bvt. Maj. 2nd Dragoons.

N. B. I have located a new post on West Fork Trinity River. My
address will be "Dallas, Dallas County Texas," a town about
thirty five miles east of me.

Northern Frontier of Texas.
Fort Worth, West Fork of Trinity River
June 18, 1849.

General.

Having seen a paragraph going the rounds of the newspapers, stating that the Dragoons above Waco Village had lost many Horses by the Indians, I have the honor to contradict such a report and to state that the two companies of Dragoons which have been under my command have not had a Horse stolen since their arrival in Texas in November last nor have I heard of any Indian depredations committed in this part of the country for several months.

About one hundred Indians of the different wild tribes are now visiting me. They brought down and delivered up some thirty five horses which they had taken from the Wichitas, horses stolen within the last year from citizens. Three Wichita chiefs are here and promise everything for the future. All is peace and quiet on this frontier.

Very Respectfully Genl.
Your most obt svt.
R. A. Arnold
Bvt. Maj 2nd Drags Comdg

Maj Genl Roger Jones
Adj Genl USA
Washington D C

N. B. Be pleased to send me twelve blank Post Returns and to address me at "Dallas, Dallas County Texas"

Northern Frontier of Texas
Fort Worth West Fork Trinity River
June 15th 1849.

General.

I have the honor to ask you to look over the enclosed roll of my company and to request that if there are any drilled recruits at the Cavalry Depot that my company be filled up. (Those assigned me from detachment brought out by Lt. Smith in November last with one exception had not even been drilled at the Carbine Manual or Saber Exercises or at least knew nothing of either).

I am building a new post at this place (the extreme Northern Frontier yet occupied) and my company is so small that I cannot keep up my scouting parties. I have represented this matter to the Col of the Regiment and have asked that I might at least have a Subaltern Officer. I require a Bugler. The boy I have is sickly and his time will expire in November next.

Very Respectfully Genl
Your Most Obt Svt
R. A. ARNOLD
Bvt Maj 2nd Dragoons
Comdg.

Maj Genl.
Roger Jones
Adj Genl USA
Washington
D. C.

Roll Call of Capt. & Bvt. Maj. R. A. Arnold's Company ("F") Second Regiment of Dragoons, stationed at Fort Worth, West Fork of the Trinity River, Texas. June 19th, 1849.

No.	Name	Rank	Remarks
1.	Jacob Dearing	1st Sergt.	
2.	Danl. McCauley	Sergt.	
3.	William Slade	do.	

1.	Joseph Noland	Corpl.	On sick furlough from May 12th 1849, for three months
2.	James R. Kepner	do.	
3.	Joseph Schaffer	do.	
4.	Nathan Zorkowsky	do.	
1.	Thomas Noland	Musician	Sick in hospital. Time expires in Nov.
2.	Anthony Kemp	Farrier	On extra duty qr. mstr. department.
1.	Anderson, Philip	Private	
2.	Beyer, Nicholas	do.	
3.	Burlage, Frederick W.	do.	
4.	Bohrman, Christian	do.	
5.	Dilcher, William	do.	On detd. serv. with Bt. Br. Genl. Harney since April 3, 1849.
6.	Dixon, William H.	do.	
7.	Durfee, George	do.	
8.	Doyle, Hugh	do.	Sick in hospital
9.	Donelly, Thomas	do.	Sick in hospital
10.	Freeman, Alphonso	do.	
11.	Fuchs, Charles	do.	Sick at Austin since Dec. 1 1848, has never done any duty since I joined and I was informed that a surgeon's certificate had been forwarded for him. Lost to the company at any rate.
12.	Gerstring, Simon	do.	
13.	Gross, Joseph	do.	
14.	Gwynne, William A.	do.	
15.	Harrison, Andrew I.	do.	
16.	Hughes, Johnston	do.	

17.	Helmering, Augustus	do.	Hospital Steward at Fort Worth
18.	Hanna, James	do.	
19.	Hannibal, John	do.	
20.	Knaar, Francis	do.	Saddler, and always at work at old equipment
21.	Kaas, Otto	do.	
22.	Keough, Peter	do.	
23.	Law, John	do.	
24.	Moser, Stephen	do.	on detd. serv. with Bt. Brig. Genl. Harney since April 3d, 1849.
25.	Miller, Blassis	do.	Sick in hospital
26.	Mendez, Anthony L.	do.	
27.	McCullough, Moses	do.	Sick since about 3rd Dec./48
28.	Porthouse, Thomas	do.	
29.	Poggenpuhl, August	do.	
30.	Patterson, Matthew M.	do.	Perfectly worthless— can't trust him with horse or equipment.
31.	Schultz, Ferdinand	do.	
32.	Senn, John	do.	
33.	Wagner, John	do.	Driving company team
34.	Weaver, Samuel	do.	
35.	Wetmore, Louis	do.	
36.	Wolbel, William	do.	
37.	Zeckler, William	do.	On extra duty as clerk in Quartermaster and Commisary Dept.

But twenty five privates for duty—building post, scouting &c. This is not a mere morning report but the roll of my entire company.

R. A. ARNOLD
Bvt. Maj. 2nd Dragoons
Commanding.

Fort Worth, Texas, April 22, 1851

General,

I have the honor to acknowledge the receipt on the 19th inst. of a circular from your office, of the 28th Dec. 1850, requiring a report upon the capacity of the country in this vicinity to furnish supplies of subsistence stores; and submit the following:

Fresh beef of a good quality can be procured in any quantity. The price paid by contract at present is 3 ¾ cents per pound. It cannot probably be contracted for much below this price.

Flour cannot be had except in small parcels of *very* inferior quality. There are no flouring mills in this section of the country. Price not easily ascertained.

Beans cannot be procured at any price. As a substitute, *Cow Pease* can be had; probable price delivered, one dollar per bushel.

Vinegar cannot be had except by importation.

Tallow, in small quantities can be procured if the trouble be taken to collect it at the scattered farm houses. Price at present, ten cents per pound. The price will increase on the increase of demand.

Candles are not procurable.

Hard soap is not procurable. *Soft soap* as a substitute has been offered to me at *eight cents per pound;* three fourths of it being water, at that price it is equivalent to *thirty two cents per pound.*

Salt is all imported from New Orleans and sells at three dollars per bushel.*

Cattle are grazed on the prairies attended with no other expense in summer than branding them. In winter, if intended for beef, it will be nice and easy to find them. The expense of herding one hundred cattle may be thus stated:

Three herdsmen at $20 per month	$60.00
Rations for these, @ 19¢	17.00
	$77.10

Supposing this command (a single company) to be kept up to the maximum strength allowed by law, viz: 3 officers and 86

243

non-commissioned officers and privates, the probable number of pounds of beef required to be slaughtered during the month, allowing beef twice a week, will be 890—Cost per pound for herding alone, about 8⅔ cents.

Corn is furnished at this post by contract at $1.15 per bushel. It can be had in any required quantity. Hereafter probably at much higher price. If Corn Meal be in part substituted for flour or hardbread, the price per 100 rations deducting 20 percent, in cost of grinding and other loss by screening, will be about $4.15. The price of flour is 7.87½ per hundred rations. The price of hard bread $9 per hundred rations.

I am, General, very respectfully,
Your obt Servant
SAM H. STARR
2nd Lt. 2nd Dragoons

Major General Geo. Gibson
    Commissary Genl of Subsistence U. S. Army
      Washington City, D. C.

* Some salt of an inferior quality is manufactured in this country. The price, delivered here, is that stated above.

S. H. STARR
Lt. 2nd Dragoons
A. A. Q. M.

Fort Worth   Lieut. Starr   2nd Drags. A. A. Q. M.

Established June 6, 1849, by Company "F" 2nd Drags. Bvt. Major R. A. Arnold Comdg. The first location was thought to be unhealthy, the post was in consequence removed to its present site about the 1st of August 1849.

BUILDINGS

There are at the post three sets of officers quarters, two rooms and a passage each, with kitchen (built of logs) and covered with clapboards.

One of these sets is hewn logs 52x17 feet for comdg. officer. One a frame 41x16 sided with sawed clapboards. These have two good stone chimneys each; and one a temporary hut 41x16 built of rough logs with a stick chimney daubed with mud.

Quarters for 120 men, built of logs and puncheons—without floors—mud and stick chimneys; with kitchen . . . of same construction covered with clapboards—very temporary.

A commodious hospital 34x17 feet and dispensary 11x11. These are frame buildings ceiled with inch boards and roofed with shingles. Hospital has a good stone chimney.

A small building 12x12 of same construction as hospital used for office purposes.

A stable 30x30 feet, built of split logs and roofed with claps, for Drags. horses, a forage room attached.

A commissary store 32x12 of rough logs and clapboard roof.

A guard house—a quartermaster store house—a blacksmith shop and a wheelwright shop made of rough logs and covered with clapboards, are embraced among the temporary buildings at the post—many of these require repairs more or less.

Nearly all the labor has been performed by the troops.

BUILDING MATERIALS
An abundance of stone and timber, suitable for building purposes is in the neighborhood of the post. Price of lumber $30 to $40 per thousand feet.

WATER
Plenty of good River and spring water within ⅛ to ½ a mile of the post—a well in the garrison furnishes a supply of good water for drinking. For other purposes it is hauled by a public wagon.

FUEL
Abundant and easily obtained and always by the troops. No claim for fuel has yet been made, nor will any be admitted, until the claimant shall produce a clear title to the land.

FORAGE
Average price of corn since the establishment of the post is about ninety cents per bushel. Price now paid is $1.15.

Hay has been procured by contract. The price last year was $3.19 per ton. Good grass for grazing purposes is plenty in the immediate vicinity of the post—but for hay: from one to three miles distant.

FRESH BEEF

Fresh beef is abundant—delivered at the post, it costs 3 ¾ cents per pound.

ROADS

Roads leading from this post are three (viz) to Austin, Houston and Shreveport. All good in favorable seasons of the year; and bad in the wet season.

SUPPLIES

Drawn chiefly from N. Orleans and forwarded via the Trinity and Brassos River or via Houston, latterly by the last named place. Transportation done exclusively by hired teams at $3.00 per hundred (average).

RIVERS

The rivers which intersect the route to Austin, are the Brassos, North, Middle and South Bosques, Leon, Lampassas, San Gabriel and Brushy—most of which have already been adverted to in the report of Fort Graham herewith.

Ferry across the Brassos at Fort Graham and ford the remainder.

The Navasoto is the principal stream crossing the road to Houston. The road crosses many of the headwaters of the tributaries of the Trinity, but these ordinarily offer no obstacle to travel upon the road.

The road to Shreveport is crossed by "Mountain Creek" a very bad but small stream having a bad bottom and rapid current.

Also the Trinity at Dallas where is a ferry but bad bottom of three miles on the west side—next the east Fork of the Trinity where is also a ferry and a bad bottom next the Sabine where is a ferry, besides many other small streams not difficult to cross excepting always after heavy rains.

Distance to Shreveport about 220 miles.

A point on Red River "Warren" is believed to be the most favorable from which to draw supplies for Forts Worth and Graham, distance about 105 miles.

County Officers
Since 1849

Below is a list of Tarrant County officers from 1849, the year the county was created. The list is complete from 1876 on. But the courthouse fire of 1876 destroyed records of office holders prior to that year. For the period 1849–76 a partial list as reported here was found in the State Archives at Austin.

Dec., 1849–August, 1850

Temporary Commissioners Vincent J. Hatton, Walling R. Rogers, Middleton Tate Johnson, Sanders Elliott, ——— Little.

1850–1852

Chief Justice Seabourne Gilmore; no commissioners shown; District Clerk Sanders Elliott; County Clerk Archibald F. Leonard; Sheriff Francis Jourdan.

1852–1854

Chief Justice Jason Watson; County Clerk Benjamin P. Ayres; Sheriff John B. York.

1854–1856

Chief Justice I. Tracey Morehead; District Clerk William Quayle; County Clerk Benjamin P. Ayres; Commissioners James Joyce, G. W. Minter, C. C. McKinney, I. L. Purvis; Sheriff John York.

1856–1858

Chief Justice Seabourne Gilmore; County Clerk Gideon Nance; Commissioners Hamilton Bennett, John W. Smith, John Farran and Isaac Y. Bowman; Sheriff W. B. Tucker.

1858–1860
Chief Justice William Quayle; Commissioners James Young, V. J. Hutton, Isaac Bowman and W. B. Bell; County Clerk Gideon Nance; District Clerk William B. Tucker; Sheriff John B. York.

1860–1862
Chief Justice William Quayle, until 1861; succeeded as chief justice by R. W. Tannahill, Nov. 5, 1861; Commissioners Allen Russell, William Poe, James M. Crawford, James R. Allen, James Young, S. B. Bowman, W. R. Bell (the number indicates that those first elected left at the outbreak of war and were succeeded by the others); County Clerk Gideon Nance; Sheriff William O. Yantis; District Clerk W. B. Tucker; Assessor-Collector Dan Mullinghaus; Treasurer W. T. Ferguson; Surveyor W. L. Lively.

1862–1864
Chief Justice Stephen Terry; Commissioners I. B. Hibbert; Joshua Cook, William Lytle, Isaac D. Parker; County Clerk Gideon Nance; Sheriff John W. Gillespie.

Aug. 1, 1864–Aug. 21, 1865
Chief Justice Stephen Terry; Commissioners L. C. Stephens, Barney B. McQuien, Joshua Cook, Lawrence Steele; County Clerk Gideon Nance; Sheriff James P. Davis.

Aug. 21, 1865–June, 1866
(Appointed by Provisional Governor Andrew J. Hamilton)
Chief Justice Stephen Terry; Commissioners Hiram Riddle, Charles Wise, Daniel McKinzie, Thomas Jefferson; County Clerk Gideon Nance; District Clerk Mark Elleston; Sheriff B. F. Arthur.

June 25, 1866–November, 1867
(First free election after the surrender of the Confederacy)
County Judge William B. Tucker; Commissioners Lawrence Steele, Joshua Cook, Thomas Jefferson, L. H. Stephens; County Clerk Gideon Nance; District Clerk I. T. Turner.

RECONSTRUCTION

When General Sheridan removed Governor Throckmorton from office in July 1867 as an impediment to Reconstruction, all of the above county officials were shorn of authority by Military Order No. 195. From Nov. 12, 1867 until May 1869 all county officials were appointed by various generals. The military and, apparently, political appointees between 1867 and 1873 appear below:

County Judge B. F. Barkley; Commissioners Newton Holland, Joseph B. Farmer who refused to qualify, William Evans who was removed by General Canby, H. C. Jefferson, William Linn, Y. W. Mann, John E. Browdon, W. H. Richardson; District Clerk I. B. Edens who refused to qualify, Eugene Arthur, A. G. Walker, W. B. Lorance, Dan Parker. County Clerk Lewis H. Brown, A. G. Walker, T. W. Mann. Sheriff M. T. Morgan, Sanders Elliott, Charles L. Loucks, J. T. Furnish, T. B. James.

POST-RECONSTRUCTION (*local elections held again*)
1873–1876 (*For unknown length of time*)
Chief Justice J. S. Morris; Associate Justices James Grimsley, James K. Allen, J. P. Lipscomb, C. W. Jones.

1876–1878
County Judge C. C. Cummings; Commissioners J. W. Chapman, J. S. W. Morrison, John Terrell, J. M. Young; County Attorney Sam Furman (first time the office was filled); County Clerk J. P. Woods; Sheriff John Henderson; District Clerk George Mulkey; Treasurer W. T. Ferguson; Assessor A. J. Chambers; Justices of the Peace A. G. McClung and George W. Jopling.

1878–1880
County Judge C. C. Cummings; Commissioners H. C. Johnson, William Harrison, J. B. Andrews and T. B. Maddox; County Clerk J. P. Woods; District Clerk J. M. Hartsfield; County Attorney W. S. Pendleton; Surveyor L. S. Leversedge; Assessor A. J. Chambers; Treasurer W. T. Ferguson; Sheriff J. M. Henderson, also tax collector.

249

1880–1882

County Judge R. E. Beckham; Commissioners John F. Zinn, William Harrison, J. B. Andrews and T. B. Maddox; Sheriff W. T. Maddox; County Clerk John F. Swayne; Treasurer W. T. Ferguson; District Clerk J. M. Hartsfield; Assessor W. D. Hall; Collector H. C. Johnson; County Attorney W. S. Pendleton; Surveyor W. G. Finley.

1882–1884

County Judge R. E. Beckham; Commissioners B. F. Latimer, L. H. Stephens, T. B. Maddox, John Terrell; County Clerk John F. Swayne; Sheriff W. T. Maddox; Tax Collector Frank Elliston; Treasurer J. B. Boyd; Assessor W. D. Hall; County Attorney W. S. Pendleton.

1884–1886

County Judge Sam Furman; Commissioners S. Terry, J. T. McKnight, T. B. Maddox, John Terrell; County Attorney N. R. Bowlin; County Clerk John F. Swayne; Sheriff W. T. Maddox; Assessor W. D. Hall; Collector Frank Elliston; Surveyor George M. Williams.

1886–1888

County Judge Sam Furman; Commissioners H. C. Holloway, J. T. Nichols, J. W. Higgins, J. T. Pulliam; County Attorney R. L. Carlock; County Clerk John F. Swayne; Sheriff B. H. Shipp; District Clerk L. R. Taylor; Treasurer W. E. Ferguson; Assessor J. W. Robinson; Collector J. E. Murrey; R. F. Moore named school superintendent May 9, 1887.

1888–1890

County Judge W. D. Harris; Commissioners J. J. Scott, M. R. Collins, J. W. Higgins, T. B. Maddox; County Clerk John P. King; Sheriff J. S. Richardson; Collector J. E. Murrey; School Superintendent W. H. Pool; Surveyor J. J. Goodfellow; Assessor Thomas Bratton.

1890–1892
County Judge W. D. Harris; Commissioners J. J. Scott, M. R. Collins, F. L. Wist, T. B. Maddox; County Attorney O. W. Gillespie; Collector J. B. Boyd; Sheriff J. C. Richardson; District Clerk L. R. Taylor; Surveyor J. J. Goodfellow; County Clerk John R. King; School Superintendent W. H. Pool; Treasurer J. B. Boyd; Assessor E. Harding.

1892–1894
County Judge R. G. Johnson; Commissioners H. C. Holloway, M. R. Collins, H. R. Wall, J. L. Mack. County Attorney O. W. Gillespie; Collector J. F. Hovenkamp; Superintendent R. H. Buck; Treasurer Thomas B. Collins; Assessor E. Harding; County Clerk John King; Sheriff E. A. Euless; District Clerk R. H. McNatt.

1894–1896
County Judge George W. Armstrong; Commissioners John Bardon, A. T. Lowe, J. W. Higgins, William M. Cross; County Attorney Burt M. Terrell; County Clerk John P. King; Sheriff E. A. Euless; Surveyor J. J. Goodfellow; Treasurer Thomas B. Collins; Collector J. F. Hovenkamp; Superintendent D. McRae; Assessor W. R. Rogers; District Clerk Robert H. McNatt.

1896–1898
County Judge George W. Armstrong; Commissioners C. G. Mitchell, A. S. Lowe, J. K. P. Hammond, W. S. Bourland; County Attorney James W. Swayne; County Clerk John P. King; Sheriff S. P. Clark; Assessor Ed Hovenkamp; Superintendent D. McRae; Treasurer J. M. Lyles; District Clerk R. H. McNatt; Surveyor John M. Blackburn.

1898–1900
County Judge M. B. Harris; Commissioners William Barr, S. W. Rudd, J. K. P. Hammond, W. S. Bourland; County Clerk W. E. Butler; Surveyor J. M. Blackburn; District Clerk W. D. McVean; Sheriff S. P. Clark.

1900–1902
County Judge M. B. Harris; Commissioners William Barr,
B. F. Ramsey, B. H. Starr, J. H. Hightower; County Attorney O. S.
Lattimore; County Clerk W. E. Butler; Sheriff S. P. Clark; Super-
intendent M. H. Moore; Assessor Ed Hovenkamp; Treasurer J. A.
Ball; Collector J. K. Winston.

1902–1904
County Judge R. F. Milam; Commissioners William Barr,
B. F. Ramsey, Edd Andrews, J. H. Hightower; County Attorney
O. S. Lattimore; County Clerk R. L. Rogers; District Clerk J. A.
Martin; Sheriff John T. Honea; Superintendent M. H. Moore;
Treasurer J. A. Ball; Collector John W. Walker; Surveyor J. J.
Goodfellow.

1904–1906
County Judge R. F. Milam; Commissioners W. Z. Castle-
berry, B. F. Ramsey, Edd Andrews, O. L. Sweet; County Attor-
ney Jeff D. McLean; Collector John W. Walker; Superintendent
George D. Ramsey; County Clerk R. L. Rogers; Assessor W. L.
Sweet; Surveyor J. J. Goodfellow; Sheriff John T. Honea.

1906–1908
County Judge J. L. Terrell; Commissioners D. H. Purvis, John
A. Hiett, T. P. Huffman, O. L. Sweet; County Clerk John A. Kee;
Sheriff T. J. Wood; Treasurer W. H. Hart; Collector R. M. Davis;
Assessor R. Lee Tillery; District Clerk John A. Martin; Superin-
tendent George D. Ramsey, resigned, and Lee M. Hammond.

1908–1910
County Judge John L. Terrell; Commissioners D. H. Purvis,
John A. Hiett, T. P. Huffman, W. O. Reves; County Attorney
R. E. L. Roy; Sheriff T. J. Wood; District Clerk E. J. Brock Jr.;
Treasurer J. P. Witcher; Superintendent Lee M. Hammond; As-
sessor R. L. Tillery; Surveyor H. M. Dickson.

1910–1912
County Judge R. E. Bratton; Commissioners R. E. Duringer,
J. H. Rodgers, Wallis Estill, W. O. Reves; County Attorney John

W. Baskin; County Clerk A. J. Beavers; District Clerk E. J. Brock Jr.; Assessor G. W. Bell; Sheriff W. M. Rea; Superintendent L. M. Hammond; Collector R. M. Davis.

1912–1914

County Judge Charles T. Prewett, civil; County Judge R. E. Bratton, criminal; Bratton resigned May 1, 1913, succeeded by Jesse Brown; Commissioners R. E. Duringer, J. H. Rodgers, Wallis Estill, W. O. Reves; Rodgers and Estill resigned May 3, 1913, succeeded by W. C. Weeks and H. R. Wall; County Attorney John W. Baskin; District Clerk E. J. Brock Jr.; County Clerk A. J. Beavers; Assessor George W. Bell; Treasurer W. E. Matthewson; Surveyor H. M. Dickson; Superintendent Sam J. Calloway; Sheriff W. M. Rea.

1914–1916

County Judge Jesse M. Brown; Commissioners R. E. Duringer, Olin W. Gibbins, H. R. Wall, Rufe Snow; County Attorney Marshall Spoonts; Collector W. E. Elliott; Sheriff N. C. Mann; Assessor G. W. Prichard; District Clerk J. M. Collins; County Clerk W. H. Logan; Superintendent G. T. Bludworth; Surveyor John H. Darter; Treasurer W. E. Matthewson.

1916–1918

County Judge Jesse Brown; Commissioners James A. Childers, Olin W. Gibbins, H. R. Wall, Rufe Snow; County Attorney Marshall Spoonts; Collector Marvin Scott; Assessor G. W. Prichard; Sheriff N. C. Mann; Superintendent G. T. Bludworth; County Clerk W. H. Logan, resigned Nov. 16, 1917, succeeded by Charles H. Rose.

1918–1920

County Judge Hugh L. Small; Commissioners James A. Childers, Olin W. Gibbins who died December, 1919, and was succeeded by Ed McRae, H. R. Wall who died same month and was succeeded by S. A. Wall, John W. Roberts; County Attorney Jesse M. Brown; County Clerk Bart Mynatt; Sheriff S. P. Clark; Surveyor John H. Darter; District Clerk Mrs. G. Frank Coffey; Treasurer Effie Redmond; Collector S. D. Shannon; Superintendent B. Carroll.

1920–1921

County Judge Hugh L. Small; Commissioners James A. Childers, who resigned October, 1921 and succeeded by W. A. Fitts, W. T. Hudson, Hugh Hightower, John W. Roberts; District Attorney (first time office filled) Jesse M. Brown; County Clerk Bart Mynatt; Sheriff Carl Smith; Treasurer W. T. Shaw; Superintendent B. Carroll; Collector Dean Bell; District Clerk Mrs. G. Frank Coffey; Assessor S. D. Shannon; Surveyor H. M. Dickson.

1922–1924

(County officials who previously served on fiscal year basis began taking office in January and serving two full calendar years.)

County Judge Emmett Moore; Commissioners H. E. Wright, W. T. Hudson, H. M. Hightower, H. E. Seyster; District Attorney R. K. Hanger; County Clerk Ed L. Sorrels; Sheriff Carl Smith; Assessor L. A. Freeman; Collector Dean Bell; Treasurer W. T. Shaw; District Clerk G. S. Williams; Superintendent B. Carroll.

1925–1926

County Judge Emmett Moore; Commissioners H. E. Wright, W. T. Hudson, S. A. Wall, H. E. Seyster; District Attorney R. K. Hanger; County Clerk Ed L. Sorrels; Collector John L. Pengilly; Treasurer John M. Moore; District Clerk G. S. Williams; Superintendent B. Carroll; Sheriff Carl Smith; Assessor L. A. Freeman; Surveyor Henry M. Dickson; First purchasing agent, W. E. Yancy, appointed Jan. 26, 1925.

1927–1928

County Judge S. D. Shannon; Commissioners H. E. Wright, J. F. Schooler, S. A. Wall, Dick Boaz; District Attorney Jesse E. Martin; County Clerk Chester Hollis; Sheriff Carl Smith; Superintendent John T. White; Assessor J. Lester Wright; District Clerk R. E. Neely; Collector John Pengilly; Treasurer John M. Moore.

1929–1930

County Judge S. D. Shannon; Commissioners H. E. Wright, Joe F. Schooler, S. A. Wall, Dick Boaz; District Attorney R. A. Stuart; County Clerk Chester Hollis; Collector L. P. Card; Superintendent John T. White; Assessor J. Lester Wright; Sheriff J. R. Wright; District Clerk R. E. Neely; Surveyor John Lipscomb; Treasurer John M. Moore.

1931–1932
County Judge C. W. Atkinson; Commissioners H. E. Wright, Joe F. Schooler, Frank T. Estill, W. W. Merrett; District Attorney Jesse E. Martin; County Clerk Orville Beall; Sheriff J. R. Wright; District Clerk W. E. Alexander; Assessor J. Lester Wright; Collector L. P. Card; Surveyor John Lipscomb; Treasurer John M. Moore; Superintendent John T. White.

1933–1934
County Judge Emmett Moore; Commissioners J. M. Mitchell, C. V. Fox, J. A. Davis who died April 13, 1933, and was succeeded by S. A. Wall, J. I. Short; District Attorney Jesse E. Martin; County Clerk W. W. Miller; Sheriff J. R. Wright; Collector John Bourland; District Clerk W. E. Alexander; Assessor J. R. Williams; Surveyor H. M. Dickson; Treasurer John M. Moore.

1935–1936
County Judge Emmett Moore; Commissioners J. M. Mitchell, Joe C. Thannisch, Frank T. Estill, W. W. Merrett; District Attorney Will R. Parker; Superintendent A. D. Roach; Treasurer Mrs. Johnnie Mitt House; District Clerk W. E. Alexander; Assessor-Collector John Bourland; County Clerk J. W. Shelton; Sheriff Carl Smith; Surveyor John H. Darter.

1937–1938
County Judge Dave Miller; Commissioners Joe C. Thannisch, Frank T. Estill, W. W. Merrett; District Attorney Will R. Parker; County Clerk Mrs. Happy Shelton; Surveyor John H. Darter; District Clerk W. E. Alexander; Treasurer Mrs. Johnnie Mitt House; Sheriff A. B. Carter; Assessor-Collector John Bourland.

1939–1940
County Judge Dave Miller; Commissioners James M. Scott, Joe C. Thannisch, H. M. Hightower, Frank Winters; District Attorney Marvin H. Brown Jr.; County Clerk Mrs. Happy Shelton;

District Clerk W. E. Alexander; Treasurer Mrs. Johnnie Mitt House; Surveyor John H. Darter; Sheriff A. B. Carter; Assessor-Collector John Bourland; Superintendent A. D. Roach.

1941–1942

County Judge Dave Miller; Commissioners J. M. Scott, Joe C. Thannisch, H. M. Hightower, Frank Winters; District Attorney Marvin H. Brown Jr.; County Clerk Mrs. Happy Shelton Wood; District Clerk W. E. Alexander; Assessor-Collector John Bourland; Superintendent A. D. Roach; Sheriff A. B. Carter; Surveyor H. M. Dickson; Treasurer Lelia Mae Smith.

1943–1944

County Judge Clarence O. Kraft; Commissioners J. M. Scott, Joe C. Thannisch, Jess Holder, Frank Winters; District Attorney Marvin H. Brown Jr.; County Clerk Mel Faulk; Superintendent A. D. Roach; Sheriff Dusty Rhodes; District Clerk W. E. Alexander; Assessor-Collector John Bourland; Treasurer Lelia Mae Smith.

1945–1946

County Judge Clarence O. Kraft; Commissioners Ed Ailes, Joe C. Thannisch, Jess Holder, Frank Winters; District Attorney Al Clyde; County Clerk Mel Faulk; District Clerk W. E. Alexander; Assessor-Collector John Bourland; Superintendent A. D. Roach; Sheriff Dusty Rhodes; Surveyor H. M. Dickson; Treasurer W. S. Tannahill.

1947–1948

County Judge Clarence O. Kraft; Commissioners Ed Ailes, W. W. O'Farrell, Jess Holder, Hap Hovenkamp; District Attorney Al Clyde; County Clerk Mel Faulk; District Clerk Lewis D. Wall Jr.; Assessor-Collector John Bourland; Superintendent O. H. Stowe; Sheriff Sully Montgomery; Surveyor Jack R. Williams; Treasurer W. B. Gurley.

1949–1950

County Judge Gus Brown; Commissioners Bryan Henderson, W. W. O'Farrell, James Owens, Hap Hovenkamp; County Clerk

Mel Faulk; District Clerk Lewis D. Wall Jr.; Assessor-Collector Reed Stewart; Superintendent O. H. Stowe; Sheriff Sully Montgomery; Surveyor Louis M. Hawkins; Treasurer W. B. Gurley; District Attorney Stewart Hellman.

1951–1952

County Judge Gus Brown; Commissioners Bryan Henderson, C. H. Wright, James Owens, and Hap Hovenkamp, who resigned September, 1952, and was succeeded by Rosco Minton; County Clerk Mel Faulk; Assessor-Collector Reed Stewart; School Superintendent O. H. Stowe; Sheriff Sully Montgomery, who resigned September, 1952, and was succeeded by Harlon Wright; Surveyor Louis M. Hawkins; Treasurer W. B. Gurley; District Attorney Stewart Hellman; District Clerk Mrs. Lewis D. Wall, Jr.

1953–

County Judge Brown; Commissioners Henderson, Wright, Owens and Minton; County Clerk Faulk; Assessor-Collector Stewart; Superintendent Stowe; Sheriff Harlon Wright; Surveyor Henry M. Dickson; and District Attorney Howard M. Fender; District Clerk Mrs. Lewis D. Wall, Jr.

Congressmen
Since 1849

These are the gentlemen who since 1849 have represented Tarrant County in the House of Representatives, United States Congress. Their homes sometimes were far removed from Fort Worth because in the earlier years great slices of Texas comprised Congressional districts.

1848 APPORTIONMENT—DISTRICT 2.
31st Congress (1849–51): Volney E. Howard, San Antonio
32nd Congress (1851–53): Volney E. Howard, San Antonio
33rd Congress (1853–55): Peter H. Bell, Austin
34th Congress (1855–57): Peter H. Bell, Austin
35th Congress (1857–59): Guy M. Bryan, Brazoria
36th Congress (1859–61): Andrew J. Hamilton, Austin
37th Congress (1861–63): No Representatives
38th Congress (1863–65): No Representatives
39th Congress (1865–67): No Representatives
40th Congress (1867–69): No Representatives

1869 APPORTIONMENT—DISTRICT 2.
41st Congress (1869–71): John C. Conner, Sherman
42nd Congress (1871–73): John C. Conner, Sherman
43rd Congress (1873–75): William P. McLean, Mount Pleasant

1874 APPORTIONMENT—DISTRICT 3.
44th Congress (1875–77): James W. Throckmorton, McKinney
45th Congress (1877–79): James W. Throckmorton, McKinney
46th Congress (1879–1881): Olin Wellborn, Dallas
47th Congress (1881–83): Olin Wellborn, Dallas

1882 APPORTIONMENT—DISTRICT 6.
48th Congress (1883–85): Olin Wellborn, Dallas
49th Congress (1885–87): Olin Wellborn, Dallas
50th Congress (1887–89): Jo Abbott, Hillsboro
51st Congress (1889–91): Jo Abbott, Hillsboro
52nd Congress (1891–93): Jo Abbott, Hillsboro

1892 APPORTIONMENT—DISTRICT 8.
53rd Congress (1893–95): Charles K. Bell, Fort Worth.
54th Congress (1895–97): Charles K. Bell, Fort Worth
55th Congress (1897–99): Samuel W. T. Lanham, Weatherford
56th Congress (1899–1901): Samuel W. T. Lanham, Weatherford
57th Congress (1901–1903): Samuel W. T. Lanham, Weatherford
(Resigned January 15, 1903, having been elected governor.)

1901 APPORTIONMENT—DISTRICT 12.
58th Congress (1903–05): Oscar W. Gillespie, Fort Worth
59th Congress (1905–07): Oscar W. Gillespie, Fort Worth
60th Congress (1907–09): Oscar W. Gillespie, Fort Worth
61st Congress (1909–11): Oscar W. Gillespie, Fort Worth
62nd Congress (1911–13): Oscar Callaway, Comanche
63rd Congress (1913–15): Oscar Callaway, Comanche
64th Congress (1915–17): Oscar Callaway, Comanche
65th Congress (1917–19): James C. Wilson, Fort Worth

1917 APPORTIONMENT—DISTRICT 12.
66th Congress (1919–21): James C. Wilson, Fort Worth
Resigned before Congress assembled (March 13, 1919.)
Fritz G. Lanham elected to fill vacancy, took seat May 19, 1919.
67th Congress (1921–23): Fritz G. Lanham, Fort Worth
68th Congress (1923–25): Fritz G. Lanham, Fort Worth
69th Congress (1925–27): Fritz G. Lanham, Fort Worth
70th Congress (1927–29): Fritz G. Lanham, Fort Worth
71st Congress (1929–31): Fritz G. Lanham, Fort Worth
72nd Congress (1931–33): Fritz G. Lanham, Fort Worth
73rd Congress (1933–35): Fritz G. Lanham, Fort Worth

1933 APPORTIONMENT—DISTRICT 12.
74th Congress (1935–37): Fritz G. Lanham, Fort Worth
75th Congress (1937–39): Fritz G. Lanham, Fort Worth
76th Congress (1939–41): Fritz G. Lanham, Fort Worth
77th Congress (1941–43): Fritz G. Lanham, Fort Worth
78th Congress (1943–45): Fritz G. Lanham, Fort Worth
79th Congress (1945–47): Fritz G. Lanham, Fort Worth
80th Congress (1947–49): Wingate Lucas, Grapevine
81st Congress (1949–51): Wingate Lucas, Grapevine

State Legislators

Since 1853

Although Tarrant County was created in 1849, no state legislators from the county are shown on the Legislature's rosters until 1853. Since that time the county has been represented by these gentlemen:

Fifth Legislature, Nov. 7, 1853 to Feb. 13, 1854: Sen. Weatherford Jefferson, Dallas County. Rep. L. J. Wilson, Birdville, for Tarrant and Ellis counties.

Sixth Legislature, Nov. 5, 1855 to Feb. 4, 1856 and July 7 to Sept. 1, 1856: Sen. Weatherford Jefferson. Rep. Isaac Parker for Tarrant and Ellis counties.

Seventh Legislature, Nov. 2, 1857 to Feb. 16, 1858: Sen. A. G. Walker, Birdville. Rep. W. R. Shannon, Buchanan, for Tarrant, Ellis, and Johnson counties.

Eighth Legislature, Nov. 7, 1859 to Feb. 13, 1860; Jan. 21 to Feb. 9, 1861; Mar. 18 to Apr. 9, 1861: Sen. Walker, Rep. Shannon.

Ninth Legislature, Nov. 4, 1861 to Jan. 14, 1862; Feb. 2 to Mar. 6, 1863: Sen. A. T. Obenchain, Weatherford; resigned, succeeded by W. Quayle. Rep. R. M. Gano, Grapevine; resigned, succeeded by J. P. Alford, Fort Worth, for Tarrant County.

Tenth Legislature, Nov. 2 to Dec. 16, 1863; May 9–28, 1864; Oct. 17 to Nov. 15, 1864: Sen. W. Quayle, Morton's Grove. Rep. J. H. Allen, Fort Worth.

Eleventh Legislature, Aug. 6 to Nov. 13, 1866: Sen. W. R. Shannon, Buchanan. Rep. Samuel Evans, Fort Worth.

Twelfth Legislature, Feb. 8–24, 1870; Apr. 26 to Aug. 15, 1870; Jan. 10 to May 31, 1871; Sept. 12 to Dec. 2, 1871: Sen. Samuel Evans, Fort Worth. Reps. J. W. Lane, Dallas, A. F. Leonard, Fort Worth, and B. S. Shelburne, Lebanon, for Tarrant, Dallas, and Collin counties.

Thirteenth Legislature, Jan. 14 to June 4, 1873: Sen. Samuel Evans, Fort Worth. Reps. K. M. Van Zandt, Fort Worth, Edward Chambers, McKinney, and J. H. Brown, Dallas, for Tarrant, Dallas and Collin counties.

Fourteenth Legislature, Jan. 13 to May 4, 1874; Jan. 12 to Mar. 15, 1875: Sen. Amzi Bradshaw, Waxahachie. Reps. A. K. Middleton, Fort Worth, John H. Cochran, Dallas, J. W. Kemble, Waxahachie, for Tarrant, Ellis and Dallas counties.

Fifteenth Legislature, Apr. 18 to Aug. 21, 1876: Sen. Thomas Ball, Jacksboro. Rep. N. H. Darnell, Fort Worth, for Tarrant.

Sixteenth Legislature, Jan. 14 to Apr. 24, 1879; June 10 to July 9, 1879: Sen. W. R. Shannon, Weatherford. Rep. W. R. Gause, Fort Worth.

Seventeenth Legislature, Jan. 11 to Apr. 1, 1881; Apr. 6 to Mar. 5, 1882: Sen. W. R. Shannon, Weatherford, Rep. B. B. Paddock, Fort Worth.

Eighteenth Legislature, Jan. 9 to Apr. 13, 1883; Jan. 8 to Feb. 6, 1884: Sen. W. R. Shannon, Weatherford. Rep. A. J. Chambers, Fort Worth, for Tarrant. Rep. J. D. Parsons, Rockwall, for Tarrant, Dallas, and Rockwall counties.

Nineteenth Legislature, Jan. 13 to Mar. 31, 1885: Sen. W. R. Shannon, Weatherford. Rep. W. S. Pendleton, Fort Worth, for Tarrant. Rep. M. S. Austin, Rockwall, for Tarrant, Dallas, and Rockwall counties.

Twentieth Legislature, Jan. 11 to Apr. 4, 1887; April 16 to May 15, 1888: Sen. James J. Jarvis, Fort Worth. Rep. E. Newton, Bransford, for Tarrant. Rep. E. C. Heath, Rockwall, for Tarrant, Dallas, and Rockwall counties.

Twenty-first Legislature, Jan. 8 to Apr. 6, 1889: Sen. James J. Jarvis, Fort Worth. Rep. Isaac Duke Parker, Birdville, for Tarrant.

Rep. J. W. Crayton, Fate, for Tarrant, Dallas, and Rockwall counties.

Twenty-second Legislature, Jan. 13 to Apr. 13, 1891; Mar. 14 to Apr. 12, 1892: Sen. A. M. Carter, Fort Worth. Rep. J. W. Swayne, Fort Worth, for Tarrant. Rep. J. W. Crayton (resigned, succeeded by W. L. Crawford, Dallas) for Tarrant, Dallas, and Rockwall counties.

Twenty-third Legislature, Jan. 10 to May 9, 1893: Sen. J. W. Savage, Fort Worth. Reps. T. B. Maddox, Fort Worth, and E. Newton, Bransford, for Tarrant. Rep. B. Wohlford, Acton, for Tarrant, Parker, and Hood counties.

Twenty-fourth Legislature, Jan. 8 to Apr. 30, 1895; Oct. 1–7, 1895: Sen. W. J. Bailey, Fort Worth. Reps. T. T. D. Andrews, Fort Worth, and R. E. L. Roy, Arlington, for Tarrant. Rep. B. W. Morris, Granbury, for Tarrant, Parker, and Hood counties.

Twenty-fifth Legislature, Jan. 12 to May 21, 1897; May 22 to June 20, 1897: Sen. W. J. Bailey, Fort Worth. Reps. B. P. Ayres, Fort Worth, and F. R. Wallace, Johnson Station, for Tarrant. Rep. W. L. McGaughey, Tolar, for Tarrant, Parker, and Hood counties.

Twenty-sixth Legislature, Jan. 10 to May 27, 1899; Jan. 23 to Feb. 21, 1900: Sen. W. A. Hanger, Fort Worth. Reps. B. P. Ayres, Fort Worth, and Clarence E. Stewart, Grapevine, for Tarrant. Rep. A. P. Gordon, Granbury, for Tarrant, Parker, and Hood counties.

Twenty-seventh Legislature, Jan. 8 to Apr. 9, 1901; Aug. 6 to Sept. 4, 1901; Sept. 5 to Oct. 1, 1901: Sen. W. A. Hanger, Fort Worth. Reps. J. Y. Hogsett, Fort Worth, and Clarence E. Stewart, Grapevine, for Tarrant. Rep. R. D. Mugg, Neri (Parker County), for Tarrant, Parker, and Hood counties.

Twenty-eighth Legislature, Jan. 13 to Apr. 1, 1903; Apr. 2 to May 1, 1903: Sen. W. A. Hanger, Fort Worth. Reps. William D. Williams, Fort Worth, and Clarence E. Stewart, Grapevine, for Tarrant. Rep. Less L. Hudson, Fort Worth, for Tarrant, Denton, Wise, and Cooke counties. Frank Mullins, Tarrant County, senate doorkeeper.

Twenty-ninth Legislature, Jan. 10 to Apr. 15, 1905; Apr. 15 to May 14, 1905; Mar. 26 to Apr. 3, 1906: Sen. W. A. Hanger, Fort Worth. Reps. W. B. Fitzhugh, Arlington, and William D. Williams, Fort Worth, for Tarrant. Rep. Charles Soward, Decatur, for Tarrant, Denton, Wise, and Cooke counties. Frank Mullins, Tarrant County, senate doorkeeper.

Thirtieth Legislature, Jan. 8 to Apr. 12, 1907; Apr. 12 to May 11, 1907: Sen. D. M. Alexander, Weatherford. Reps. A. J. Baskin and W. P. Lane, Fort Worth, for Tarrant. Rep. W. H. O'Beirne, Gainesville, for Tarrant, Denton, Wise, and Cooke counties.

Thirty-first Legislature, Jan. 12 to May 11, 1909; July 19 to Sept. 10, 1910: Sen. D. M. Alexander, Weatherford. Reps. W. B. Fitzhugh, Arlington, and Louis J. Wortham, Fort Worth, for Tarrant. Rep. F. F. Hill, Aubrey (Denton County), for Tarrant, Denton, Wise, and Cooke counties.

Thirty-second Legislature, Jan. 10 to Mar. 11, 1911; July 31 to Aug. 28, 1911: Sen. O. S. Lattimore, Fort Worth. Reps. Marvin H. Brown and Louis J. Wortham, Fort Worth, for Tarrant. Rep. A. W. Walker, Fort Worth, for Tarrant, Denton, Wise, and Cooke counties. J. C. Stanberry, Tarrant County, senate calendar clerk.

Thirty-third Legislature, Jan. 14 to Apr. 1, 1913; July 21 to Aug. 19, 1913; Aug. 24 to Oct. 22, 1914: Sen. O. S. Lattimore. Reps. H. P. Lane, B. B. Paddock and Louis J. Wortham, Fort Worth, for Tarrant. Rep. Sam T. Hunter, Fort Worth, for Tarrant and Denton counties. J. C. Stanberry, Tarrant County, senate calendar clerk.

Thirty-fourth Legislature, Jan. 12 to Mar. 20, 1915; Apr. 29 to May 28, 1915: Sen. O. S. Lattimore, Fort Worth. Reps. Charles A. Burton, H. P. Lane and Louis J. Wortham, Fort Worth, for Tarrant. Rep. I. T. Valentine, Fort Worth, for Tarrant and Denton counties.

Thirty-fifth Legislature, Jan. 9 to Mar. 20, 1917; Apr. 18 to May 17, 1917; Aug. 1 to Sept. 29, 1917; Feb. 26 to Mar. 27, 1918: Sen. O. S. Lattimore, Fort Worth. Reps. Charles A. Burton, R. L. Carlock, Fort Worth, and C. E. Walker, Grapevine, for Tarrant. Rep. I. T. Valentine, Fort Worth, for Tarrant and Denton counties.

Thirty-sixth Legislature, Jan. 12 to Mar. 19, 1919; May 5–9, 1919; June 23 to July 22, 1919; May 20 to June 18, 1920; Sept. 21 to Oct. 2, 1920: Sen. R. L. Carlock, Fort Worth. Reps. Ben F. Dwiggins (died, succeeded by G. T. Bludworth), Wallace Malone, and A. B. Curtis, Fort Worth, for Tarrant. Rep. Marvin H. Brown, Fort Worth, for Tarrant and Denton counties.

Thirty-seventh Legislature, Jan. 11 to Mar. 12, 1921; July 18 to Aug. 25, 1921; Sen. R. L. Carlock, Fort Worth. Reps. O. L. Sweet, Wallace Malone, and A. B. Curtis, Fort Worth, for Tarrant. Rep. John M. Adams, Fort Worth, for Tarrant and Denton counties.

Thirty-eighth Legislature, Jan. 19 to June 14, 1923: Sen. Robert A. Stuart, Fort Worth. Reps. George C. Kemble, Frank B. Potter, O. L. Sweet, Fort Worth, and H. S. McNatt, Arlington, for Tarrant. Rep. John M. Adams, Fort Worth, for Tarrant and Denton counties.

Thirty-ninth Legislature, Jan. 13 to Mar. 19, 1925; Sept. 13 to Oct. 8, 1926: Sen. Robert A. Stuart. Reps. Harry C. Jordan, George C. Kemble, Charles T. Rowland, Fort Worth, and H. S. McNatt, Arlington, for Tarrant. Rep. G. R. Lipscomb, Fort Worth, for Tarrant and Denton counties.

Fortieth Legislature, Jan. 11 to Mar. 6, 1927; May 9 to June 7, 1927: Sen. Robert A. Stuart, Fort Worth. Reps. Walter H. Beck, J. C. Duvall, A. E. Harding, and George C. Kemble, Fort Worth, for Tarrant. Rep. G. R. Lipscomb, Fort Worth, for Tarrant and Denton counties.

Forty-first Legislature, Jan. 8 to Mar. 14, 1929; Apr. 22 to May 21, 1929; June 3 to July 29, 1929; Jan. 20 to Mar. 20, 1930: Sen. Robert A. Stuart (resigned, succeeded by Julian C. Hyer, Fort Worth). Reps. Walter H. Beck, J. C. Duvall, A. E. Harding, and George C. Kemble, Fort Worth, for Tarrant. Rep. Frank Patterson Jr., Fort Worth, for Tarrant and Denton counties.

Forty-second Legislature, Jan. 13 to May 23, 1931; July 14 to Aug. 12, 1931; Sept. 8 to Oct. 3, 1931; Aug. 30 to Sept. 21, 1932; Nov. 3 to Nov. 12, 1932: Sen. Frank H. Rawlings, Fort Worth. Reps. Walter H. Beck, J. C. Duvall, Clarence E. Farmer, J. Greathouse, Fort Worth, for Tarrant. Rep. Frank Patterson Jr., for Tarrant and Denton counties.

Forty-third Legislature, Jan. 10 to June 1, 1933; Sept. 14 to Oct. 13, 1933; Jan. 29 to Feb. 27, 1934; Aug. 27 to Sept. 25, 1934; Oct. 12 to Nov. 12, 1934: Sen. Frank H. Rawlings, Fort Worth. Reps. J. C. Duvall, J. F. Greathouse, Thomas J. Renfro and S. D. Shannon, Fort Worth, for Tarrant. Rep. Frank Patterson Jr., Fort Worth, for Tarrant and Denton counties.

Forty-fourth Legislature, Jan. 8 to Apr. 15, 1935; Sept. 16 to Nov. 14, 1935: Sen. Frank H. Rawlings, Fort Worth. Reps. J. C. Duvall, Clarence E. Farmer, J. F. Greathouse and J. W. Youngblood, Fort Worth, for Tarrant. Rep. Lonnie Smith, Fort Worth, for Tarrant and Denton counties.

Forty-fifth Legislature, Jan. 12 to May 22, 1937; May 27 to June 25, 1937; Sept. 27 to Oct. 26, 1937: Sen. Frank H. Rawlings, Fort Worth. Reps. Alvin E. Amos, Clarence E. Farmer, H. A. Hull, and B. T. Johnson, Fort Worth, for Tarrant. Rep. Lonnie Smith, Fort Worth, for Tarrant and Denton counties.

Forty-sixth Legislature, Jan. 10 to June 21, 1939: Sen. Jesse E. Martin, Fort Worth. Reps. Ed Bradford, H. A. Hull, B. T. Johnson, and Obel L. McAlister, Fort Worth, for Tarrant. Rep. W. N. Corry, Keller, for Tarrant and Denton counties.

Forty-seventh Legislature, 1941: Sen. Jesse E. Martin, Fort Worth. Reps. Obel McAlister, Jack Love, Lester Boone, and Marvin Simpson Jr., Fort Worth, for Tarrant. Rep. Virgil Goodman, Fort Worth, for Tarrant and Denton counties.

Forty-eighth Legislature, 1943: Sen. Jesse E. Martin, Fort Worth. Reps. H. A. Hull, Obel McAlister, Jack Love, and Marvin Simpson Jr., Fort Worth, for Tarrant. Rep. Virgil Goodman, Fort Worth, for Tarrant and Denton counties.

Forty-ninth Legislature, 1945: Sen. Jesse Martin. Reps. H. A. Hull, Obel McAlister, Jack Love, and Marvin Simpson Jr., Fort Worth, for Tarrant. Rep. A. B. Smith, Fort Worth, for Tarrant and Denton counties.

Fiftieth Legislature, 1947: Sen. Keith Kelly. Reps. Joe Pyle, Bill Abington, Doyle Willis, and John Wallace, Fort Worth, for

Tarrant. Rep. W. C. Cowan, Fort Worth, for Tarrant and Denton counties.

Fifty-first Legislature, 1949: Sen. Keith Kelly. Reps. H. A. Hull, Joe Pyle, Bill Abington, and Doyle Willis, Fort Worth, for Tarrant. Rep. Joe Shannon, Fort Worth, for Tarrant and Denton counties.

Fifty-second Legislature, 1951; Sen. Keith Kelly; Reps. Pyle, Abington, Hull, Willis, and Shannon.

Fifty-third Legislature, 1953: Sen. Doyle Willis; Reps. Pyle, Abington, Hull, Scot Sayres, Don Kannard, Gene Smith, and Warren Cowan.

City Officials
Since 1873

These are the gentlemen who have served Fort Worth as mayors, councilmen, commissioners, and aldermen since the city was incorporated in 1873:

1873
Mayor W. P. Burts. Councilmen M. B. Loyd, M. D. McCall, A. Blakeney, W. J. Boaz, J. P. Alexander.

1874
Mayor Burts. Aldermen R. H. King, A. B. Frazier, W. H. Overton, W. H. Williams, Joseph Kane. Burts resigned and G. H. Day was elected mayor Nov. 9, 1874.

1875
Mayor Day. Aldermen J. J. Jarvis, P. J. Bowdry, W. T. Maddox, I. Dahlman, D. R. Crawford.

1876
Mayor Day. Aldermen D. W. C. Pendery, W. A. Huffman, C. B. Daggett Jr., P. J. Bowdry and John Nichols.

1877
Mayor Day. Aldermen Nichols, Pendery, B. C. Evans, C. M. Peak, J. M. Davis, W. J. Allen.

1878
Mayor R. E. Beckham. Aldermen George Jackson, S. H. Holmes, Thomas Aston, Evans, Allen and Nichols.

1879
Mayor Beckham. Aldermen S. Terry, R. M. Hatcher, E. W. Morton, Jackson, Holmes, Aston.

1880

Mayor John T. Brown. Aldermen Isaac W. Rouse, E. M. Orrick, W. A. Darter, C. L. Pigman, John A. Thornton, S. Terry.

1881

Mayor Brown. Aldermen Jesse Jones, H. P. Shiel, H. B. Pitts, L. A. Trimble, Rouse and Orrick.

1882

Mayor J. P. Smith. Aldermen Max Elser, H. S. Broiles, Sam Seaton, J. T. Hickey, Jones, N. C. Brooks. Broiles resigned and W. R. Haymaker succeeded him Aug. 30, 1882.

1883

Mayor Smith. Aldermen T. T. D. Andrews, J. R. Adams, J. B. Askew, J. T. Hickey, Haymaker, and Elser. With increase from three to four wards, W. H. Aldridge and Richard Flanigan were elected aldermen Aug. 14, 1883.

1884

Mayor Smith. Aldermen J. P. Alexander, Julian Feild, Aldridge, John P. Hughes, Flannigan, Askew, Adams, Andrews.

1885

Mayor Smith. Aldermen George Mulkey, W. A. Darter, John Brownson, C. B. Daggett Jr., Alexander, Feild, Aldridge, Hughes. Feild resigned and W. R. Haymaker was elected Nov. 17, 1885. Aldridge resigned, C. N. Ferguson was elected Dec. 29, 1885.

1886

Mayor H. S. Broiles. Aldermen George W. Hill, Haymaker, J. L. Cooper, F. J. Tatum, Brownson, Darter, Mulkey, Daggett.

1887

Mayor Broiles. Aldermen J. L. Ward, Darter, E. B. Daggett, John G. Reilly, Hill, Haymaker, Cooper, Tatum.

1888

Mayor Broiles. Aldermen S. M. Fry, Haymaker, J. P. Nicks, William Jackson, W. W. Trippett, Tatum, William Barr, George Neis, George Mulkey, Ward, Reilly.

1889
Mayor Broiles. Aldermen Jesse Jones, Nicks, Daggett, W. J. Bailey, Trippett, T. B. Smith, A. B. Fraser, J. T. Clements, Fry, Jackson, Neis, Haymaker.

1890
Mayor W. S. Pendleton. Aldermen James Ryan, T. P. Martin, Jackson, G. H. Day, Neis, Clements, Jones, Fraser, Nicks, Smith, Bailey, W. L. Rail.

Mayor Pendleton resigned, J. P. Smith elected Aug. 4, 1890. S. M. Furman replaced Bailey as alderman. George W. Armstrong and Arnold Gertler elected aldermen July 22, 1890, when seventh ward created.

1891
Mayor Smith. Aldermen Jones, W. A. Darter, John F. White, John T. Montgomery, C. T. Matkin, C. C. Drake, J. H. Tiller, Ryan, Martin, Jackson, Day, Neis, Clements, Armstrong.

Aldermen H. R. Early, J. J. Massie, S. O. Moodie, R. H. Orr elected July 14, 1891, when two new wards created.

1892
Mayor B. B. Paddock. Aldermen W. H. Ward, J. P. Nicks, N. LaCroix, Day, Neis, W. B. Tucker, M. J. Lewis, M. C. Bowles, J. C. Terrell, W. K. Byrom, Jones, Drake, White, Darter, Montgomery, Tiller, Early, Orr.

1893
Mayor Paddock, Aldermen F. W. Chiles, H. Tully, B. F. Wallis, Montgomery, William Barr, Drake, Tiller, M. A. Spoonts, Fry, Nicks, Terrell, Byrom, Ward, Lewis, Day, Neis, Bowles, LaCroix.

1894
Mayor Paddock, Aldermen Ward, K. M. Van Zandt, Martin McGrath, I. N. McCullouch, W. S. Essex, Clements, W. E. Williams, J. B. Roberts, W. S. Head, Fry, Tiller, Barr, Spoonts, Tully, N. H. Lassiter, B. F. Wallis, C. C. Drake.

1895
Mayor Paddock. Aldermen W. H. Fisher, C. W. Hudgins, LaCroix, H. Canto, Lassiter, Barr, George Mulkey, Tiller, Spoonts,

Fry, Ward, Van Zandt, McCullouch, Essex, Clements, Williams, Roberts, Head.

1896

Mayor Paddock. Aldermen Ward, Van Zandt, J. F. Moore, W. W. Trippett, Essex, Clements, J. F. Henderson, R. H. Orr, A. M. Scott, F. S. Boulmare, Mulkey, Spoonts, LaCroix, Lassiter, Barr, Tiller, Fisher, Hudgins. Barr and Van Zandt resigned, succeeded Nov. 5, 1896, by R. H. Tucker and J. P. Nicks, Hudgins resigned, succeeded Nov. 17, 1896, by B. L. Waggoman.

1897

Mayor Paddock. Aldermen W. H. Ward, J. P. Nicks, J. F. Moore, W. W. Trippett, W. S. Essex, J. T. Clements, J. F. Henderson, R. H. Orr, A. M. Scott.

1898–1900

Mayor Paddock. Aldermen Ward, Nicks, Moore, W. F. Stewart, R. H. Tucker, T. N. Edgell, Henderson, M. A. Spoonts, Scott. Nicks died, T. J. Powell elected April 21, 1899.

1900–1902

Mayor T. J. Powell. Aldermen W. H. Ward, B. L. Waggoman, T. F. Murray, J. F. Lehane, R. H. Tucker, W. G. Newby, J. F. Henderson, E. C. Orrick, H. T. Moreland.

1902–1904

Mayor Powell. Aldermen Ward, Waggoman, Murray, Lehane, M. M. Lydon, Newby, Henderson, Orrick, Moreland.

1904–1906

Mayor Powell. Aldermen Ward, Waggoman, W. R. Parker, Lehane, Lydon, Newby, Henderson, J. F. Zurn, Moreland, Newby resigned, E. P. Maddox elected May 17, 1905.

1906–1907

Mayor W. D. Harris. Aldermen Ward, Waggoman, R. F. Cook, Lehane, Lydon, Maddox, R. L. Armstrong, Zurn, E. G. Harrold.

1907–1909

Mayor Harris. Commissioners George Mulkey, G. H. Colvin,

Sam Davidson, Lee Stephens. John F. Grant became special commissioner March 15, 1909, to represent recently annexed North Fort Worth.

1909–1911
Mayor W. D. Williams. Commissioners Mulkey, W. J. Gilvin, J. H. Maddox, Thomas J. Powell, Grant. Mayor Williams resigned April 27, 1909, to take a seat on the Railroad Commission and W. D. Davis was elected May 29, 1909.

1911–1913
Mayor Davis. Commissioners Allen, Gilvin, Maddox, Powell, Grant.

1913–1915
Mayor R. F. Milam. Commissioners Allen, W. H. Smith, R. M. Davis, L. H. Blanke, Grant.

1915–1917
Mayor E. T. Tyra. Commissioners M. W. Hurdleston, Smith, R. G. Littlejohn, Blanke, C. F. Crabtree. Blanke resigned, Hugh Jamieson elected Oct. 6, 1915.

1917–1919
Mayor W. D. Davis. Commissioners Ed Parsley, E. C. Manning, Charles D. Wiggins, J. C. Lord, Selwyn Smith. Police Commissioner Parsley was killed in September 1917 and O. R. Montgomery elected Oct. 12, 1917.

1919–1921
Mayor Davis. Commissioners Montgomery, Manning, C. D. Wiggins, Lord, Smith.

1921–1923
Mayor E. R. Cockrell. Commissioners John Alderman, W. B. Townsend, Paul Gilvin, Lord, R. A. Hunter.

1923–1925
Mayor Cockrell. Commissioners Alderman, Townsend, Gilvin, Lord, Hunter. Townsend died, Chester L. Jones elected Oct. 23, 1923. Mayor Cockrell resigned Oct. 8, 1924, to become president of William Woods College, Fulton, Mo., and Willard Burton was appointed mayor.

1925–1927
Councilmen H. C. Meacham (mayor), Willard Burton, T. B. Hoffer, A. E. Thomas, William Bryce, E. T. Renfro, William Monnig, W. E. Austin, L. P. Card.

1927–1929
Councilmen Bryce (mayor), Burton, Hoffer, Thomas, Renfro, Monnig, Austin, Van Zandt Jarvis, J. N. Sparks.

1929–1931
Councilmen Bryce (mayor), Burton, Sparks, Dr. W. R. Thompson, Renfro, Thomas, Monnig, J. R. Penn, Jarvis. Sparks resigned, J. B. Davis elected.

1931–1933
Councilmen Bryce (mayor), Burton, Davis, Thompson, Renfro, Thomas, Monnig, Penn, Jarvis. Thomas resigned, S. J. Callaway elected.

1933–1935
Councilmen Bryce (mayor), Burton, Davis, Thompson, Callaway, Jerome C. Martin, Monnig, Penn, Jarvis. Bryce resigned Dec. 13, 1933, Jarvis elected mayor and T. J. Harrell elected to council.

1935–1937
Councilmen Arthur Brown (mayor), Burton, W. J. Hammond, Thompson, Roy C. Murphy, Harrell, Martin, Monnig, Jarvis. Martin resigned, W. T. Ladd appointed June 17, 1936.

1937–1938
Councilmen Hammond (mayor), J. P. Elder, Herbert L. Hull, E. S. Hooper, Harrell, Jerome C. Martin, D. M. Rumph, George A. Seaman, George B. Eagle.

Harrell resigned Sept. 9, 1937, John W. Oglesby appointed Feb. 17, 1938. Rumph resigned Dec. 15, 1937, Orville E. Tunstill appointed April 13, 1938. Elder resigned, succeeded by R. H. W. Drechsel March 9, 1938. Eagle resigned, succeeded by A. B. Smith March 30, 1938.

Hammond resigned as mayor but remained on council, Drechsel elected Mayor May 11, 1938. Hammond resigned from council, Jack Carter appointed July 6, 1938.

273

1938–1939
A recall election of July 23, 1938, made these changes: T. J. Harrell (mayor) for Carter; Ward B. Powell for Hull; Ross Trimble for Hooper; Marvin D. Evans for Oglesby; Henry L. Woods for Martin; George B. Eagle for Seaman.

Powell resigned, I. N. McCrary elected Dec. 7, 1938.

1939–1941
Councilmen Harrell (mayor), Drechsel, McCrary, Trimble, Evans, Woods, Tunstill, Eagle, Smith.

Harrell resigned, Roscoe Carnrike elected July 10, 1940. McCrary elected Mayor July 17, 1940.

1941–1943
Councilmen McCrary (mayor), Drechsel, Carnrike, Trimble, Evans, Woods, Tunstill, Eagle, Malvern Marks. Drechsel resigned, Roy C. Murphy appointed. Trimble resigned, Bradley Burks appointed Nov. 19, 1941. Burks resigned, J. R. Edwards appointed July 22, 1942. Woods resigned, Clay Berry appointed Feb. 10, 1943.

1943–1945
Councilmen McCrary (mayor), Murphy, Carnrike, Edwards, Evans, Berry, Tunstill, Eagle, Marks. Evans resigned Dec. 20, 1944, F. Edgar Deen appointed.

1945–1947
Carnrike elected mayor, others re-elected.

1947–1949
Councilmen Deen (mayor), Murphy, McCrary, Carnrike, Edwards, Berry, Tunstill, Eagle, Marks. Carnrike resigned, succeeded by Bob McKinley. McCrary died, succeeded by R. E. Cowan.

1949–1950
Councilmen Deen (mayor), Edwards, Cowan, M. M. McKnight, George Bennett, McKinley, Ed Baker, Ray Crowder, L. T. Martin.

1951–1953
Councilmen J. R. Edwards (mayor), George B. Bennett, F. Edgar Deen, R. E. Cowan, R. B. McKinley, Ray Crowder, Ed L. Baker, M. M. McKnight, L. T. Martin.

274

1953–
Councilmen F. Edgar Deen (mayor), M. M. McKnight, Joe
B. Ellis, Jess F. Tarlton, Edd Kane, Joe Spurlock, Tom A. McCann,
J. D. Thompson, T. L. Carleton.

CITY MANAGERS
O. E. Carr, 1925–1931; George D. Fairtrace, 1931–1937; S. B.
Edwards, May 20–July 7, 1937; Dudley Lewis, 1937–1939; Sam H.
Bothwell, 1939–1946; W. O. Jones, since 1946.

CITY ENGINEERS
I. C. Terry, 1873–1874; Zane-Cetti, 1874–1878; I. C. Terry,
1878–1879; C. C. Hyde, 1879–1882; J. J. Goodfellow, April–July
1882; E. K. Smoot, 1883–1885; W. B. King, 1885–1889; F. W. Kane,
1889–1890; I. E. Reis, 1890–1891; H. H. Kerr, 1891–1893; T. E. Cop-
page, 1893–1897; John B. Hawley, 1897–1907; E. C. Woodward,
1907–1908; J. D. Trammell, 1908–1911; F. J. Von Zuben, 1911–
1919; D. L. Lewis, 1919–1937; W. O. Jones, 1937–1946; C. Milo
Thelin, since 1946.

POLICE CHIEFS
E. S. Terrell, April–October 1873; T. M. Ewing, April–No-
vember 1874; H. P. Shiel, 1874–1875; T. P. Redding, 1875–1876;
John Stocker, February–April 1876; T. I. Courtright, 1876–1879;
S. M. Farmer, 1879–1883; W. M. Rea, 1883–1887; S. M. Farmer,
1887–1891; J. H. Maddox, 1891–1897; W. M. Rea, 1897–1905; J. H.
Maddox, 1905–1909; L. J. Polk, 1909–1911; J. W. Renfro, 1911–
1913; O. R. Montgomery, 1913–1915; Cullen Bailey, 1915–1917;
O. R. Montgomery, April–October 1917; R. R. Porter, 1917–1921;
Harry Hamilton, 1921–1922; W. H. Lee, 1923–1933; Henry Lewis,
1933–1937; A. E. Dowell, 1937–1938; Karl M. Howard, 1938–1942;
T. G. Curry, 1942–1945; R. E. Dysart, 1945–1949; George Hawkins,
1949–1951; R. R. Howerton, since 1951.

CITY ATTORNEYS
Frank W. Ball, 1873–1874; J. S. Chapman, 1874–1877; Henry
Feild, 1877–1881; Robert McCart, 1881–1883; J. W. Swayne, 1883–
1885; William Capps, 1885–1887; Ed F. Warren, 1887–1889; T. J.
Powell, 1889–1893; C. M. Templeton, 1893–1897; W. D. Williams,

275

1897–1903; E. C. Orrick, 1903–1907; Sidney Samuels, 1907–1909; W. H. Slay, 1909–1913; H. C. McCart, 1913–1915; T. A. Altman, 1915–1917; T. J. Powell, 1917–1921; R. B. Ridgeway, 1921; Rhinehart Rouer, since 1921.

CITY TREASURERS

W. T. Ferguson, 1873–1874; John Loving, 1874–1883; John Nichols, 1883–1885; K. M. Van Zandt, 1885–1891; Max Elser, 1891–1895; J. Morton Logan, 1895–1899; W. B. Harrison, 1899–1907; A. C. Alexander, Walter H. Wallerich, between 1907 and 1919. Others not shown in the city council minutes. Since 1925, the post of treasurer has been combined with that of city secretary.

CITY SECRETARIES

John F. Swayne, 1873–1874; Theo Hitchcox, 1874–1875; C. McDougall, 1875–1883; Stuart Harrison, 1883–1885; Henry R. Early, 1885–1891; H. V. Burns, 1891–1893; James M. Collier, 1893–1895; John T. Montgomery, 1895–1907; W. J. Estes, 1907–1913; M. P. Harwood, Jr., 1913–1917; H. A. Lawrence, 1917–1925; I. L. Van Zandt Jr., 1925–1932; Henry Keller, 1932–1937; E. S. Birdsong, since 1937.

CITY AUDITORS

F. S. Johnstone, 1889–1893; E. W. Pressley, 1893–1895; James M. Collier, 1895–1896; J. J. Nunnally, 1896–1913; W. B. Martel, 1913–1915; George S. Adams, 1915–1920; E. B. Cheatham, 1920–1925; H. C. Michael, since 1925.

CITY JUDGES

The first officially designated city judge was O. M. Kerr who served from April 21, 1891 until Sept. 17, 1892. Prior to that time there had been police recorders and the mayor's court. Since Kerr's tenure ended:

R. W. Flournoy, 1892–1895; H. T. Smith, 1895–1897; J. W. Jackson, 1897–1899; W. W. Stewart, 1899–1903; C. T. Prewett, 1903–1907; George Steere, 1907–1909; Hunter P. Lane, 1909–1911; B. D. Shropshire, 1911–1913; Hugh Bordin, 1913–1915; Shropshire, 1915–1917; T. J. Powell, 1917–1919; H. O. Gossett, 1919–1922; Cullen W. Bailey, 1922–1930; Arthur S. Haddaway, 1930–1931;

M. T. Boynton, 1931–1937; W. H. Gilmartin, February–April, 1937; W. L. Coley, 1937–1938; Gilmartin, since 1938.

FIRE CHIEFS

William T. Field, 1873–1875; John Nichols, 1875–1876; J. F. Beall, July–October 1876; John Nichols, 1876–1877; J. W. Monica, 1877–1879; W. T. Maddox, 1879–1880; Richard Wilkes, 1880–1881; F. L. Twombly, 1881–1882; George Mulkey, 1882–1884; R. Matkin, 1884–1886; John T. Wilkes, 1886–1887; Don B. Adams, 1887–1888; R. Matkin, 1888–1889; Don B. Adams, 1889–1892; Ben U. Bell, 1892–1893; John Cella, 1893–1901; James H. Maddox, 1901–1905; W. E. Bideker, 1905–1919; Standifer Ferguson, 1919–1939; Cecil Killian, 1939–1945; Claude L. Ligon, 1945–1948; Paul C. Fontaine, since Jan. 1, 1948.

FIRE MARSHALS

A. W. Penninger, 1911–1913; W. H. Lennon, 1913–1915; R. M. Harris, 1915–1917; Tom McClure, 1917–1921; T. F. Cottar, 1921–1925; Claude L. Ligon, 1925–1945; H. A. Owens, 1945–1948; Cecil Killian, since 1948.

PURCHASING AGENTS

J. M. Collins, 1909–1913; F. N. Graves, 1913–1915; P. Floyd Maben, 1915–1917; H. W. Wentworth, 1917–1919; Howard Parsley, 1919–1921; Frank R. Graves, 1921–1924; G. L. Cline, since 1924.

WATER DEPARTMENT SUPERINTENDENTS

A. W. Scoble, June–September 1885; J. H. Kerr, September–November 1885; Robert De Haven, 1885–1888; M. H. Milburn, 1888–1892; Scoble, 1892–1894; F. W. Chiles, 1894–1895; Scoble, 1895–1911; D. G. Griffin, 1911–1913; H. O. Gossett, 1913–1915. After Gossett, city commissioners designated as water commissioners headed the department. L. A. Quigley was appointed superintendent April 15, 1925 and served until his death on Oct. 30, 1942. Uel Stephens has been superintendent since.

Bibliography

Manuscripts

Anon. "Summary of History of the Fort Worth and Denver City Railway Co." Ft.W. and D.C. files, Fort Worth.

Goerte, Anne Lenore. "Some Phases of the Development of the Fort Worth Public School System, 1854–1930." Thesis, University of Colorado, 1930. Typescript on file in the Fort Worth Public Library.

Stephens, Uel. "An Improvement Program for the Fort Worth City Water Department." Fort Worth Water Department.

Texas Writers Project. "Research Data, Fort Worth and Tarrant County." 26 vols. Typescript in the Fort Worth Public Library.

Tidwell, D. D. "A History of the West Fork Association." Th.D. thesis, Southwestern Baptist Theological Seminary, 1940. Southwestern Baptist Theological Seminary Library, Fort Worth.

Wallace, Edward S. "General William Jenkins Worth, the American Murat." Ph.D. thesis. Boston University, 1948. Typescript on file in the Fort Worth Public Library.

Government Documents and Records

United States

Fort Worth, Texas. Historical Summary. Records of the War Department, Office of the Adjutant General, April 11, 1924. The National Archives.

"Fort Worth—Lieutenant Starr, Second Dragoons, Acting Assistant Quartermaster," 32 Cong., 1 sess., *House Exec. Doc. 2.*

Letters from Brevet Maj. R. A. Arnold to Maj. Gen. Roger Jones, adjutant general, June 15, June 18, October 6, December 27, 1849. The National Archives.

Letter from Brevet Maj. R. A. Arnold to Maj. George Deas, assistant adjutant general, 8th Mil. Dept., July 30, 1849. The National Archives.

Orders No. 9, Headquarters, 8th and 9th Mil. Depts., February 8, 1849. The National Archives.

Orders No. 13, Headquarters, 8th and 9th Mil. Depts., February 14, 1849. The National Archives.

Post Return for Fort Worth, June, 1849. The National Archives.

Report of Inspection by Col. Samuel Cooper of the 8th Mil. Dept., 1851. The National Archives.

Report of Inspection by Lt. Col. W. G. Freeman, October 1, 1853. The National Archives.

Report of Brevet Brig. Gen. William S. Harney, May 1, 1849. The National Archives.

Williams, Assistant Surgeon Thomas H. "Medical Topography and Diseases of Fort Worth," 34 Cong., 1 sess., *Senate Exec. Doc. 96.*

FORT WORTH

Minutes and Ordinances of the City Council from 1873 to 1949. Fort Worth.

TARRANT COUNTY

Minutes of the Tarrant County Commissioners Court from 1876 to 1949.

TEXAS

Journals of the House of Representatives of the State of Texas, Third Session, 1849. Members of the Legislature of the State of Texas from 1846 to 1939. Chief Clerk of the House of Representatives, Austin.

Texas Newspapers

Austin Daily Statesman, 1886–88.
Austin State Gazette, September 22, 1860.
Corpus Christi Star, December 16, 1848.

Dallas Herald, December 5, 1860.
Fort Worth Chief, March 7, 1860.
Fort Worth Democrat, 1873–81.
Fort Worth Democrat-Advance, 1881.
Fort Worth Gazette, 1884–87.
Fort Worth Mail-Telegram, 1902.
Fort Worth Register, 1897, 1901, 1902.
Fort Worth Standard, 1876–77.
Fort Worth Star-Telegram, 1909–49.
Fort Worth Telegram, 1902–1903.
Texas State Gazette, November 15, 1853.

Books

Baillio, F. B. *A History of the Texas Press Association.* Dallas, Southwestern Printing Company, 1916.

DeShields, James T. *Border Wars of Texas.* Tioga, Texas, The Herald Company, 1912.

Henry, Robert Selph. *The Story of the Mexican War.* Indianapolis, Bobbs-Merrill Company, 1950.

Kirkpatrick, A. Y. *The Early Settlers' Life In Texas and the Organization of Hill County.* Hillsboro, Texas, n.d.

Little, Charles C., and James Brown. *American Almanac for 1849.* Boston.

———. *American Almanac for 1850.* Boston.

McConnell, J. C. *West Texas Frontier.* Jacksboro, Texas, Gazette Print, 1933.

Mitchell, Edwin V. *Encyclopedia of American Politics.* Garden City, Doubleday and Company, Inc., 1946.

Paddock, B. B. (ed.). *A Twentieth Century History and Bibliographical Record of North and West Texas.* Chicago and New York, Lewis Publishing Company, 1906. 2 vols.

———. *History of Texas; Fort Worth and the Texas Northwest Edition.* Chicago and New York, Lewis Publishing Company, 1922. 4 vols.

Richardson, R. N. *Texas, Lone Star State.* New York, Prentice-Hall, Inc., 1943.

Riegel, Robert E. *Young America, 1830–40.* Norman, University of Oklahoma Press, 1949.

Rodenbough, Theo. F. *From Everglades to Canyon with the Second Dragoons.* New York, D. Van Nostrand Company, Inc., 1875.

Terrell, J. C. *Reminiscences of the Early Days of Fort Worth.* Fort Worth, Texas Printing Company, 1906.

Thoburn, Joseph B., and Muriel H. Wright. *Oklahoma, A History of the State and Its People.* New York, Lewis Historical Publishing Company, 1929. 4 vols.

Toulouse, Joseph H. and James R. *Pioneer Posts of Texas.* San Antonio, The Naylor Company, 1936.

Articles

Holden, W. C. "Frontier Defense," *West Texas Historical Association Yearbook,* Vol. VI (June, 1930), 35–64.

Koch, Lena Clara. "Federal Indian Policy in Texas 1845–1860," *Southwestern Historical Quarterly,* Vol. XXIX, No. 1 (July, 1925), 19–35.

Norton, A. B. "A History of the Early Newspapers of Texas," incorporated in Baillio, *A History of the Texas Press Association,* q.v.

Index

Abernathy (first photographer): 68
Abilene, Kan.: 60, 61
Adams, John D.: 102–103
Adams, Col. Wirt: 65
Adelphi Theater: 88
African Methodist Church: 162
Air Force, U. S.: 209, 218, 224, 227
Alabama: 27
Albritton, E. P.: 69
Alexander, J. P.: alderman, 73, 268, 269; postmaster, 102; leads stagecoach parade, 103
Alford, J. B.: 205
Alford, J. P.: 116, 261
Alford, Miss Jennie: 110
Allen, W. J.: 119, 268
Allison, William: 135
All Saints Hospital: 201
American Airlines: 210
American Broadcasting Co.: 203
American Federation of Labor: 145, 204
American LaFrance Fire Extinguisher Co.: 183
American Petroleum Institute: 222
Anchor Mills: 138, 178
Anderson, John Murray: 212
Anderson, Lt. Richard: 23
Andrews, J. H.: 139
Andrews, Kitty: 56
Annexations: see government, city
Arlington Heights: 192, 206
Arlington Heights Traction Co.: 176
Arlington Inn: 206

Armistead, Mrs. Mary: 39
Armour & Co.: 173 f.
Armstrong, George: 175, 251, 270
Army, Confederate: Tarrant County units, 51; Tarrant Rifles, 51; Sul Ross Brigade, 51; Seventh Texas Cavalry, 51; Ninth Texas Cavalry, 51; Seventh Texas Infantry, 54
Army, U. S.: Second Dragoons, 6, 9, 10, 19, 22, 23, 240–42; strength in 1849, 6; Eighth Infantry, 6, 13, 18, 22; Eighth and Ninth Mil. Depts., 6, 7; First Infantry, 6; Indian policy of, 6, 231–33, 237; frontier districts, 8; Army of Occupation in Texas, 13, 14; forts, 15, 16, 25; Reconstruction occupation troops, 56; weather service, 159; county units in Spanish-American War, 165; Second Texas Volunteer Infantry, 165; First Texas Cavalry, 165; 36th Division, 192; see also Fort Worth, as military post
Arnold, Gen. H. H.: 225
Arnold, Kate: 21, 15 n.
Arnold, Maj. Ripley: repulses Indian attack, 3–5; commands Camp Thornton, 9; establishes Fort Worth, 11–12; biographical data, 14–15; as disciplinarian, 17; at play with children, 21; transferred to Fort Graham, 22–23; killed by Steiner, 23–24; buried in Fort Worth, 25; correspondence, 238–42
Arnold, Mrs. Ripley: 14, 21, 25

Arnold, Sophie and Willis: 22
Ashmore, Will: 157
Askew, Fred: 72, 155
Audemars, Edmond: 180
Auditorium: *see* Will Rogers Memorial
 Auditorium and Coliseum
August Clothing Store, A. and L.: 141
Ault, John T.: 69
Ault and Connor's Band: 145
Austin, Tex.: 7, 8, 19, 140, 186
Automobiles: 169–73
Aviation: first flights, 178–82; World
 War I airfields, 192; companies,
 209; first air passengers, 209; mu-
 nicipal airport, 209; air traffic, 210;
 in World War II, 215; aircraft man-
 ufacture, 215; B–36, 217; global
 non-stop flight, 227; *see also* Air
 Force
Ayres, B. P.: 44, 247, 263

Bailey, Joe Weldon: 198
Bailey, W. A.: 49
Bailey, W. J.: alderman, 140, 270; real
 estate developer, 206; state senator,
 263
Bailey Addition: 206
Bain, C.: 102
Baldridge, W. H.: 161
Bamberg, B. F.: 58
Bands: 89, 103, 110, 145
Banks: 62, 68, 104–105, 142, 199–200
Baptist Church: 21; first in county,
 35–36; Fort Worth church, 36; mis-
 sionaries, 36; West Fork Association,
 36; services, 109; First Baptist
 Church, 162, 203; Seminary, 189
Barkley, B. F.: 77, 105, 249
Barkley, Lon: 187
Barksdale, H.: 69
Baseball: 220
Bateman, K. D. and W. Q.: 58
Bates, Rev. William: 34
Baton Rouge, La.: 7, 14
Baugh, Sammy: 212
Baxter Springs Trail: 60, 62, 125
Beall, J. F.: 113, 277

Beckham, R. E.: lawyer, 69; mayor,
 115f., 268; district judge, 158;
 school trustee, 161; county judge,
 250
Beggs Agency, George: 100
Behrens, Ella: 192f.
Bell, Ben: 156, 277
Bell, Harvey: 155
Bell, James: 55
Benbrook, Tex.: 173
Benbrook Field: 192
Berkley Addition: 206
Berliner, B.: 57
Berney, Morris E.: 201
Berry, P. B.: 155
Bevan, Lionel W.: 201
Bewley, Murray P.: 138, 178
Bewley Mills: 138, 178
Bideker, W.: 155, 277
Bigger, J. C.: 120
Biggs, Electra Waggoner: 225
Billings, Josh: 88
Bird, Col. Jonathan: 16
Birdville, Tex.: 15, 16, 22, 36, 40, 41,
 42–44, 50, 52, 77
Bishop, F.: 155
Blackstone Hotel: 200
Blackwell, Ella: 134
Blakeney, A.: 73, 268
Blandin, William T.: 81
Blanton, T. N.: 155
Blue Back Speller: 56
Blue Mound: 56
Blue Network: 203
B'nai B'rith: 190
Board of Trade: 100, 159, 201
Boaz, Marklee and Co.: 105
Boaz, Tuck: 88
Boaz, W. J.: alderman, 73, 268; busi-
 ness interest, 105, 138
Bold, Lt. John: 19
Bolt Works: 177–78
Bomford, Capt. J. V.: 22
Botanic Garden: 16, 38
Bowen, H. G.: 69
Bowen, R. Mayo: 201
Bowel, Mrs. Temple: 210

Boy Scouts: 190
Bradner, Jim: 60
Brant, Maj. Gen. Harry C.: 215
Brazendine, W. L.: 44
Breckenridge, Tex.: 196
Brerris, Harvey: 106
Brinson, Jack: 43
Brinson, M. J.: merchant, 37; school
 trustee, 39; on courthouse bond, 44;
 in Civil War, 51
Broiles, H. S.: 136, 269, 270
Brooks, Dr. W. B.: 100
Brotherhood of Locomotive Engi-
 neers: 145
Brown, F. O.: 153
Brown, J. M.: 161
Brown, John C.: 84
Brown, Joseph H.: 67
Brown, Louis: 55
Brown, O. M. and Associates: 75
Brownwood, Tex.: 102, 103, 127, 172
Brunswig, L. H.: 58
Bryce, William: 206, 273
Buckholtz, Charley: 169
Buena Vista Heights: 205
Buffalo hunters: see trade, western
Buley, Rev. Anthony: 48–49
Burchill, Mrs. Belle M.: 110, 159
Bureau of Animal Husbandry: 137
Burkburnett, Tex.: 196–97
Burnett, Burk: 101, 168
Burnett, R. H. H.: 109
Burnham, Clara: 162
Burns, Henry: 90
Burrus Mills: 178, 214
Burton, J. H.: 155
Burton, J. S.: 79
Burton, Noel: 31
Burton, Will G.: 88
Burts, Dr. W. P.: arrives in Fort
 Worth, 27; mayor, 73, 268; opening
 of telegraph line, 78–80
Burwell, Col. Harvey: 209
Business conditions: 67, 98–107, 124–
 25; see also trade, retail
Business district: 37, 185, 204
Bus service, city: 177

Butler, H. H.: 162
Byars, Noah T.: 36
Byers, A. T.: 137, 205

Cabell, W. L.: 79
California and Texas Bank: 68
Calloway, Hiram: 42
Cameron Mill and Elevator Co.: 145
Campbell, W. M.: 69
Camp Bowie: 192, 206
Camp Colorado, Tex.: 102
Camp Thornton, Tex.: 9, 236
Capps, William: pleads with mob, 131;
 sells land to city, 154; city attorney,
 275
Carlock, R. L.: 136, 250, 264, 265
Carnegie, Andrew: 166
Carpetbaggers: 62
Carrico, Thomas: 63
Carroll, Rev. B. H.: 190
Carswell, Maj. Horace S.: 218
Carswell Air Force Base: 218, 227
Carter, Amon G.: in aviation, 178,
 182; on Fort Worth Star, 186; buys
 Fort Worth Record, 199; Chamber
 of Commerce president, 201; starts
 radio station, 202; biographical data,
 219–26; Shady Oak hats, 225
Cary, Dan: 98
Casa Mañana: 212
Casey, James: 132
Casey, Martin: 178
Castle, Vernon and Irene: 192
Catchpole, John: 89
Catholic Church: 63, 109
Cattle: 136, 137; see also trail drives,
 packinghouses, stockyards
Cattle Exchange Saloon: 90, 113
Cattlemen: 62, 105, 202
Cella, John: 155, 277
Centennial Theater: 114
Chalk, Rev. John W.: 34
Chamber of Commerce: 201; see also
 Board of Trade
Chamberlain, H. B.: 206
Champion, Frank: 196
Chapman, J. W.: 44, 249

Charity: 190–91
Chase, Ed: 207
Cheltenham: 206
Chidester, J. D.: 102–103
Chisholm Trail: 61
Christian Church: *see* Disciples of Christ
Churches: first organized, 33; sexes segregated, 63; number of, 69, 70, 125; services, 108–109; *see also by name of sect*
Cigar manufacturers: 139
Circuit riders: 33, 34
Cisco, Tex.: 196
Citizens Hotel Co.: 200
Citizens Light and Power Co.: 176
Citizens Railway and Light Co.: 176
City: *see* government, city
City-County Hospital: 201
City Mills: 81, 138
City National Bank: 105, 138,
City Railway Co.: 156
Civil Aeronautics Administration: 219
Civil War: 18, 22; county units in, 51; battles, 51, 54; civil law superseded during, 52; effects of, 52; Fort Worth attitude toward, 53; Indian raids, 55; *see also* secession
Clark, Addison and Randolph: 57, 59, 189
Clark, George: 148
Clark, Ida: 57
Clark, Joseph: 59
Clark House: 101
Cleburne, Tex.: 55, 99, 102, 117, 126, 127, 177
Cleveland, J. W.: 64
Clifford, George H.: 201
Clothing: 28, 29, 37, 123
Club Room: 100–101
Cobb, Harry: 91
Cobb, Ty: 220
Cochran, William M.: 20
Cody, Buffalo Bill: 103
Coffins: 99
Cogley, Peter: 98
Coker, J. W.: 156

Cold Springs: 27, 32, 42, 59
Coleman, A. C.: 44
Coleman, P. E.: 44
Coleman, Tex.: 102
Collier, John B., Jr.: 201
Colorado and Southern Railroad: 127
Comanche, Tex.: 102
Commerce: *see* trade
Community Chest: 191
Concho Wagon Yard: 103
Confederacy: 18; *see also* Army, Confederate
Congress, U. S.: railroad subsidy, 66; airport issue, 218–19; Congressmen listed, 258–60
Congress of Industrial Organizations: 204
Connally, Tom: 223
Conner's Station: 7, 8, 9
Connor, J. W.: 44
Connor, W. D.: 44
Consolidated-Vultee Aircraft Corporation: 215, 217
Constitutional Union Party: 47
Consumers Heat and Light Co.: 175
Continental Bank and Trust Co.: 200
Continental Meat Packing Co.: 137
Continental National Bank: 200
Cook, Frederick A.: 198
Cook, Josiah: 50
Cook Memorial Hospital: 201
Cooke, Jay: 76
Copher, D. T.: 103
Corbett, James J.: 168
Corley, Dan B.: 69
Costan, R. E. L.: 178
Cotton: 88, 108
Cotton Belt Railroad: 127, 177
Courtenay, John J.: 43
Courtright, T. I. (Long Hair Jim): city marshal, 91–92, 275; in railroad strike, 128; arrested by Rangers, 130; escape from Rangers, 131–34; killed by Short, 134–35
Courts: first session, 22; during Reconstruction, 62, 64; length of argument, 105; municipal, 115; districts estab-

lished, 158–59; criminal, 191–92; judges of, 278
Covey, Homer: 201
Cowan, E. P.: 152
Cowart, Robert E.: 82
Cowboys: 60, 89
Cox, R. E.: 201
Craig, G. H.: 157
Crawford, L. W.: 68
Crebbins, Alfred: 206
Crime: 91–95, 113, 114–15, 136
Crockett, John M.: 33
Cromer, H. R.: 169 f.
Croswell, Ambrose: 58
Cummings, C. C.: 69, 120, 249

Dade, Dabney C.: 28, 30, 51
Daggett, C. B.: 27
Daggett, E. B.: 76, 269
Daggett, E. M.: arrives in Fort Worth, 27; merchant, 37; on courthouse bond, 44; in secession, 50; pleads for Mathews, 52–53; city seal in likeness of, 74; stockyards interest, 137; gives land to newcomers, 205
Daggett, E. M., Hose Co.: 154
Daggett, Henry: 18, 27, 36, 37
Dahlman Bros.: 100
Dallas, Tex.: 8, 27, 38, 56, 64, 78, 93, 126, 140, 142, 159, 163, 171, 177, 214, 222; postoffice for Fort Worth, 12, 18; rivalry with, 28, 218, 224
Dark Lantern Party: 146
Darnell, N. H.: 84, 262
Davenport, A. G.: 44
Davenport, G. W.: 156
Davis, J. W.: 68
Davis, T. B.: 162
Davis, William: 184
Davis, William H.: 58
Davis & Walker: 99
Dawson, A. G.: 186, 187
Day, G. H.: as mayor, 81, 113, 115–16, 268; brings railroad pay to Fort Worth, 86; alderman, 270
Dean, Rev. A. M.: 34
Dearing, Hill: 157

Decatur, Tex.: 102, 127
Dees, Tom: 197
Delaney, Floyd: 205
Delaware Hotel: 102
Delmonico Restaurant: 91
Democratic Party: 32, 146, 147
Denison, Tex.: 9, 62, 126, 181
Denison and Pacific Railroad: 126
Dentists: 34, 63
Denton County, Tex.: 15, 20 f., 34 ff., 49
Depression: 76, 210–11
Desdemona, Tex.: 197
Dial, Lula: 162
Disciples of Christ: First Christian Church founded, 34; ministers open school, 57; church moved, 63; services, 109
Divorces: 169
Dodd & Co.: 98
Dodge, Gen. Grenville M.: 66, 127
Doolittle, James: 225
Dragoons: see Army, U. S.
Drake, J. S.: 152
Driving Park: 178
Dublin, Tex.: 127, 213
Dugan, H.: 103
Duke, Joe: 197
Dulaney, R. O.: 201
Dunn, W. H.: 102
Dunwoody, E. L.: 155
Durrett, Uncle Jack: 31, 32

Eagle Ford, Tex.: 76, 83
Eagle Mountain Lake: 186
Eagles Hall: 186
East Fort Worth Town Co.: 207
East Texas: 54, 56, 111
East-West Broadcasting Co.: 203
Eastern Star: 190
Eastern Trail: 61
Eastland, Tex.: 196
Eastland County, Tex.: 195
Echols, W. B.: 11
Ederle, C. F.: 139
Edwards, L. J.: 44
Education: see Schools and Colleges

Eisenhower, Dwight D.: painting in Carter office, 224; unveils Rogers statue, 225
Ellis, James F.: 138
Ellis, M. G.: 137
Ellison and Dewees: 106
Elections: *see* government
Electricity: 139–40, 175–76, 211
Elks: 190
Elliott, Sanders: 20, 247, 249
Elliott and Roe Lumber Co.: 67
El Paso Hotel: 92, 101, 102
Elser, Max: 269, 276; telegrapher, 78, 80; merchant, 98
Episcopal Church: first services, 34–35; established, 109; Fort Worth Mission, 109
Equitable Life Assurance Society: 100
Evans, B. C.: merchant, 67–68; opens Evans Hall, 88; alderman, 268
Evans, Ben C.: 156
Evans, Sam: 64, 261, 262
Evans and Martin: 98
Evans Bros.: 158
Evans Hall: 88
Evarts, G. A.: 105
Everman Field: 192
Ewing, T. M.: 81, 275

Fairfax, C. K.: 101
Fairtrace, George: 210–11, 275
Fakes & Co.: 99
Farmer, J. D.: 205
Farmer, Press: 17, 44, 57, 205
Farmers Alliance: 146
Farmers and Mechanics National Bank: 142, 200
Farrar, Simon B.: 11
Faut, D. R.: 106
Federal Communications Commission: 203
Federal Radio Commission: 202
Feild, Dr. J. R.: 150
Feild, Julian: merchant, 27; Mason, 33; miller, 37–38; school trustee, 39; on courthouse bond, 44; postmaster, 159; alderman, 269

Feild, Dr. Theodore: 63
Ferguson, Jess: 32
Ferguson, N. K.: 74
Ferguson, Standifer: 155, 184, 277
Ferguson, W. I.: 58
Ferguson, W. T.: 73, 248–50, 276
Fields, Henry: 105
Fire Department: predecessors, 71; stations, 72, 119, 154, 155; volunteers, 72, 154–55; alarms, 72, 154; salaries, 117; horses, 117, 183–84; equipment, 117, 118, 154, 183; companies, 117, 118, 154; uniforms, 118; chiefs, 118, 154, 277; cisterns, 118f.; fires, 71, 118; bell, 154; modernized, 154–55; paid department, 155; motorized, 183–84; civil service for, 208; fire marshals, 277
Fire Extinguisher Manufacturing Co.: 154
First and Last Chance Saloon: 32
First National Bank: 101, 105, 142
First National Bank of Handley: 200
Fisher, O. L.: 163
Fitzgerald, A.: 36
Fitzgerald, Parson: 81–82
Flenner, Frank: 104
Food: 29, 31; *see also* restaurants
Football: 164, 212
Forest Park: 208
Forney, John W.: 66
Fort Belknap, Tex.: 25, 102
Fort Concho, Tex.: 102
Fort Graham, Tex.: 10, 11, 15, 18, 22, 23
Fort Griffin, Tex.: 82, 96, 102
Fort Sill, Okla.: 92
Fort Washita, C. N.: 9, 236
Fort Worth, as military post: established, 5, 12; designated as fort, 12; building materials, 15, 245; fort moved to bluff, 15; buildings, 15, 244–45; discipline, 17; garrison, 17, 18, 22, 23, 25; patrols, 17; garrison duty, 17; sutler, 17; soldier pay, 18; mail, 18; description of, 19, 22; supplies, 19, 243–44, 246; rations, 19,

25, 243–44, 246; inspections, 22, 25; abandoned, 25; weather reports, 159; orders and correspondence, 231–46; muster roll of Co. F., Second Dragoons, 240–42; forage, 243–44, 245–46; fuel, 245; water, 245; transportation, 246; roads, 246
Fort Worth and Albuquerque Railroad: 177
Fort Worth and Arlington Heights Street Railway Co.: 144, 156
Fort Worth and Denver City Railroad: 127, 130, 177
Fort Worth and New Orleans Railroad: 127, 177
Fort Worth and Rio Grande Railroad: 127, 177
Fort Worth and Rosen Heights Railway: 176
Fort Worth Auto Bus Co.: 177
Fort Worth Auto Livery: 172
Fort Worth Benevolent Association: 190
Fort Worth Brass Band: 103
Fort Worth Brewing Co.: 138
Fort Worth Broadcasting Co.: 203
Fort Worth City Co.: 205
Fort Worth Club: 223
Fort Worth Dressed Meat and Packing Co.: 137
Fort Worth Electric Light and Power Co.: 139, 140
Fort Worth Fencibles: 165
Fort Worth Gas Co.: 175, 176
Fort Worth Gas Light and Coke Co.: 97
Fort Worth Gas Light Co.: 139
Fort Worth Grocer Co.: 140
Fort Worth Light and Power Co.: 176
Fort Worth National Bank.: 68, 142, 200; see also Tidball, Van Zandt and Co.
Fort Worth Power and Light Co.: 176, 210
Fort Worth Relief Association: 190
Fort Worth Street Railway Co.: 97, 143

Fort Worth Telephone Co.: 178
Fort Worth Trades Assembly: 145
Fort Worth Transit Co.: 177
Fort Worth University: 163–64, 188, 189
Fort Worth Wagon and Plow Co.: 108
Fort Worth Water Co.: 152, 155
Fort Worth Water Works Co.: 75
Fort Worth–Fort Yuma Stage Line: 102
Foster, J. E.: 216
Foute, Bessie: 162
Fowler, A. Y.: 42, 50
Fowler, S. L.: 196
Fox, R. R.: 194
Fox, Valerie: 213
Fraser, A. B.: 140, 270
Fraternal organizations: 33, 190
Freeman, Rev. John A.: preaches first sermon at Fort Worth, 21; arrives in Texas, 35; founds Lonesome Dove Church, 35; founds Mount Gilead Church, 36
Freeman, Lt. Col. W. G.: 25
Frisbee, John, Jr.: 179
Frisco Railroad: see St. Louis and San Francisco Railway
Frontier Centennial: 212
Frost, C. L.: 80
Fry, S. M.: 161, 269
Fuller, William G.: 209
Fundamental Baptist Bible Institute: 214
Funeral directors: 104
Furman, E. E.: 118
Furman, Henry M.: 105
Furman, Sam: 105, 249, 250, 270

Gainesville, Tex.: 49, 52, 126
Galaspie, Robert: 49
Galveston, Tex.: 7, 51, 126, 133
Gambling: 74, 91–92, 112, 113, 116, 123, 191
Garner, John Nance: 223, 225
Garnett, W. H.: 38
Garrett, Rev. Alexander C.: 109
Garros, Roland G.: 179

Gas: artificial, 96, 97; rates, 96; companies, 96, 97, 175–76; plants, 97, 176; fixtures, 99; natural, 175
Gause, George L.: 104
Gause, W. R.: 104, 262
Gause-Ware Funeral Home: 104
Gholson, John M.: 195
Gibson, James: 35
Giddings, George H.: 172
Gilliam, J. M.: 203
Gilmore, Seabourne: 44, 247
Ginnochio Hotel: 130
Glenwood and Polytechnic Street Railway Co.: 156
Goff, A. G.: 155, 156
"Golden Goddess": 198
Goldstein & Co., A.: 99
Good, John J.: 21, 69
Gordon, W. K.: 195
Gould, Jay: 128
Gounant, Adolphus: 21, 24, 44
Government, city: formed, 73–74; officials listed, 73, 268–77; elections, 73, 81, 112 f., 115, 116, 175, 183, 208, 210, 216, 268, 269, 270, 271, 272, 274; fees, 74; corporate seal, 74; ordinances, 74, 96, 114, 116, 117, 156, 170; corporate area, 74, 207, 216; officials serve without pay, 80–81; reform, 112 f.; aldermanic system, 113; wards, 113, 156, 270; business regulation, 114; taxes, 114, 155; poundkeeper, 116; building regulations, 116, 155, 185; City Halls, 119, 156, 162, 174, 211; public power, 140; modernization of services, 150–57; public health, 150–52; acquires water works, 153; salaries, 155, 211; zoning, 156; scavenger, 156; public utilities, 156, 210; City Council, 160, 161, 211; automobile regulations, 170; River Plant, 176; City Commission, 176, 184; commission form adopted, 183; movie censorship, 185; annexations, 204–207, 216; manager form adopted, 207–208; home rule, 208; civil service, 208;

recall, 211; *see also* police, fire, water, recreation, streets
Government, county: first commissioners, 20; elections, 22, 40, 120, 146–47; county seat elections, 40–45; courthouses, 44, 157–58; courthouse fire, 118; telephone, 157; jail, 157, 192; Commissioners Court, 157, 158; children's home, 158; road bonds, 173; gallows, 192; officials listed, 247–57; county attorney's office created, 249; purchasing agent added, 254; district attorney's office created, 254; *see also* roads
Government, federal: 159–60; presidential elections, 119 f., 121; depression expenditures, 211; *see also* Post Office, Army, Congress, Presidents
Government, state: elections, 77, 147–49; Constitutional Convention, 82–83; *see also* courts *and* legislature
Granbury, Tex.: 102, 127
Grand Saline, Tex.: 27
Grange: 78
Grant, A. W.: 185
Grant, George: 49
Grant, U. S.: 103, 120
Grapevine, Tex.: 35, 51, 173, 193
Great Train Robbery, The: 168
Greater Fort Worth International Airport: 218–19
Green, H. R.: 148
Green, Hetty: 148
Green and Beall: 105
Greenback Party: 146
Greene, S. P.: 72
Greene, W. W.: 139
Gregg, Rt. Rev. Alexander: 34
Griffeth & Co., A.: 98
Griffin, James: 63
Gunmen: 91, 108, 123
Gunn and Curtiss: 157
Gurley and Co.: 96

Haas, J. E.: 155
Halford, James: 35
Halifax, Lord: 215

Hall, B. F.: 34
Halsey, Admiral: 225
Hamilton, A. J.: 54, 248, 258
Hangings: 48, 192
Hanna, John: as schoolmaster, 56; lawyer, 57; financier, 64; Sunday-school superintendent, 109; school trustee, 161
Hanna and Hogsett: 69
Harding, R. E.: 201
Hardtgen, Fritz: 145
Harney, Brig. Gen. William S.: commands Second Dragoons, 8; report of North Texas survey, 9–10, 223, 235–38; establishes Fort Graham, 10; orders establishment of Fort Worth, 11–12; commands frontier district, 233; locates area for Fort Worth, 234
Harper, Charles: 19
Harrell, J. M.: 155
Harris, Abe: 4–5, 26, 44
Harris Hospital: 201, 223
Harrison, Robert: 205
Hart, Judge Hardin: 62
Hatton, Vincent J.: 20, 247
Hawley, John B.: 153, 275
Hayes, Rutherford B.: 46, 102 f.
Haywood, Bob: 130
Haywood, Eva: 162
Headlight Bar: 89
Health, public: see government, city
Hearses: 104
Hearst, William Randolph: 199, 222
Hedgecoke, Henry O.: 21
Helium plant: 199
Hell's Half Acre: 115, 136
Henderson, W. A.: 44
Hendricks, H. G.: 76, 105
Hendricks, Thomas A.: 119 f.
Henley, J. S.: 44
Henry, O.: 129
Herbert, Larry: 155
Herman, H. M.: 152
Herring, B. F.: 135
Hibernians: 167
Hicks Field: 192

Hides: 96
High Vigilance Committee: 52
Highways: see roads
Hildebrand, Emma: 162
Hill, G. W.: 117
Hillcrest: 206
Hirschfield, John S.: 83
Hodges, Rev. Joshua: 35
Hodge Station: 127
Hofle & Co.: 99
Hogan, Ben: 213–14
Hogg, Alexander: 161, 163
Hogg, James Stephen: 147–49
Hogs: 88, 116
Holly Plant: 184–85
Holly Water Works Co.: 153
Homes: 29, 30, 87, 110–11, 124
Honea, B. N.: 221
Hoover, Herbert: 202
Horse cars: see streetcars
Hosey, George: 192
Hospitals: 143, 201, 223
Hotels: 27, 92, 101, 102, 118, 130, 151, 200, 224
Hough, Harold: 202
House of Representatives, Texas: 223
House of Representatives, U. S.: 121
House-raisings: 31
Houston, Sam: 32–33, 50
Houston, Tex.: 19, 37, 140
Houston and Texas Central Railroad: 163
Howard, Jennie: 162
Howard, W. C.: 98
Hoxie, John: 137, 142
Hoyt, Robert L.: 188
Hubbard, Mrs. T. O.: 205
Hudson, W. T.: 254
Huffman, Sue: 56, 161
Huffman, W. A.: 83, 97, 268
Hunter and Sheridan's Saddle Rock Oyster Saloon: 91
Hurd, Leo F.: 86
Hurley, Tom: 206
Hurley Building: 206
Hyde Park Street Railway Co.: 144

Ice: 68
Illinois: 138
Illumination: 88, 97, 99, 102, 140
Indiana: 38
Indians: threaten Fort Worth, 3–5; threat to northern Texas, 8; on Brazos River, 10; visit Fort Worth, 31, 101–102; camp near Fort Worth, 39; trade, 55; raids, 55–56, 239
Indian Territory: 8, 51, 96, 101, 140
Industry: 37–38, 81, 108, 136–40, 175–76, 177–78, 215–16
Influenza: 193
Inman, Jack: 44
Insurance: 100
International and Great Northern Railroad: 176
International Aviators: 178
International Butcher Workers Union: 203
International Typographical Union: 145
Interstate Association of Livestock Boards: 138
Interurbans: 177
Ireland, Governor: 129, 131
Isaacs, Max: 118
Isbell, Paul: 44, 49

Jacksboro, Tex.: 56, 102
Jackson, J. M.: 55
Jacobs, Henry: 99
Jarvis, J. J.: 262, 268; business interests, 8, 64, 68, 100; lawyer, 105; home, 110–11; school trustee, 161
Jefferson, Tex.: 37, 58, 64
Jennings, Hughey: 220
Jennings, Thomas J.: 76, 105
Jews: 165
Johnson, A. D.: 39, 44
Johnson, Byron G.: 105
Johnson, J. W.: 162
Johnson, Jake: 134
Johnson, Rev. James G.: 34
Johnson, M. T.: Helps pick fort site, 11; county commissioner, 20, 247; host to Hardin Runnels, 32; in

county seat election, 43–44; on courthouse bond, 44; in secession, 50–51; as Indian fighter, 55; gives land to newcomers, 205
Johnson, M. T., Hook and Ladder Co.: 72, 117, 135
Johnson, Maud P.: 162
Johnson, Miss Sallie: 72
Johnson, Tom: 43
Johnson Station: 11, 16, 17, 32, 41, 52, 56
Jones, Jesse (financier): 200
Jones, Jesse (politician): 74, 269–70
Jones, Morgan: 84, 152
Jones, Pinka: 162
Jose Maria Village: 10, 235

Kahn, Otto: 225
Kamp, Roy E.: 172
Kansas: 51, 55, 138
Kansas Pacific Railroad: 60
Kasan, Billy: 169
Keating, Paul W.: 74
Keeler, Mrs. D. B.: 166
Keg Saloon: 88
Keith, Ben E.: 201
Kelk Bros.: 104
Kellis Park: 216
Kenedy and Scott: 104
Kennedy, M. D.: 39
Kentucky: 27, 38
Kerr, George: 155
Kessler, George: 185
Key Saloon: 118
Kidder, George and John: 44
Kinder, Johnny: 30
King, John P.: 206, 250
King's Foundry: 80
Kinkle, W.: 155
Kitts, Richard: 156
Knaar, Francis: 26, 44, 242
Kneeland, W. E.: 100
Knights of Columbus: 190
Knights of Labor: 128, 146
Knights of Pythias: 190
Knudsen, W. S.: 225
Kuhn, E.: 99

Ku Klux Klan: 55
Kuzzatz, Herman: 90

Labor: jobs, 70; unions, 128, 145, 203, 204; strikes, 128, 203; in politics, 146–47
Labor Day: 45–46
Lacey, J. N.: 162
Ladies Ice Cream Parlor: 68
Lafayette Restaurant: 90
Lake and Nash: 63
Lake Bridgeport: 186
Lake Como: 206
Lake Como Pavilion: 144
Lake Erie (Handley): 177
Lake Worth: 186, 225
Lake Worth Amusement Park: 177
Lamplighters: 97
Lantery, F.: 90
Lard, S. S.: 201
Lark, A.: 109
Lattimore, Hal S.: 159
Lawrence, Cetti & Brewer: 80
Lawrence, Oscar J.: 57
Lawrence, W. H.: 97
Lawyers: 19, 27–28, 68–69, 105
Leach, H. S.: 155
Ledford, G. M.: 155
Leer's Stables: 101
Legislature, Texas: creates Tarrant County, 19–20; orders county seat elections, 40, 43–44; charters Fort Worth's city government, 73; attitude toward T&P, 83–85; outlaws gambling, 191; annexation legislation, 205, 207; home-rule legislation, 208; Tarrant County senators and representatives listed, 261–67
Leonard, Archibald F.: 18, 247, 262
Leonard, Marvin: 201, 219
Leonard, O. P.: 201
Leonard Bros.: 201
Lester, A. Y.: 73
Library: established, 166; Theodore Roosevelt plants tree, 169; new building, 211
Life of America Building: 199

Light Guards: 165
Lindbergh, Charles: 209, 225
Line, Dr. R. F.: 85
Lipscomb, Will: 162
Little, W. H.: 139
Livery stables: 101, 103–104
Lockett, Elder: 109
Lockwood, John: 96, 97
Lonesome Dove Baptist Church: 21
Longstreet, Lt. James: 18
Lorantz, Bird: 77
Louisiana: 51, 69
Love Field: 219
Lovett, Robert S.: 225
Loving, George G.: 142
Loving, J. P.: 44
Lowe, Joe: 114
Loyd, M. B.: first banker, 62; partnership with Marklee, 68; alderman, 73, 268; incorporates First National Bank, 105; volunteer fireman, 118; interest in water company, 152
Loyd, Marklee and Co.: 68
Loyd Rifles: 165
Lucas, Wingate: 194, 260
"Lucky Lady II": 227
Lund, A. A.: 201
Luther Construction Co.: 216
Lydick, Dan: 200

Maben, N. M.: 73
McAdams, Rev. George: 190
McArthur Bros.: 153
McCaleb, D. C.: 186, 187
McCall, M. D.: 73, 268
McCart, Robert: 135, 154, 275
McCart, W. L.: 155
McCauley, Sgt. Daniel: 4, 240
McCleskey, John: 196
McCormick, S. C.: 108
McCoy, Joseph G.: 60
McDonald, Gooseneck Bill: 148
McDougal, C.: 118, 276
McDowell, Red: 197
McElroy, F. D.: 178
McGinley, Michael: 221
McGrath, P.: 155

McGraw, John: 168, 220
McGuffey's Reader: 56, 161
McIntire, Jim: 129
McIntyre, O. O.: 224
Mack, Connie: 220
McLaughlin, H.: 152
Maclay, Capt. Robert P.: 18, 22
McLean, Jeff: 191, 252
McNaught, C.: 155
McNulty, Caleb J.: 47
Madame Rentz's Female Minstrels: 88
Madder, R.: 162
Maddox, J. M.: 104
Maddox, James: 130, 185
Maddox, R. E.: 137, 139
Maddox, W. T.: 104, 118, 250, 268, 277
Maddox, Web: 201
Mail: *see* post office
Malone, Wallace: 207, 265
Malone, Walter: 142–43
Man, R. S.: 37–38
Mansfield, Tex.: 56, 158, 173
Mansion Hotel: 102
Manuel & Co.: 98
Marine Creek: 56, 137
Marklee, Clyde P., Sr.: 68
Marshall, Everett: 212
Martin, Bennett H.: 22
Masonic Hall: 33, 40, 56
Masonic Home and School: 190
Masons: 25, 33
Massengale, F.: 155
Massie, William: 201
Masten, W. J.: 27
Mather, M. D.: 152
Mathews, Dr. Mansell: 34, 52–53
Matkin, R.: 154, 277
Mauck, David: 37–38, 44
Maury's Geography: 161
Mayfield, Dr. W. D.: 63
Mayors, J. B.: 155
Meacham, H. C.: 200–201, 208, 273
Meacham's: 200–201
Medlin Milling Co.: 178
Merchants Restaurant: 132

Merrill, Maj. Hamilton W.: 23, 25
Mesquite, Tex.: 93
Methodist Church: Fort Worth Mission, 34; Fort Worth District, 34; Grapevine Mission, 34; Texas Conference, 34; minister hanged, 48; services, 109; Methodist Episcopal Church, 163; St. Paul's Methodist Church, 190
Metropolitan Hotel: 102
Meyers, Joe: 74
Miller, Henry: 99
Miller, Melvin J.: 201
Miller's Musical Emporium: 110
Millican, J. K.: 69, 79, 108
Milling: 37–38, 81, 138–40, 145, 178, 199
Milner Hotel: 102
Milwee, W. H.: 56
Mississippi: 51, 62, 65
Missouri: 28, 35, 49, 138
Missouri-Kansas-Texas Railroad: reaches Denison, 61–62; builds into Fort Worth, 126–27; strike, 128; route of Cal Rodgers, 181
Missouri-Pacific System: 176
Missouri Wagon Yard: 104
Mister, W. F.: 110
Mistletoe Heights: 205
Mitchell, John A.: 31
Mitchell, Rev. W. W. 36
Mitchell & Thompson: 99
Mitchell Bros.: 103
Mobley, C. L.: 205
Money: 37, 52, 57, 62, 96
Monnig, George: 141
Monnig, William: merchant, 141; heads hotel company, 200; Chamber of Commerce president, 201; city councilman, 273
Monnig's: 141
Monteith's Geography: 56
Moore, Dan D.: 199
Moore, Dr. H. W.: 151
Moorman, Cull: 195
Moody, Thomas O.: 39, 44
Moreland, Mrs. Q. T.: 190

Morris Plan Bank: 200
Morton, E. W.: 108, 146, 268
Moslah Temple: 190
Mosley, William: 39, 44
Movies: 168, 185
Mulecars: *see* streetcars
Municipal: *see* government, city
Music: 21, 31, 110
Myers, David: 35, 36
Myers and Souders Carriage Manufactory: 108
My Theater: 88

Nash, Charles: 67
Nash, Z. E. B.: 67
Nash Hardware Co.: 67
National Air Transport: 209
National Bank of Commerce: 200
National Broadcasting Co.: 203
Navarro County, Tex.: 12, 20
Nebraska: 138
Neely, M. E., and Co.: 154
Neis, George: 140, 269
New Deal: 210
New Hampshire: 19
Newman, G. M.: 75
Newman, George: 97
Newspapers: *Birdville Union,* 43; *Birdville Western Express,* 43; *Dallas Herald,* 44, 82; *Fort Worth Chief,* 46, 48; *Austin Intelligencer,* 46, 47; *The White Man,* 49; *Fort Worth Democrat,* 64, 67, 69, 70, 71, 73, 75, 78–79, 85, 97, 100–101, 106, 107, 109, 110, 117; *Dallas Union Intelligencer,* 64; *Fort Worth Chieftain,* 64; *Fort Worth Enterprice,* 64; *Fort Worth Epitomist,* 64; *Fort Worth Exponent,* 64; *Fort Worth Times,* 64; *Fort Worth Whig Chief,* 64; *Jefferson Union Intelligencer,* 64; *Quitman Herald,* 64; *Philadelphia Chronicle,* 66; *Fort Worth Standard,* 69, 79, 100, 106, 107–108, 112, 117–19, 120; editorial campaigns, 71, 75, 106, 108, 112–13, 117–18, 120–21; first daily, 107; *Fort Worth Ad-*vance, 107; *Fort Worth Democrat-Advance,* 107, 124, 142, 151; telegraphic dispatches, 108; *Fort Worth Gazette,* 124, 142–43, 187; *New York Daily Chronicle,* 124; *Austin Statesman,* 142; (*Fort Worth*) *Livestock Journal,* 142; modernization, 142; *Dallas Morning News,* 143, 186, 224; *Fort Worth Register,* 143, 186; (*Fort Worth*) *Greenback Tribune,* 146; (*Fort Worth*) *National Texas,* 146; *Fort Worth Tribune,* 146; *Fort Worth Telegram,* 171, 186–88, 222; *Fort Worth Star Telegram,* 172, 181, 182, 188, 189, 199, 202, 222; *Fort Worth Record,* 186, 199, 222; *Fort Worth Record-Register,* 186; *Fort Worth Star,* 186–88, 221, 222; advertising, 187; *Fort Worth Mail,* 187; *Fort Worth Mail-Telegram,* 187; *Fort Worth Press,* 199; *Fort Worth Record-Telegram,* 199
Newsstands: 91
New York Store: 100
Nichols, John: 118, 268, 276–77
Nichols and Monica: 117
Niles, L. V.: 206
Niles City: 206–207
Nimitz, Admiral: 225
Norgaard, Victor A.: 137
Norris, Rev. J. Frank: 203, 214
North, J. M., Jr.: 182, 221
North Fort Worth: 183, 205
North Fort Worth State Bank: 200
North Side Coliseum: 169
North Side Street Railway Co.: 144
Northern Texas Traction Co.: 177
Norton, Anthony Banning: establishes *Fort Worth Chief,* 46–47; biographical data, 46–50; disposes of *Chief,* 49; *Jefferson Union Intelligencer,* 63–64; mobbed, 64; establishes *Fort Worth Whig Chief,* 64; *Dallas Union Intelligencer,* 64; politician, 64; tutor of Malone, 142
Nugent, Thomas L.: 148

Nutt, J. R.: 175, 176

Oberhoff, G.: 155
O'Brien, Davey: 212
O'Brien, J.: 155
O'Daniel, W. Lee: 201, 214–15
Odd Fellows: 71, 190
Odeon Theater: 168
O'Flaherty, D.: 119
Oil: Ranger field, 195–96; boom, 195–99; frauds, 198; companies, 199, 222
Oil Workers International Union: 204
Oklahoma: 97, 138
Oklahoma City University: 189
Old Reliable Jewelry Store: 99
Oliver, Jennie: 162
Oliver Bros.: 106
Orton, M. D.: 152
Ousley, Clarence: 186
Overton, W. H.: 64, 268

Pacific Hotel: 101
Packinghouses: 106; early companies, 137; major packers, 173; strike, 203
Paddock, Capt. B. B.: arrives in Fort Worth, 65; as editor, 65, 69, 70, 107, 142; forms first fire company, 71–72; in formation of city government, 73; receives first telegram, 79; buys first railroad ticket, 86; deals with Santa Fe, 126–27; urges industrialization, 136; forms water company, 152; mayor, 156; school census, 161; state representative, 262, 264, 270–71
Panther City, origin of name: 81–82
Panther Fire Co.: 118
Parades: 145, 147, 149, 169
Parks: 167, 168, 184–85
Park Street Railway Co.: 144
Parker, Isaac: 40, 248, 261
Parker, Joe: 11
Parker, Quanah: 101
Parking meters: 211
Pavilion: 147
Peak, Clara: 56; *see also* Walden
Peak, Dr. Carroll M.: 268; arrives, 27; church service in home, 34; furthers

education, 39, 56, 160, 161; in county seat election, 41; on courthouse bond, 44; starts mail service, 159
Pearcy, Mrs. M. L.: 162
Peers, J. M.: 115
Peers House: 101
Pemberton, J. W.: 156
Pendery and Wilson: 67
Pendery's Sample Room: 90
Pendleton, W. S.: 105, 133, 249–50, 262, 270
Pennsylvania Hospital: 201
Perrier, Rev. Vincent: 63, 109
Peters Colony: 8, 20
Peterson, R.: 172
Petrolia, Tex.: 175
Pettus, J. J.: 172
Petty, G. T.: 44
Petty, J. N.: 44
Philbin and Jackson: 153
Phillips, J. S.: 168
Physicians: 27, 54, 63
Pickwick Hotel: 102
Pier, W. L.: 201
Pierce, Franklin: 159
Pierce Oil Co.: 222
Pittsburgh Filter Manufacturing Co.: 186
Police Department: organized, 74; jails, 74, 92; patrols, 91–92; uniforms, 92, 108, 157; conduct of, 117; mounted, 156, 184; permanent force, 156; regulations, 157; motorcycles, 172; motorized, 183–84; bicycle detail, 184; civil service in, 208; radio, 212; chiefs listed, 275
Politics: 32, 77, 78, 146–49
Polk, James K.: 47
Polytechnic: 207
Polytechnic Street Railway Co.: 144
Population: 21, 51, 71, 123, 136, 161, 169, 175, 199, 216, 217
Populist Party: 148
Post Office: military mail, 18; mail in Civil War, 52; mail service, 106, 159;

home delivery, 159; building, 159; airmail, 182, 209
Powell, A. J.: 212
Prairie City Street Railway Co.: 143
Prairie House Hotel: 118
Presbyterian Church: services, 109; established, 122
Presidents, U. S., visits: 168, 214
Preston and Co.: 154
Prindle, Tom: 32
Probst Construction Co.: 157
Prohibition: 138
Prostitutes: 112, 113, 116
Public Health Service Hospital, U. S.: 223
Public Works Administration: 210
Purvis, Charles: 155
Purvis, Duff: 206
Purvis, Joe: 44

Quality Hill: 167
Quayle, William: 51, 247–48, 261
Queen City Street Railway Co.: 143

Rachal Bros.: 106
Radio: 201–203, 213
Railroad Commission: 148, 272
Railroads: 60, 61, 70, 125–29, 163, 176–77; boom in Fort Worth, 66–67; first train, 85; train robberies, 93–94; refrigerator car, 106; strikes, 128 f.; bonuses, 177
Railroad Store: 98
Rainey, Dr. and Mrs. Frank P.: 190
Ramey, Maj. Gen. Roger: 218
Rand, Sally: 212
Ranger, Tex.: 195
Rangers, Texas: 7–9, 129
Ravenscroft, E. M.: 160
Ravey, Emmanuel and Lee: 190
Ray, Rev. Fountain P.: 34
Real estate: prices, 69; rents, 70; agents, 80; auctions, 87; salesmen, 104; developments, 204 f.
Record, James R.: 221
Reconstruction: insecurity of government, 54; occupation troops, 55, 56, 77; conditions during, 55, 62; voting during, 77; orders changing county officers, 249; see also Indians
Red Cross: 190
Red Light Saloon: 89
Red Network: 203
Red River: 6, 9, 17, 56, 61
Reid Auto Co.: 183
Reimers, C. D.: 187
Remington, Frederick: 226
Republican Party: 49, 64, 146, 148
Restaurants: 90–91, 132
Rich, Ida: 162
Richardson, Sid: 224
Richmond, Harry: 129, 132
Ridglea Addition: 216
Rivercrest: 206
Riverside: 177, 207
Riverside State Bank: 200
Riverside Street Railway Co.: 144
Roads: 19, 158, 173
Roberts, O. M.: 22
Robinson, Flora: 56
Robinson, Milt: 56
Robinson, W. M.: 44
Roche Brothers and Tierney: 83
Rockett, D.: 155
Rock Island Lines: 127
Rodgers, C. P.: 181
Roe Lumber Yard: 191
Rogers, R. W.: 185
Rogers, W. R.: 20, 247, 251
Rogers, Will: 225
Roosevelt, Elliott: 214
Roosevelt, Franklin D.: 212, 221, 225
Roosevelt, Theodore: 168–69, 214
Rose, Billy: 212
Rosedale Street Railway Co.: 43
Rosen Park: 168
Ross's Station: 7, 9
Rouse, Fred: 203
Royal Canadian Flying Corps: 192
Rucker, Tony: 77
Rufner, J. F.: 155
Runnels, Hardin: 32–33
Rushing, W. L.: 156
Russell, Charles M.: 226

St. Andrew's Episcopal Church: 109
St. Joseph's Hospital: 201
St. Louis, Mo.: 29, 60, 100, 173, 176
St. Louis and San Francisco Railway: 127, 176
St. Louis Hide Depot: 96
St. Patrick's Day: 167
Saloons: 31, 32, 88, 89, 90, 100, 108, 116, 118, 123, 168, 191, 195
San Angelo, Tex.: 63, 102, 169, 172
San Antonio, Tex.: 6, 8, 11, 16, 61, 140, 181, 209
Sanger Bros.: 98
Santa Fe Railroad: arrives, 126–27; bonus, 177
Santee, James: 226
Scalawags: 62
Scharbauer, John: 200
Schermerhorn, W. B.: 141
Schools: teachers, 27, 39, 56–57, 110, 161, 162; E. M. Daggett School, 38; first school, 39; description of, 39; private, 39–40, 110; tuition, 39, 110; elections, 39, 160–61; Male and Female schools, 39; trustees, 39, 161; Masonic Institute, 40, 57; closed in Civil War, 52; textbooks, 56, 161; exercises, 57; public, 69, 160–61; Male and Female Institute, 110; Weaver Male Institute, 110; Arnold Walden Institute, 110; tax, 161; superintendent, 161–62; high schools, 162; Paschal High School, 163; household arts, and manual training, 163; Technical High School, 205; Amon G. Carter Riverside, 223
Scoble, A. W.: 153, 277
Scott, Mrs. E. J.: 146
Scott, Mrs. Louise: 63
Scott, Milton: 132
Scott, Thomas: 66, 76
Scott, Walter B.: 201
Scott, Winfield (cattleman): 102, 168
Scott, Gen. Winfield: 13
Scribner, Mrs. E. S.: 110
Scripps-Howard: 199

Secession: 49–51
Seminaries: 189–90, 214
Senate, Texas: 20
Senate Bar: 186
Settlers: 25, 26, 236
Sewers: 155
Shepard, Seth: 147
Shipp, J. R.: 155
Shiels, Henry: 74, 269
Short, Luke: 123, 134–35
Sidewalks: 89, 108, 113, 125
Silsby Manufacturing Co.: 118
Silver Cornet Band: 110
Simmons, W. T.: 158
Simon, René: 180
Simpson, G. W.: 137
Sinclair, E. W.: 222
Sinclair Building: 199
Sinclair Oil Co.: 222
Slaughter, J. A.: 37
Slauter, George: 43
Slavery: 48
Smallpox: 151–52
Smith, George: 46
Smith, I. N.: 155
Smith, John Henry: 109
Smith, John Peter: arrives, 27, 38; schoolteacher, 27, 39; in county seat election, 43; in secession, 50, 51; business interests, 68, 97, 100, 137, 270; mayor, 150f., 269; furthers public schools, 160, 161, 162; death, 169
Smith, John Peter, Hose Co.: 154
Smith, Junius W.: 64, 69
Smith, Mrs. Leo F.: 110
Smith, Mrs. Ralph P.: 190
Smith, Rev. Thompson L.: 35
Sneed, C.: 155
Sneed and Howard: 99
Snow, David: 53
Solon, John: 98
Sons of Hermann: 167
South, Rev. Walter: 34
Southern Air Transport: 210
Southern Pacific Railroad: 127, 181
Southern Pacific mail route: 28

South Fort Worth State Bank: 200
South Side: 38, 204–205
Southwestern Baptist Theological
Seminary: 189–90
Southwestern Bell Telephone Co.:
178
Southwestern Exposition and Fat Stock
Show: 137, 191
Spaatz, General: 225
Spanish-American War: 165
Speaker, Tris: 220
Speck, J. H.: 203
Springer, J. W.: 174
Stagecoaches: 78; robberies, 92;
routes and companies, 102; equip-
ment, 103
Stag Saloon: 191
Standifer, Dr. J. M.: 17
Stark, Admiral: 225
Starr, Lt. Samuel H.: 19
Stedman, Alex: 135, 158, 278
Steele, Lawrence: 27, 44, 73, 248
Steele's Tavern: 32
Steiner, Dr. Josephus: 23–24
Stephenville, Tex.: 102, 127, 172, 201
Stewardsville, Tex.: 21
Stillman, W. O.: 108
Stockyards: 137, 174
Stone, B. B.: 201
Stone, Gaylord: 201
Stone, Seymour: 225
Stonestreet, W. C.: 200
Stores: see trade, retail
Stratton and White: 176
Streetcars: mule car, 97–98; com-
panies, 97, 143–44, 156, 177, 211;
fare, 97; motormen, 144; electrifica-
tion, 144; see also bus service
Streets: 26, 57, 108, 113, 167, 173;
condition of, 81; paving and mainte-
nance, 81, 155; lights, 97, 140;
houses numbered, 108; overpasses,
211
Strikes: see labor
Sullivan, John L.: 168
Swayne, James: 138
Swayne, John F.: 69, 73, 250, 276

Swayne Bros. and Crane: 100
Swift & Co.: 173 f.
Swingley, L. J.: 86
Sycamore Creek: 84
Sylvania Addition: 207
Symington, Stuart: 226

Taft, William Howard: 214
Tarantula Map: 70, 107
Tarleton, B. D.: 159
Tarrant, Gen. Edward H.: 19–20
Tarrant County: see government,
county
Tarrant County Construction Co.: 83–
84
Tarrant Field: 215, 217–18
Tarrant Rifles: 51, 165
Tatum, E. D.: 110
Taylor, Dan: 102
Taylor, Gen. Zachary: 7
Taylor, Tom: 157
Teague, Mrs. Elizabeth: 37
Telegraph: 78–80
Telephone: 100–101, 178
Television: 203
Templeton, John: 64
Templeton, John D.: 152
Templeton, W. D.: 152
Tennessee: 17, 31
Terrell, Alexander: 55
Terrell, Ed: 16, 32, 73–74, 81, 275
Terrell, I. M.: 162
Terrell, J. G.: 27–28, 30, 270; in
county seat election, 43; in Civil
War, 51; in Reconstruction, 54–55;
lawyer, 62
Terry, I. C.: 74, 82, 275
Terry, Col. Nathaniel: 27, 32, 34, 44,
50, 53
Terry, Stephen: 28, 248, 250, 268, 269
Texas, Republic of: 8, 20
Texas & Pacific Railroad: 70, 125;
construction of, 66; in panic of 1873,
76; builds into Fort Worth, 82–86;
first station, 86; reservation, 96;
Trans-Continental Division, 126;
strike, 128; bonus, 177

Texas A&M: 163
Texas Air Transport: 210
Texas & Pacific Coal Co.: 195
Texas Clothing House: 99
Texas Christian University: 57, 189, 205, 223, 226
Texas Dressed Beef and Packing Co.: 137
Texas Electric Service Co.: 210
Texas Hotel: 200, 223, 224
Texas Midland Railroad: 148
Texas Steel Co.: 178
Texas Technological College: 223
Texas Wesleyan College: 189
Texas Wesleyan University: 163
Theater Comique: 88, 89
Theaters: 88–89, 114, 168
The Fair: 141
Thomas and Werner: 157
Thomason, W. D.: 99
Thompson, Ben: 123
Thornton, John A., Hose Co.: 154
Throckmorton, J. W.: 119
Throop, Charles: 35
Thurmond, P. J.: 73
Thurmond, P. M.: 69
Tidball, Thomas A.: 68
Tidball, Van Zandt and Co.: 68, 100, 142
Tilden, Samuel J.: 119 f.
Tillar, Benjamin T.: 102
Tillar, Mrs. Genevieve: 215
Tiller, J. P.: 118
Tivoli Saloon: 90
Tomlinson, William: 191
Towash, Chief: 3–5
Towash Village: 9, 10
Traction companies: *see* streetcars
Trade, retail: 30; stores, 18, 27, 36–37, 57–58, 63, 67–68, 98–100, 140–41, 200–201; barter, 37; revives after Civil War, 57; drygoods, 67–68; cattlemen, 62
Trade, western: wagon trains, 6; activity, 82; buffalo hunters, 82, 96; freighters, 82, 96; wagon freight, 92

Trade, wholesale: apple peddlers, 37; houses, 67; volume, 140
Trail drives: 59–62, 92, 105
Transcontinental Hotel: 101
Trans-Continental Railroad: 70; *see also* Texas & Pacific
Transportation: *see* wagons, railroads, aviation, roads
Travilla, J. C.: 173
Trinity Guards: 165
Trinity River: 10, 12, 38, 39, 96, 152, 155, 186, 224
Trinity State Bank: 200
Trowbridge, C. A.: 155
Truman, Harry S.: 214, 225
Tucker, W. B.: 44
Turf Exchange: 168
Turner, Charles: 11, 37
Turner, J. J.: 157
Turner, J. T.: 39–40
Turner, R. L.: 99
Twiggs, Gen. David: 7, 13
Typhoid fever: 150

Union Bank and Trust Co.: 200
Union Pacific Railroad: 66
Union Sabbath School: 109
United Edison Manufacturing Co.: 140
United States: *see* government, federal, *and* Public Health Service
United States Mail Line: 102
Universal Mills: 199
University State Bank: 200

Van Winkle, G.: 68, 75
Van Zandt, Dr. I. L.: 54
Van Zandt, K. M.: 262, 270, 271; arrives, 54; furthers education, 56, 160–61; merchant, 57; buys church site, 63; financier, 64; hires Paddock, 65; banker, 68; legislator, 73; furthers railroad construction, 76, 83, 127; streetcar company, 97
Variety houses: 88
Videttes, National Order of: 147
Village Creek, battle of: 20

Virginia: 38
Virginia House: 101, 151

Waco, Tex.: 8, 17, 18, 140, 189, 190, 201
Waco Tap: 89
Waggoner, Tom: 168
Waggoner Building, W. T.: 199
Wagon freight: *see* trade, western
Wagon yards: 103–104
Wainwright, Jonathan: 225
Waitresses, first: 101
Walcott, Myron W.: 81
Walden, Mrs. Clara Peak: 162
Walker, A. G.: 43f., 249, 261
Walker, Glen: 185
Walker, Nannie: 196
Walker, S.: 155
Walla Walla, Wash.: 134
Wallerich, Dr. N.: 63, 139
Want and Hartsfield Confectionery: 91, 99
Waples, Col. Paul: 187
Ware, George: 89
Washburn, D. W.: 84
Washer, Jacob: 141
Washer, Nat: 141
Washer Bros.: 141
Water: companies: 75, 152–53; demand for waterworks, 108, 113; wells, 150, 153, 185; Holly Plant, 153; mains, 153; municipal system, 153; treatment, 186
Waverly Hotel: 101
Waxahachie, Tex.: 52, 127
Wear, W. D.: 109
Weather Bureau: 159–60
Weatherford, Tex.: 92, 56, 102, 121, 152
Weaver (W. T.) Male Institute: 110
Webb Motor Fire Apparatus Co.: 183
Wells, J. B.: 98
West, Sol: 106
West Fort Worth Street Railway Co.: 144
West Side State Bank: 200
West Texas: 62, 103, 140, 223

Westbrook Hotel: 63, 111, 102, 197
Western Trail: 61
Western Union: 80
Westland, J. E.: 139
Wetmore, Louis: 26, 242
Wharton, A. B.: 172
Wheat Building: 167
Wheeler, C. A.: 201
White Elephant Saloon: 123, 134, 168
Whiteman, Paul: 212
Whitesboro, Tex.: 126, 182
White Settlement: 31
Wichita, Kan.: 96
Wichita Falls, Tex.: 130, 175
Wilburn, E.: 44
Wilkes and Barber: 206
Wilkinson, J. G.: 200
Willard, Jess: 196
Williams & Co.: 98
Willingham Bros.: 98
Will Rogers Memorial Auditorium and Coliseum: 169, 211, 223, 225
Wilson, Frank: 219
Wilson, Jeff: 155
Wilson, John: 68
Wilson, L. J.: 261
Wims and Johnson: 104
Winders, Bob: 90
Wise and McDonough: 103
Wise County, Tex.: 41, 220
Women: in railroad strike, 128; clubs, 164–65; library, 166
Wood, Gov. George T.: 20
Woods, Dr. M. L.: 31
Woods, J. P.: 118, 249
Woody, Abram: 133
Woody, H. C.: 117
Woody, Sam: 41
Wool: 37
World Wars: 192f., 215f.
Worth, Gen. William Jenkins: commands in Texas, 5; organizes frontier defense, 8; orders survey for new fort, 9; Fort Worth named for, 12; biographical data, 12–14
Worth Broadcasting Co.: 203
Worth Hills: 208

Worth Hotel (old): 67, 200
Worth Hotel (present): 200
Wortham, Louis J.: as editor, 186, 187, 221; state representative, 264
Wright, Rev. Lewis J.: 34

Yellow Bear: 101–102

YMCA: 190, 206
York, John B.: 43, 247, 248
YWCA: 190

Zane-Cetti, Jesse: 83, 97, 152
Zweifel, Henry: 198

 *University of
Oklahoma Press*
NORMAN